THE REFERENCE SHELF

Vol. 17   No. 6

COMPULSORY ARBITRATION
OF LABOR DISPUTES

Compiled by
JULIA E. JOHNSEN

THE H. W. WILSON COMPANY
NEW YORK   1945

Copyright, 1945
by The H. W. Wilson Company
All Rights Reserved
Published January 1945

Printed in the United States of America

PREFACE

The problem of industrial disputes that has so widely affected the public convenience, if it has not caused actual hardship in many cases, is a matter of increasing national concern. This has been the more marked in immediate past years by reason of the severe strains brought on by World War II and the urgent needs to which it has given rise, especially in all-out wartime production. Among the various remedies that have been proposed to check the recurring strikes, and the disruption of life incident to them, the suggestion of compulsory arbitration has had serious consideration.

Arbitration is a method long in use for reconciling differences between men and groups, and its practice has extended over divergent fields, including notably commercial interests and international affairs, as well as the contentions between labor and capital. In its voluntary aspect arbitration has been widely accepted; it is in the proposal for compulsory arbitration that differences have become keen. Objectors see in it a reactionary and extreme remedy, and labor and industry have both opposed it by reason of what they regard as its potential menace to their respective freedom and rights. To groups which include the long-suffering public and aggravated public officials it has seemed to offer an eventual, neccessitous and much desired, recourse, but not always one to be articulately and freely discussed.

The present Federal Administration has endeavored in many ways, through its agencies of conciliation, mediation, and voluntary arbitration, to resolve industrial disputes where required. In January 1942 a new medium, the National War Labor Board, was created to augment this effort. Industrial peace not being adequately attained, in spite of these efforts and the no-strike pledges given by some labor leaders at the outset of the war, more drastic legislation, the Smith-Connally bill, was passed by Congress in June 1943 over the veto of the President and became known as the War Labor Disputes Act. This anti-labor act established, among other things, a cooling-off period of thirty days during which strikes would be illegal, and also authorized the President to take over plants where strikes or lockouts threatened to cause work stoppages in industries essential to the war.

The labor disputes problem is not primarily a war one, although this aspect is immediately prominent. It was prominent in the pre-war era and gives indication of becoming a major postwar problem as well, both during the reconversion period and after. A permanent policy which would work in the interests of industrial harmony and peace presents itself as highly desirable to the nation. The problems of industrial disputes concern not only the specific interests of the groups and classes concerned; they relate ultimately to the whole of labor and industry and to the balanced interadjustments of the whole of our society.

This number of the *Reference Shelf* is supplementary to the earlier number entitled *Arbitration and the National Labor Relations Board,* compiled by Egbert Ray Nichols and James W. Logan and published in December 1937. It is therefore limited for the most part to materials that have appeared since that earlier compilation. The endeavor has been made here to present material of variety and without bias, for the general reader and debater. A bibliography offers choice for more selected and extensive reading.

The compiler acknowledges the many courtesies extended in giving permission for the use of copyright materials, and in otherwise facilitating the work of the preparation of this book.

JULIA E. JOHNSEN

January 24, 1945

CONTENTS

CONTENTS

GENERAL DISCUSSION

DIVIDE AND CONQUER [1]

Divide within, then conquer from without. This is the technique of modern warfare. It is a technique that makes civil defense of the highest importance, for it reverses the sequence of warfare. The first attack is upon the populace of a nation and only afterwards do the armed forces arrive. To instill fear, confusion, hatred, loss of hope and faith in the country to be attacked, to undermine morale and soften up a people—these make it easy to defeat the army and navy and to render conquest certain.

The prevalence of disputes, differences, grievances and misunderstandings within a country offer vulnerable points for such undercover attack. Their fomentation and magnifying out of proportion to their real importance are matters of skill and time in the hands of expert manipulators.

A dispute, whether of an economic or personal nature, is so deadly today because it is a revelation of underlying conflict. It is the tangible evidence of maladjustment. It is the exposure of misunderstandings, suspicion and impaired confidence. It is a symptom of mental and moral confusion. Even though it reveals only emotions and ambitions, it brings to the surface an undercurrent that indicates goodwill to be on the decline, cooperation giving way to conflict and confidence being corroded by suspicion.

In a world where the total destruction of goodwill seems to be the objective, every dispute in the United States and on the Western Hemisphere—whether large or small, civil, industrial or commercial, prevailing in a great city or hidden in the remotest hamlet—is of the utmost importance. For every such dispute and its disputants are the center of careful cultivation

[1] By Frances Kellor, First Vice President, American Arbitration Association. *Arbitration Journal.* 5:132-9. April 1941.

to cause confution, unrest, suspicion and all of the qualities which undermine national unity and impair the inner defense line upon which a nation must depend for its morale and for its supplies for army, navy and land forces.

Yesterday, so to speak, a commercial or industrial dispute was the private affair of the individuals who made it; today every such dispute is the concern of the whole nation. Why?

Every such dispute makes the American inner defense line vulnerable to attacks from enemies within its borders at the vital points of production, manufacture and distribution, at a time when the army, navy and air defenses depend upon them for maximum speed and efficiency.

Every such dispute escapes the boundaries of the factory and the shop and penetrates to the home and personal and social life of the community. There it furnishes the unrest and ill-will that make that community fertile ground for inciting people to revolt against their own institutions through the instillation of doubt and hate and revenge.

An economic dispute, in the present state of world affairs, is as infectious and menacing as a contagious disease. That it attacks more directly the spirit of a people makes it no less dangerous. Even when it does not destroy, a dispute leaves a trail of ill-will which any hound of enmity can uncover for its master.

Every dispute, if allowed to go unchecked or unsettled, becomes a pestilential spot. It multiplies itself and in a short time, it slows up production, impedes manufactures, retards deliveries, upsets business confidence, delays payments, impairs credit, and in a thousand infinitesimal and obscure ways hampers national defense.

But such disputes have an even graver, because more insidious, influence. They sap morale, they divide loyalties, they are dry rot in the roots of patriotism. Nothing so instills hate and fear as disputes and their underlying causes of fancied or real injustice, inequalities or discrimination on the one hand and greed for power and ruthless competition on the other. Once started, hate grows fast and is soon out of bounds. The public portrayal of this unrest gives encouragement to the enemy ever on the watch for such manifestations of weakness.

Such economic disputes have enormous capacity to expand. They are, if one may so put it, a disease called ill-will. Like other malignant diseases, they multiply themselves. First, they consume the finer processes of mind and spirit in the disputants; then the dispute grows out of all proportion to its original shape and size as each party seeks to expand his grievance or claim. Misstatement and even perjury are brought to the rescue; then witnesses are sought and sometimes corrupted; then appear the opposing experts for each side, who, under other circumstances, might agree. Flowing through this mass of ill-will is claim and counter-claim, accusation and denial, attack and defense, until friends and neighbors and business associates are driven to take sides and the whole industrial group, if not the community, becomes concerned with the outcome.

What may have started out as a disagreement over facts, or a difference of opinion, or vagueness as to understanding, or a mere question as to quality, price or time of delivery of merchandise, has now become so exaggerated, through the influx of ill-will, that it takes a whole battery of lawyers on each side to extricate fact from fiction and reality from illusion, or it takes violence to settle the issue. However it ends, scars will be left and there will be bitter memories which will outlive the lifetime of the original parties.

Imbed enough of these quarrels in defense industries and the whole machinery creaks. Instill enough ill-will into the normal commercial life of a nation and its economy goes sour. For economic production is made up of thousands of parts—each dependent upon the other. So is an automobile built. It takes, however, but one small screw or bolt to put it out of commission or lead to a crash. So a dispute may well be the small screw or loose nut in our defense mechanism.

There is a prevailing idea that only big disputes cause great damage and are dangerous. It is time Americans discarded this idea. One of the reasons for the success of the Nazis is that they overlook nothing. In their penetration of countries by so-called tourists and other visitors, before they make war upon them, every weak spot is uncovered and every man or situation likely to break in their favor is carefully recorded. One cannot doubt that within our own land, a similar check-up is being made and that our small as well as great disputes, and big or little dissatisfied disputants, are not escaping notice.

The eastern world is in mortal combat because for the last two decades disputes went unsettled and the hatreds growing out of them were unchecked. Hate is now let loose upon the world.

Although this fact has been hammered into our consciousness day by day, Americans are not yet fully aware of the menace of their own internal disputes. Every other danger signal of a maladjustment in human and economic relations receives almost immediate attention. But let a dispute run up its red signal flare of warning and it is immediately nobody's business. Every other economic risk carries some kind of check or insurance or some safeguards are imposed by public policy—but not for disputes. They must still run their wasteful and menacing course of delay; they must still be allowed to destroy the things that men hold dear—friendships, happiness, respect, confidence and security.

Why has the western world so long lain under this spell of indifference? Why has the litigation of commercial disputes attained such proportions that the Chief of the Division of Commercial Laws had this to say in 1924:

> The aggregate economic loss to the nation through the necessity of referring to courts the trial of disputes arising in the course of trading would stagger imagination if it could be accurately computed both as to actual cost and to the indirect drain upon national resources. Next to war commercial litigation is the largest single item of preventable waste in civilization.

Why have Americans so long tolerated a belief in the inevitability of disputes, in that they must, like other infectious diseases, be allowed to run their course? Why is it that only since the first World War has it dawned upon men that disputes may be foreseen and checked even before they have arisen? Why is it that but so recently have economic disputes been made the subject of exhaustive research and analysis?

The answer takes us deeply into the philosophy and psychology of the American people.

First, the average American is an incurable optimist and, therefore, believes himself to be immune. It is well that this faith should exist, but not to the point of blindness. This faith is typified by the business man who says: "Why worry? I have never had a dispute." This proud boast in the strongholds of industry may have sufficed for yesterday but not for today, when disputes are not always of his making but are being made to order for him. So, also, is the industrialist blind who takes no precautions because he never has had a strike. So must his forefathers have regarded tuberculosis or pneumonia which ravaged the community but which are today foreseen and checked. In the world today, there is no immunity for any man or industry; there are only precautions and vigilance.

Second, the American, being an individualist, has long regarded disputes, when they come to him, as his own personal problem, different from those of anyone else and, therefore, his own affairs. Typical of this attitude of mind is the man who asserts: "I will have no interference from outsiders in my business." Who are these outsiders and what is their business in a world at war? Where is the individualist of yesterday in Europe, and what of his business after Nazi tanks have run over it? In a time of national defense, when all American resources are being called into action, all problems, including disputes, are the common property of a people defending itself. The isolationist in disputes is as unreal today as is the isolationist nation. Both are ostriches with their heads buried in the sand. They may awaken to find themselves captives of government regulation unless they themselves lead the way out by their own self-regulation.

Confidence in his own immunity and perpetuity of individual isolation has bred in the American a complacency toward disputes. He takes them for granted and believes they must run their course. Therefore, he is in no hurry to settle them and is tolerant of long and expensive court trials, long delayed adjustments and interminable bickerings. Since his forefathers have followed that course, it is good enough for him. But these same forefathers had no axis powers to reckon with; they had no invaders of America on the horizon; they had no enemies burrowing from within to whom a long drawn-out dispute was a bonanza.

Lastly, it may be observed, it takes size to attract the American mind and to challenge his attention. Unless it is a big dispute, with thousands of people or thousands of dollars involved, or unless those involved have big names, or have big power, his notice is not attracted. How different this viewpoint is from the totalitarian mind, which sees an opportunity in every small dispute, in every dismissed workman, in every dissatisfied injured person, in every fraudulent mail order, in every business mistake and which is ready to capitalize incipient ill-will into antagonism to American institutions. Nothing is too small or inconspicuous to escape notice or to invite contempt for American government proceedings.

One of the reasons for regarding a dispute with indifference was that Americans, individually, could afford them. The enormous profits and reserves of industry have enabled them to pay the costs of disputes. They could afford to shut down their plants; they could afford the high costs of litigation; they could regard indifferently adverse publicity. They could afford delays and maladjustments, for they held power.

Today industry cannot afford disputes; neither can the nation. Increasing taxes, higher costs of production and higher wages cut the reserves for disputes. The demands for defense and the publicity of disputes that reveal points of attack for the surreptitious invader, put the risks too high.

Nor can the nation afford the risks of disaster to its own inner defense line. Any individual, engaged in a public acrimonious controversy, is in a state of confusion concerning his rights and his proofs. He is obsessed with the chance of winning to the exclusion of much else that is urgent. He is concerned with the effect of the dispute upon his reputation, his business or his family. He is in doubt about his future relations with his adversary. He is torn between the desire to retain a friend and to win at all costs, with pride playing an enormous role in his decision. He is open to whispers and suggestions and points of view concerning his country which at another time he would not tolerate. For the time being, he is certainly a less useful member of society and perhaps an actual liability.

A dispute, however small or local, is, therefore, a matter of public concern. It is possible that, though the individual industry can afford to continue the quarrel, the country cannot afford it. It is possible that, when disputes give aid to enemies within a nation, it is a primary duty of the country, in its own defense, to see that this aid is no longer given. It is possible, when a war contract is let to a company and it lets sub-contracts, that these activities become so integral a part of national defense that the government and nation are partners in those concerns and disputes are no longer private affairs.

Owing to their optimism and individualism and opulence, Americans have not found a common interest in disputes. Each one has tended to regard a strike in another's plant as strictly that other's affair; each one has regarded another's lawsuit as strictly the litigants' business. Each one has come to regard an accident as solely the affair of the injured person and the insurance company.

But Hitler's emissaries do not so regard them. To their keen minds and clear eyes each one fits into the pattern of "divide and conquer"; each has a place in their scheme of totalitarianism; each is seen in relation to the other as swelling the volume of discontent and ill-will.

In the first World War, which was a battle between men and where war was formally declared and hostilities began from the outside, disputes and grievances and mismanagement within a nation were not so important. The war was far from our own shores and there was no defense problem. Today, the situation is wholly different. The invasion of America by subterraneous, circuitous methods has been going on for a decade with no declaration of war. The real attack has first been made upon American institutions and the American way of life. This change shifts the menace of disputes from the individual to the nation, no matter where it originates, what it concerns or who are the participants.

Today, disputes are to be found everywhere—in the home, the office, the factory, the salesroom—in our transportation, warehousing and financing systems. They are brought there by ourselves, through our own practices, through complex racial relations, through the activities of enemies within the country.

Wherever men seek power, riches, advantages or preferment, disputes are to be found, more acutely than they existed in 1914. But they are also fomented deliberately and purposely by others who know their disastrous effect upon national unity.

But, observing the new techniques of war and the causes of the downfall of other nations and the part disputes and grievances have played in them, Americans are awakening to the fact that disputes bear a vital relation to the inner American defense line. In 1914 there were no instruments for the control, isolation and correction of disputes; today they exist. Today there are whole new mechanisms for dealing with industrial disputes; and there are hemisphere-wide facilities for dealing with commercial disputes. We can prevent as well as control disputes. We have wholly new instruments of self-regulatory control and for clearing whole industrial groups of disputes. The Consent Decree for the motion picture industry offers an illustration. Both governmental and voluntary efforts have modern techniques if they will but use them.

The question is, are we too late so to mobilize these resources as to make a dispute-free America an asset to national defense, or is there still time? The answer is, nothing is too late for America in action.

ADJUSTMENT OF LABOR DISPUTES [2]

Employer-employee disputes in a democratic, industrial country fall into four general categories: (1) Those caused by conflicting interpretation or the nonobservance of the terms of an employer-union agreement; (2) those concerning conditions of employment—wages, hours, working rules, etc.—when such have not already been agreed upon and the terms embodied in a collective agreement; (3) jurisdictional disputes or controversies between two or more unions as to which shall have jurisdiction over certain jobs or kinds of work; (4) disputes concerning the rights of workers to organize and to bargain collectively with their employer, including such incidental issues as protest against discrimination for union activity, etc.

[2] By Florence Peterson, Bureau of Labor Statistics. *Monthly Labor Review.* 49:1023-44. November 1939.

Until very recently there was no legal acknowledgment in the United States of any distinction in the kinds of disputes which arise between employers and employees. The Railroad Labor Act in 1926, section 7 (a) of the National Industrial Recovery Act in 1933, and the National Labor Relations Act in 1935 gave to workers certain statutory rights and protections in their bargaining relations with their employers. These laws thereby distinguished disputes arising over union recognition and the right to bargain collectively from all other kinds of employer-employee disputes. The laws established special quasi-judicial agencies to make determinations on the basis of facts revealed by investigations and hearings.

The National Labor Relations Board and the several state labor relations boards which are patterned along similar lines cannot strictly be called arbitration or conciliation agencies, although certain phases of their work approximate that of conciliation and arbitration. When a complaint is first made to a representative of the National Labor Relations Board, he may, and frequently does, act as a mediator in an attempt to get the parties to agree to obey the law. While the terms of the law are explicit and cannot be compromised, settlement of questions over specific application and adaptations necessarily have to be made. In such a capacity the representative of the Board serves more as a peace officer than as a conciliator. If the matter is not settled through mutual counsel and formal charges are issued, then the agency must exercise its judicial powers and make a decision on the basis of facts as related to the law. Insofar as such decisions are final —subject to court review—they resemble arbitration awards. However, the function of the Labor Relations Board differs vitally from that of an industrial arbitrator, for the Board makes its determinations solely on the legality or illegality of a matter in dispute, while the industrial arbitrator bases his decision on the provisions of a contract which has been mutually accepted, or upon conflicting proposed terms of a new agreement. In the latter case, the arbitrator considers the economic interests of the several parties, taking into account their relative bargaining strength, the ability of either to carry on under given or proposed conditions, etc.

Since this article is concerned only with arbitration and conciliation, the work of the national and state labor relations boards and similar functions of the National Mediation Board will not be discussed here. The conciliation activities of the latter will, however, be referred to.

In general, it may be said that conciliation and arbitration are concerned with disputes: (1) Where the collective-bargaining relationship has been established but where there is a controversy over the interpretation, application, or observance of certain terms in an agreement already entered into by the employer and the union. (2) Where there is a controversy over the terms of a new agreement under negotiation, or where there is no collective bargaining but where the right to bargain collectively is not the issue. The matter in dispute, as under a collective-bargaining situation when a new agreement is under consideration, is a question over particular issues such as wages, hours, or other employment conditions. Such disputes are rare in an unorganized plant, because it is difficult for a number of individuals without leadership or financial backing to express their grievances in an overt act of protest. (3) Over rights between two or more unions to perform a certain job. There is a distinct difference between jurisdictional disputes and disputes between rival unions. A dispute between rival unions is likely to come under the jurisdiction of a labor relations board, since it is a matter of determining which union a majority of the workers in a certain trade or plant wish to have represent them. In a jurisdictional dispute, it is a question of which union has jurisdiction over a certain trade or kind of work, the workers themselves already having chosen their bargaining agency.

Disputes arising over the interpretation, application, or enforcement of an agreement already in force are more amenable to arbitration, since the basic terms of the employment relationship have been negotiated and embodied in the collective agreement. The arbitrator's sole duty is to clarify ambiguous clauses, to relate a general rule to a specific situation, or to determine whether or not the accused party has actually violated any of its terms. In theory, such disputes would not be subject to conciliation, since conciliation implies compromise and a give-and-take kind of adjustment.

Disputes arising over terms to be included in a new agreement are of an altogether different nature. These are controversies over what general wages, hours, and working rules should be adopted. They are not controversies over rights accruing from the terms of a contract, although each side may feel that "moral" or "natural" rights are at stake. The union, for instance, may contend that the workers have a moral right to what they consider to be a fair wage; the employer, on the other hand, may contend that the wage asked for will interfere with his natural right to engage in profitable business. The question of what is "fair," however, has not been mutually determined and this is the basic cause of the dispute.

While either one or both parties may ask for the assistance of an outside mediator in such a dispute, employers and unions are less likely to have such questions arbitrated, especially at the beginning of a dispute. When one side finds its position relatively weak, it may seek arbitration, but the other party is not likely to agree. If the dispute has been prolonged into a stalemate, both sides may be willing to have the matter arbitrated. In such instances, both sides have given evidence that their bargaining strength, their withholding power, is about equal, and an outsider's decision is sought merely to bring to a speedier conclusion a settlement which, it is assumed, would result if the dispute were prolonged. It does not necessarily mean that a strike or lockout must take place before such arbitration is sought. If both sides are aware that their bargaining strength is about equal, they may seek arbitration in order to avoid a stoppage of work.

In the case of jurisdictional disputes, if both the unions concerned belong to the same affiliated organization, this organization usually attempts settlement. In many instances the city or national federation, such as the City Trades Council or Building Trades Department of the American Federation of Labor, has established special machinery for the adjustment of jurisdictional disputes. At the request of one or both parties, government agencies may intervene. When they enter such disputes, however, they usually serve as conciliators and not arbitrators, since organized labor has been averse to having governmental agencies impose final awards in controversies arising among its various groups.

There are two main channels through which labor disputes in this country are adjusted: (1) Committees of private citizens or individual arbitrators who are appointed directly by the parties concerned in the disputes. These may be permanent joint boards or impartial chairmen, who function continously for an industry or area, or a person or agency temporarily selected to mediate or act as arbitrator upon specific occasion. (2) Governmental agencies, federal, state, and local. These may be permanent boards established by law, or they may be ad hoc committees appointed by the President, governor, or mayor in pursuance of a law which permits or requires such appointment when certain occasions arise.

Union-Employer Arrangements

In industries where both the employers and workers are well organized there may be joint boards or an impartial chairman appointed and financed by the employers and unions concerned. In some instances a government agency may have helped to establish such a joint board and even appointed its first chairman. Thereafter, however, the joint board is what its name implies— an agency maintained by the employers and the unions. The jurisdiction of such boards is usually confined to the plants of an industry located in one city or market area, although some function over an entire industry. Most frequently, the impartial chairman is an economist or labor-relations specialist who devotes his full time to the adjusting of disputes and "policing" the industry. In some instances he not only serves as umpire between the two factions but has become a consultant and research agent for general problems affecting the industry. Illustrations of employer-union arrangements for handling disputes are found in the clothing, printing, mining, and other industries.

Whenever disputes are referred to such joint industry boards or impartial chairmen, it is expected that their decisions shall be final. Through such machinery employers and unions voluntarily adopt a means for mandatory adjustment of disputes. Obviously, such an arrangement can exist only where there is collective bargaining, for its functioning is contingent upon the presence of a collective agreement. At the lapse of an agreement the arrangement automatically ceases, although both sides may tentatively agree to continue the office if there is a desire or hope that the terms of a new agreement can soon be agreed upon. Indeed, the impartial chairman may be an important factor in getting a new agreement signed. In this capacity, however, he serves as a mediator and not as a referee or umpire. His decisions are not binding and the parties concerned may decide to call a strike or a lock-out rather than accept his suggestions for peaceable settlement.

A common procedure under collective-bargaining arrangements is the appointment of a disinterested private citizen or committee to arbitrate a particular dispute after it rises. As is the case with the permanent joint boards, it is usually only those disputes arising over questions of interpretation or enforcement of an agreement which are referred to such an impartial arbitrator. Very seldom is an outsider given the responsibility of deciding the basic terms to be included in a new contract. When such is done the arbitrator is usually hedged in with certain limitations or restrictions as, for example, on the question of a wage scale, when he is instructed to make a determination on some such specific basis as the wages prevailing in the industry or area, or a change in the cost of living, etc.

American Arbitration Association

Since 1937, when it established an Industrial Arbitration Tribunal, the American Arbitration Association, a nonofficial agency, has arbitrated a number of employer-union disputes. The Tribunal offers a panel of arbitrators from which the two parties make the selection. Only disputes arising over the interpretation or application of a labor contract are accepted. Either party may apply for arbitration if such permission is already provided for in the collective agreement; otherwise both parties must voluntarily submit the case. In contrast to the joint boards in a particular industry, the Tribunal is not a permanent board of arbitrators to hear and determine any and all cases which arise. It is a mechanism by which arbitrators are selected for each dispute in accordance with its peculiar requirements. The method in which hearings are held and evidence taken is more formal than is usually the case with the joint boards, since it is intended that the awards can be legally enforceable should either party resort to such enforcement measures.

LOCAL COMMITTEES

In a number of cities certain individuals or groups have organized committees whose primary function has been the settling of disputes and improvement of employer-employee relations within the community. Usually these committees have orginated with some employer group—the local chamber of commerce, the manufacturers' association—which has then asked labor to cooperate. Sometimes the mayor has initiated the movement by calling together representatives of employers, unions, and the public. In other cases an outstanding citizen has assumed leadership. The urge for the establishment of such local committees has usually come at a time when the community has experienced a serious strike or a series of strikes.

The experience of local nongovernmental conciliation committees has revealed that they function under some very severe handicaps. Citizens having no direct interest in the dispute must of necessity be represented on such committees, and it is frequently difficult to get qualified persons who are willing to spend the time necessary for the tedious task of mediation. Also, a private citizen is loathe to enter into a dispute between two factions in his own community, particularly if he himself is engaged in a local business. Persons from outside the community are likely to have more prestige and carry greater confidence, even though they may not be any better qualified than local citizens.

In spite of these handicaps, local committees of private citizens in a number of communities have proved very helpful in settling disputes, particularly those which occur in the service and local transportation industries.

GOVERNMENT CONCILIATION AND ARBITRATION

Federal and state agencies for the adjustment of labor disputes vary greatly in their mechanical arrangements—the type of personnel, by whom appointed and to whom responsible, the formality or informality of their investigations, etc. Much more significant, however, are the possible differences in degree of voluntarism or compulsion exercised throughout the progress of the dispute, from the first threat to call a strike or lockout to the final termination or settlement.

A purely voluntary arrangement exists when the adjustment agency has neither the power to compel the parties to the dispute to submit the matter to it, nor to accept any decision it might make. The agency exists for the convenience of either or both parties to use, so long as they desire, but there is no compulsion or even implied obligation to ask for its assistance. This is commonly referred to as voluntary mediation.

A second type is a procedure which permits or requires the conciliation agency to investigate any or all disputes, even though the parties concerned have not asked for such intervention. The agency may or may not have the power of subpoena. On the basis of this investigation it may recommend terms of settlement. Neither party, however, is obligated to accept its recommendations. This procedure may be termed compulsory investigation and voluntary acceptance. It implies the foregoing of strike action during a limited time while investigation is under way. A variant of these two types exists when neither party is obligated to refer the dispute to the outside agency, but, after both parties have once submitted the matter, acceptance of its recommendations is mandatory. This is usually called voluntary submission with compulsory acceptance.

The most extreme form of procedure for the settlement of labor disputes exists where a government agency is given the power to investigate and to make an award which must be accepted. This is compulsory arbitration and is generally accompanied by the requirement that there be no stoppage of work. Compulsory arbitration usually implies, therefore, that strikes and lockouts are illegal. It must be noted that reference here is to compulsory arbitration established by law, which is totally different from compulsory arbitration established by agreement between employer and union. The latter is voluntary acceptance of an arbitration process of settling certain carefully defined kinds of disputes after basic terms in the working contract have been mutually agreed upon.

Legal compulsory arbitration does not at present exist anywhere in the United States. By court decision, as well as preponderance of public opinion, it is held to be contrary to a free, democratic form of government. In only rare instances have government agencies been given the authority even to investigate or to make recommendations if neither party has asked for such outside intervention. Predominantly in this country legislation dealing with the settlement of labor disputes has clearly indicated that any government intervention shall be voluntarily agreed upon by the parties concerned, and that acceptance of the findings or recommendations shall be optional unless both parties have voluntarily agreed in advance to accept an arbitrator's decision.

WAR-TIME ADJUSTMENT

Even during the critical years of the World war, when the government adopted the general principle of "no strikes in wartime," there was no Federal legislation compelling either employers or workers to submit their disputes to any government agency. The government, however, could exercise certain pressures: Many of the contracts let by the War Department contained a labor clause requiring disputes to be submitted to any person or agency nominated by the Secretary of War; through the powers conferred upon the War Industries Board and the Fuel Administration, the government could shut off raw materials to a recalcitrant employer; the President might even take over the plant if there was a serious stoppage of work. In the case of the workers the government could threaten to draft the strikers, and refuse to them the assistance of the United States Employment Service. All such powers and threats were used upon only a very few occasions.

Chief reliance for the settlement of disputes during the war was placed upon conciliation and mediation. A separate board was created for each of the more important industries, and a National War Labor Board was established for disputes in essential war industries and as a supreme tribunal for appeals from the industry boards. These boards settled many strikes and threatened strikes. Whatever results they accomplished were due to their conciliatory efforts and to the pressure of public opinion, which opposed serious stoppages in production during the war. The boards had no legal power to compel either employers or employees to submit any matter of dispute to them, nor to compel either side to accept their decisions once they had intervened. The prestige of the boards enabled them to obtain compliance in most of the disputes in which they intervened during the time the war was in progress. After the armistice was signed, however, employees refused to carry out their recommendations. The industry boards soon ceased to function and in August 1919 the National War Labor Board was formally dissolved.

Kansas Court of Industrial Relations

The only experience this country has had with compulsory arbitration was that of the Kansas Court of Industrial Relations, which functioned from 1920 to 1923. This court was given jurisdiction in disputes arising in the public utilities, coal, food, and clothing industries, wherein strikes were altogether prohibited in Kansas. The 3-man court, appointed by the governor, had power to fix wages and conditions of employment in these industries. Proceedings before the court could be started by the court on its own initiative, by employers, by unions, or by a specified number of unorganized workers, or the public. Its decisions were binding and violations were punishable as criminal offenses.

Labor, particularly the Kansas district of the United Mine Workers, bitterly opposed the establishment of the court. Several of the union leaders were given jail sentences when they defied the anti-strike clause of the act by calling a number of strikes. Some employers also refused to put into effect its wage and hour decisions. The United States Supreme Court sustained these employers, when such cases were presented to it, by declaring the entire scheme of compulsory arbitration to be unconstitutional for industries not peculiarly affected with the public interest, thus depriving the Industrial Relations Court of jurisdiction in manufacturing and transportation industries. The Supreme Court held that the fixing of wages and hours, rules and regulations by such an agency was contrary to the due process clause of the fourteenth amendment in that it "curtailed the right of the employer, on the one hand, and of the employee, on the other, to contract about his affairs."

Before even the first of these Supreme Court decisions was rendered, the Industrial Relations Court had practically ceased to function, because of the increasing opposition and indifference of the employers, workers, and public. In 1925 the court was abolished altogether.

The short-lived experiment of Kansas with compulsory arbitration was one of the aftereffects of the war psychology. It was inaugurated after the state had taken over the operation of the mines in order to end a coal strike. The returning soldiers who filled the strikers' places, as well as the general public, were prone to consider all strikes as unpatriotic and to welcome a device which would make them illegal. Within a few months many of the court's most ardent supporters began to question the implications of such legal compulsion in the employer-employee relationship and to oppose specific actions and decisions of the court.

COLORADO COMPULSORY INVESTIGATION

Except for the brief experiment in Kansas, no government unit in the United States has passed legislation for the compulsory arbitration of labor disputes. Before this experiment, however, Colorado had provided for the compulsory investigation of disputes. The Colorado Industrial Relations Act, passed in 1915 following the bitter coal strike of the previous year, prohibits strikes and lockouts in industries affected with a public interest, pending investigation and report by the Industrial Commission. Employers and employees are required to give to the Commission 30 days' notice of any "intended change affecting conditions of employment or with respect to wages or hours." It is "unlawful for any employer to declare or to cause a lockout, or for any employee to go on strike, on account of any dispute prior to or during an investigation, hearing, or arbitration of such dispute by the Commission."

Although investigation is compulsory, the findings of the Commission are not binding unless the parties have agreed in advance to abide by the award. "Nothing in this act shall be held to restrain any employer from declaring a lockout nor any employee from going on strike, in respect to any dispute, after the same has been duly investigated, heard, or arbitrated under the provisions of this act."

The Colorado Industrial Relations law, passed almost 35 years ago, is still in effect. During the 4-year period 1934-38, the Commission received 524 notices of changes in wages and hours and working conditions. In only 74 instances were formal arbitration awards made. Although the Commission's reports do not indicate what happened in the other cases, presumably they were settled through conciliation or, if such failed, developed into a strike or lockout. During this period there were at least 41 strikes, involving 13,000 workers. A number of these, no doubt, were outside the jurisdiction of the law as not being "affected with the public interest." In some, the law was not applied or enforced. During the general bituminous coal stoppage in May 1939, over 7,000 Colorado miners participated, with no legal action taken against them except the denial of unemployment compensation.

RAILROAD MEDIATION

Because of the importance of railroads in the nation's economic life, the government very early began to concern itself with railroad labor relations. An arbitration act providing for the voluntary investigation of disputes was passed in 1888, but never used. The Erdman Act of 1898 provided for mediation and arbitration by the Commissioner of Labor and the chairman of the Interstate Commerce Commission. The Newlands Act of 1913 created a permanent, full-time Board of Mediation and Conciliation. Under both of these acts, if government mediators failed to obtain a settlement, they were to try to get the parties to agree to arbitration. Special triparite arbitration boards were appointed for each dispute, the government appointing the neutral members if the others failed to come to an agreement. Awards made by the arbitration boards were binding.

When, in 1916, the railroads refused to accede to the employees' demand for an 8-hour day, the employees threatened a general strike and refused to submit the matter to arbitration,

The Railroad Brotherhoods' refusal was based on the belief that the public representatives on previous arbitration boards, who actually determined the cases, were unsympathetic toward labor and that such awards as were favorable to labor were not obeyed by the railroads. This strike was averted by the enactment of the Adamson Act establishing a basic 8-hour day.

During the Federal control of the railroads in 1917-20 railway boards of adjustment were established, composed of an equal number of management and employee representatives, which had authority to make decisions in all disputes over the interpretation and application of existing agreements.

When the railroads were returned to private ownership in 1920 a Railroad Labor Board was established, composed of nine members appointed by the President. This Board was to investigate all disputes and to publish its findings and recommendations. Compliance with its decisions, however, was not obligatory. The Railroad Labor Board was never popular with railroad labor, especially after the Pennsylvania Railroad was successful in ignoring the Board's decision that it should deal with the regular labor unions instead of its company union. When the case was appealed to the Supreme Court the court held that the act had provided for no stronger means of enforcement than public opinion.

The 1926 act reestablished mediation as the basic method of government intervention. Although arbitration was not compulsory, having once been accepted, awards were binding. Supplementary to the central Board of Mediation were bipartisan boards of adjustment for single systems or groups of lines to interpret and apply agreements voluntarily entered into by carriers and employees.

Labor relations on the railroads at the present time are governed by the 1934 amendments to the 1926 act. These created a 3-man National Mediation Board, appointed by the President, and a National Railroad Adjustment Board, consisting of 18 carrier representatives and 18 union representatives. The Adjustment Board, with headquarters in Chicago, is divided into four separate divisions, each of which has jurisdiction over a distinct class of employees, viz., train and yard service, shop craft, etc. . . .

FEDERAL CONCILIATION SERVICE

The act passed in 1913, which created the United States Department of Labor, provided among other things: " . . . that the Secretary of Labor shall have the power to act as mediator and to appoint commissioners of conciliation in labor disputes whenever in his judgment the interests of industrial peace may require it to be done. . . . " Under this provision the present United States Conciliation Service was established. This now has a staff of 60 commissioners actively engaged in efforts to settle questions in dispute before strikes and lockouts occur, or to bring them to a speedy settlement if they have already started. The Conciliation Service may enter a case at the request of either party to the dispute, or at the request of some representative of the public—mayor, governor, congressman. It may also intervene upon its own motion, but this is done only in the more serious disputes when it is believed that a public interest is involved.

Although the original act gave power to mediate in any kind of dispute, the Conciliation Service has no power of coercion or means to enforce its recommendations. When the National Labor Relations Act was passed, giving to workers the legal right to organize and to bargain collectively with their employers, the enforcement of this act was turned over to the National Labor Relations Board which exercises quasi-judicial power. When requested, however, the Conciliation Service intervenes in union-recognition disputes to the extent of supervising consent elections to determine the collective-bargaining agency. Thus the responsibilities of the two Federal agencies, the Department of Labor Conciliation Service and the National Labor Relations Board, are clearly distinguished between the judicial and enforcement function of deciding and maintaining rights under a given law, and conciliation or mediation which implies voluntarism and compromise.

The United States Conciliation Service is primarily concerned, not with the rights and mechanics of collective bargaining as such, but with the disputes which arise over the terms to be included in a collective agreement, or the interpretation and application of the provisions of the agreement after it is once made. Also, a conciliator may intervene in a dispute in an unorganized plant where the employees are seeking not collective-bargaining arrangements but only a settlement of a specific question of wages, hours, and working conditions. The Service is also frequently called upon to settle jurisdictional disputes, most of these being in the construction industry.

A Commissioner of Conciliation has no set formula of procedure when he is called in to help settle a dispute. Whenever possible he tries to get the parties concerned to discuss their differences in conference, in which case he acts as a conciliator. Frequently, especially during the early stages, either or both parties refuse to meet together. He then acts as a mediator, holding separate conferences with the respective sides, adjusting the minor points of misunderstandings or differences, and getting each to agree upon what major points can be or shall be further negotiated. If either or both sides still refuse to discuss together these major points, the commissioner may draft a plan of settlement independently and submit it to the parties as a recommendation, or he may obtain the approval of both sides to have the matter arbitrated, in which case he assists in making the plans and selecting the arbitrator. An increasing number of union agreements specify that the Conciliation Service act as arbitrator or select an arbitrator when disputes arise which cannot be adjusted by the parties concerned.

Whatever the exact procedure may be, only purely conciliatory methods are used. Acceptance of the commissioner's service is optional, and his recommendations may or may not be adopted. The results he obtains are dependent entirely upon the prestige of his office, the assistance he can render by reason of his knowledge of the facts involved in the dispute, his skill as a negotiator, and the willingness of the opposing parties to come to terms of agreement.

Maritime Labor Board

In pursuance to an amendment to the Merchant Marine Act, the President, in July 1938, appointed a 3-member Maritime Labor Board. One of the duties of this Board is to act as mediator upon request of either party in any dispute over the interpretation of an agreement or over the terms of a new agreement. If mediation services are unsuccessful, the Board is to use its best efforts to secure the assent of both parties to arbitration.

Since its establishment the Maritime Board has intervened in a number of disputes between shipping interests and maritime unions on the Pacific, Gulf, and Atlantic coasts. It has followed much the same procedure as the United States Conciliation Service. This Board, however, is temporary and will cease to function after June 1941 unless legislative provision is made for its continuation. [It was discontinued in 1942—Ed.]

State Arbitration and Conciliation Service

State machinery for the adjustment of labor disputes antedates Federal conciliation services, that in Massachusetts and New York, for instance, having been created as early as 1886. The concern of most state governments with employer-employee relations, however, has fluctuated with the increase and decline of labor disputes. In only a few states has there been any continuing, consistent program for the prevention and settlement of strikes and lockouts. More generally, when there has been a sharp rise in union activity and workers have shown a disposition to make known their discontent and desires, the state government has hastily passed legislation in an attempt to meet the situation. During periods when there have been few disputes, such legislation has been all but forgotten and many agencies which had been formed have become moribund through lack of interest and financial support.

Around the turn of the century, when strikes trebled in number, the majority of the states passed some kind of legislative provision for the mediation or arbitration of industrial disputes. Thirty years later most of these state agencies were inactive. Some states had repealed the laws entirely. In others the original, independent board was abolished but the duties were nominally turned over to another department in the state government.

With the recent increase in union activity and industrial disputes, many states again have interested themselves in employer-employee relations. Following the example of the Federal Government, most of the state legislation passed in 1935 and 1937 was concerned with defining more clearly labor's "rights" and providing means for the protection of those rights. Five states, for instance, passed state labor relations acts which more or less followed the pattern of the National Labor Relations Act. Many more passed anti-injunction laws similar to the Norris-LaGuardia Act, which restricts court injunctions in labor disputes and makes "yellow-dog" contracts unenforceable in Federal courts.

Subsequent to the peak in strike activity in 1937, states which had passed protective legislation for labor, as well as others which had not already passed such legislation, turned their attention to ways and means for settling strikes and lockouts. Inactive conciliation services were revived and new mediation and arbitration boards created. At the present time the majority of the states have some kind of legislative provision for the handling of employer-employee disputes. Most of them have designated conciliation and arbitration agencies. In some, however, there is merely enabling legislation permitting the establishment of boards of conciliation and arbitration, but no such boards have been appointed.

When discussing state mediation agencies, the role of the governor must not be ignored. With or without other formal state machinery, the governor is likely to be called in whenever a serious labor dispute occurs. Sometimes his intervention follows a request by local officials for the assistance of the state militia "to maintain law and order." Always reluctant to take such a drastic step, the governor will personally intervene or appoint a "governor's committee" to attempt settlement. When a threatened stoppage of work clearly threatens the public interest, even though there is no request for calling the militia, the governor frequently appoints a temporary committee to undertake settlement. Such intervention by the governor is, necessarily, limited to the larger and more important disputes. Even though his

services have proven valuable upon occasion, they do not take
the place of a permanent, trained staff of conciliators. . . .

City Conciliation Boards

While it would seem that city governments would be as
concerned as the state and Federal governments in providing
means for the prevention and settlement of industrial disputes,
few cities in the United States have established any conciliation
machinery. Probably one reason for the lack of formal arrangements is the tendency to rely upon the mayor, especially in disputes in the service and trade industries which are most likely to
affect the comfort and convenience of the public. Other disputes, such as those in manufacturing, are more likely to be
taken to higher government agencies.

Although all mayors of necessity would intervene in disputes
which were likely to interrupt the public services, some individual mayors have entered into the field of industrial relations
much more than others. If both sides feel that a mayor is
unbiased and concerned only with the public good, and if he
is an astute mediator, a mayor is in a position to accomplish a
great deal in the prevention and settlement of disputes. A public
official who is dependent upon the popular vote, however, is
somewhat reluctant to intervene in disputes when any decision
which he might make may alienate certain portions of his con-
stituency.

For this and other reasons, the mayor usually prefers to
appoint a committee of private citizens instead of taking part
in the negotiations himself. Several cities at the present time
have continuing mayor's committees to which disputes may be
referred. Others have been appointed, served for a short time,
and then disbanded when the number of disputes declined.
Some have been created with a distinctly partisan make-up and
were, therefore, ineffective from the start.

Two cities, Toledo, Ohio, and Newark, N. J., now maintain
labor boards which can be considered a part of the regular
municipal government. The members of these boards are private
citizens who serve without pay, an equal proportion representing

employers, the union, and the public. In each case the city maintains the paid director and staff. The Toledo board has been in operation since the summer of 1935; the Newark board was established in the spring of 1937. They have handled hundreds of cases and have been effective both in the prevention and in the settlement of employer-employee disputes.

THE SCOPE OF ARBITRATION IN LABOR DISPUTES [3]

There has been a great increase during the past few years in the use of the so-called peaceful methods of settling major labor disputes. However, there is still a great deal of misunderstanding among labor leaders, employers, and the public regarding the essential characteristics of collective bargaining, mediation, conciliation, and arbitration. It should be remembered that, when the parties to a labor dispute seek to mediate or conciliate their differences, the pole star that guides them in their negotiations is that of reasonable compromise.

The principal job of the mediator and conciliator, when there is a strike or lockout or threat thereof, is to make to the employer and to the union concrete, reasonable suggestions and proposals which will result in a sensible compromise of their differences. That does not mean that, when one party or the other is clearly wrong, the party in the right must necessarily give up a portion of his rights whenever he agrees to participate in mediation or conciliation. There have been instances in which mediators and conciliators have enjoyed the respect of the parties to such an extent that they have been able to convince one side that it is entirely at fault in the dispute and that, therefore, it should agree to drop its claim.

However, experience shows that in most labor disputes of any consequence neither side is "lily white" when its claims are considered from the standpoint of the abstract test of right and wrong. If the parties in a dispute can be persuaded to sit down and, in the presence of a conciliator or mediator, discuss their

[3] By Wayne L. Morse, Dean, University of Oregon School of Law; United States Senator from Oregon, 1945. *Commonwealth Review.* 23:1-19. March 1941.

differences, there is a strong chance that reason and calm reflection will prevail against emotional thinking and bad feelings. In such an atmosphere a mediator has an opportunity to use his good offices to effect a reasonable compromise.

Of course, the ideal is for the parties, through collective bargaining by mutual agreement, to draft a labor contract which will not give rise to disputes requiring the services of a mediator or conciliator. Nevertheless, it is almost impossible for contracting parties to use language so precise and accurate in its meaning that it is subject to but one interpretation. Frequently the parties themselves, at the time they sign a complicated labor contract, are not perfectly clear in their own minds regarding just what they do mean by certain provisions that they have insisted shall be written into the contract. The human factor, which quite naturally manifests itself sometimes in an industrial dispute, often leads one party to seek an advantage over the other fellow in the selection of terminology in a contract. When such tactics are successful, the result is usually ambiguity of meaning.

The voluminous subject of contract law demonstrates that from time immemorial men have discovered frequently, after they have signed a contract which they thought was mutually agreeable to them, that in many respects they were thinking of entirely different rights and obligations to be created by the contract, from those which the language of the instrument, in fact, established legally. When such a situation exists, it would appear to be only good common sense for the parties, through the orderly process of mediation and conciliation, to attempt to compromise their differences over what they intended by the language of the contract.

There are many agencies which offer mediation and conciliation services. To mention a few, there is the conciliation and mediation division of the United States Department of Labor. This division has made a splendid record for itself by way of assisting in the settlement of literally hundreds of labor disputes. In many of these disputes, the parties through mediators have compromised their differences without resorting to the use of economic force.

The mediation services of the Maritime Labor Board is another good example of a governmental agency attempting to assist in the settlement of labor disputes by the process of mediation, whenever the parties voluntarily seek the services of the Board. Likewise, the mediation services of the National Labor Relations Board and of many similar states agencies result in the "reasonably peaceful settlement" of hundreds of labor disputes each year. Frequently the public is not even aware that a serious dispute has been threatened until it has been mediated, and many times no information at all reaches the public about many successful mediation settlements of labor disputes.

The work of the mediator and conciliator is much more difficult than the work of the arbitrator. Often when a dispute reaches the mediation stage there is such a state of bad feeling and "high blood pressure" that the parties will not even sit down in the same room together. On such occasions the chief job of the mediators and conciliators seems to be that of running back and forth between the two groups carrying messages in the form of proposals and counterproposals. A tactful mediator and conciliator, in spite of the difficulties of such situations, is frequently able to make a commonsense suggestion which results in the parties agreeing to settle their differences on a reasonable give-and-take basis. Don't forget that mediators and conciliators must think and act in the very midst of the heat of an industrial debate between the parties. They must search out the reasons which have resulted in the differences of opinion. They must be judges of men and of the various motives which compel men into action. They must be able "to take it," so to speak, and never hesitate "to give it" when they are sure of their facts.

The work of the arbitrator and the process of arbitration are entirely different from the work of the mediator and conciliator and the process of mediation and conciliation. Arbitration is a judicial process. The arbitrator sits as a private judge, called upon to determine the legal rights and the economic interests of the parties, as those rights and interests are proved by the record made by the parties themselves. An arbitrator is bound entirely by the record presented to him in the form of evidence and argument at the arbitration hearing. His job is the same as that performed by a state or Federal judge who has been called upon to decide a case between party litigants.

The principle of compromise has absolutely no place in an arbitration hearing. The moment an arbitrator compromises one of the issues involved in a case, that moment he disqualifies himself as an arbitrator. Therefore, an arbitrator should not take judicial notice of anything which is not presented by the parties in the record of the case. Hence it is of the utmost importance that the parties to an arbitration case prepare their evidence very thoroughly. It should be remembered that argument, no matter how persuasive, unsupported by evidence and facts, is of little value to an arbitrator when he is called upon to decide a typical labor dispute.

One essential to fair arbitration is orderly arbitration procedure, although many laymen seem to be critical of legal procedure. Undoubtedly there is a need for some reform in court procedure, pleading, and the rules of evidence, but the need is not as serious as the average layman would sometimes make out. There is a great deal of loose thinking about trial by orderly procedure. It should be kept in mind that it is impossible to separate substantive rights from procedural rights. Usually, when laymen insist, in argument, that cases and disputes should be decided upon the basis of their merits—and their merits only—they really mean that cases should be decided by someone unchecked by any rules of procedure.

Of course, if the time ever comes in this country when legal, substantive rights are determined by a judge who is checked in his action only by his own discretion concerning the merits of a given case, then we shall live under a government of men and not of law. Unless the person who is empowered to decide a dispute between A and B is required to decide that dispute in accordance with reasonable rules of procedure, then the rights of A and B are at the mercy of the arbitrary discretion of the judge. Such a judicial system would truly result in a dictatorship by the judiciary.

One of the great strengths of our American system of law is that those who are empowered to determine our respective legal rights must mold their decisions within the bounds of procedural guarantees. These procedural guarantees are so important to the protection of substantive, legal rights, that labor and employers should refuse any agreement to arbitrate a labor dispute until they first investigate the rules of procedure which are to be applied in the proposed arbitration hearing.

A sound criticism of labor arbitration as it functions in many cases is that too few arbitrators have grasped the full significance of arbitration as a judicial process. Too many arbitrators still take judicial notice of interests and facts not established in the record of the hearing. Too many arbitrators still try to apply the principle of compromise in their decisions. It is not difficult to understand their good intentions and motives and their desire to please both sides, at least a little bit. But, when they yield to the principle of compromise, they not only wrong both parties to the dispute, but they impair the effectiveness of arbitration as a judicial method of settling labor disputes.

A few years ago an arbitration award was handed down in a major dispute on the Pacific Coast, and in that award the arbitrator discussed at length many observations pertaining to the industry which he had made during the past twenty years. The language of his decision made perfectly clear that he had decided the case, not on what the parties had proved in the record, but on the basis of what he believed he knew from his own observations. The union refused, and rightly so, to be bound by that arbitration award, because it obviously was not a decision based on the record but a decision born of the prejudices, preconceived notions, and the arbitrary conclusions of the arbitrator. Unfortunately, this case is not a singular example of the misuse of arbitration. However, the recognition of arbitration as a strictly judicial process is gaining wide acceptance among arbitrators in all parts of the country.

Some union leaders and members still criticize arbitration as being too technical and legalistic. As they come to understand the importance of protecting the procedural rights of the union, this criticism will be minimized. As the number of cases have increased, familiarity with the procedural rules has resulted in a certainty and definiteness in the trial of the cases, and the parties have appreciated these advantages. In arbitration cases under the longshore contract the accepted and proven rules of procedure, applied in a court of record, are followed. Of course, it is recognized in the hearings that reasonable flexibility should be allowed in applying the rules of evidence and that the arbitrator should be permitted a reasonable latitude of discretion in applying the usual court rules of procedure to the arbitration case. . . .

The next point that should be stressed is that arbitration should not be used too much. It is no cure-all for the settlement of industrial disputes. It is subject to very definite limitations and shortcomings. Arbitration can be overused and, on occasion, arbitration cases which should never have been brought to an arbitrator for decision have been held under the arbitration provision of many labor agreements. The most satisfactory settlement of a dispute between employers and employees is a settlement which is reached by mutual agreement of the parties. It is always difficult for all concerned when a third-party arbitrator is called into a dispute and is empowered to tell the parties what they are bound to do under their own contract. When too-frequent use of arbitrators is made under a given contract, there is a tendency on the part of the parties to resent being continually subjected to the dictates of the arbitrator.

On the other hand, arbitration should be resorted to in a very large percentage of labor disputes as a last resort before making use of economic force by way of lockouts or strikes. That is, employers and labor should make a sincere, good-faith effort to settle their differences by way of collective bargaining, conciliation, and mediation. When those processes fail, then it is in the interests of all concerned to make use of arbitration.

It must be granted that employers and unions should have the right to resort to the lockout and the strike if they want to use those methods of settling their differences, especially when a great major issue is at stake—an issue which involves the right of employers to manage and control their plant or one which involves the right of the union to exist. Usually, under such circumstances, the parties have practically no choice but to resort to a lockout or strike. In other words, there are certain rights which are not arbitrable, such as the inherent rights of management and the inherent right of labor to organize and function as a union. But cases involving major issues are few compared with the total number of labor disputes in which an attempt is made to settle minor differences through the use of economic force.

In various sections of our country there is a growing agitation for legislation which will provide for compulsory arbitration. However compulsory arbitration is opposed generally by both unions and employers—and rightly so. A realistic approach to labor problems forces the conclusion that the most powerful argument against compulsory arbitration is that it obviously will not work. It will not work for many reasons. It is bound to meet with vigorous opposition on the part of employer groups whenever it is applied in a manner that endangers their interests, because they will be quick to recognize that its application is bound to threaten the managerial rights of the employers. It will always be opposed by labor because labor recognizes that compulsory arbitration places in the hands of the arbitrator the power to determine the very existence of the union itself.

Compulsory arbitration, no matter how plausible it may be made to sound theoretically, does, in fact, place in the hands of the arbitrator the power to destroy the employer or the union. If compulsory-arbitration legislation is passed, then every effort should be made to enforce it. It is at the point of enforcement that such legislation is bound to break down. It would constitute a type of social legislation which would be so opposed by large minorities within our country that it would fail because of its unenforceability. Then, too, many are opposed to compulsory arbitration because they recognize that in the long run through the decades a much sounder social and economic system will be developed if we do not attempt to place such arbitrary checks upon social trends. No third party, be he arbitrator, judge, or superman, can stem the tide of advancing, social phenomena. In this country the struggle between employer and labor has gone on since colonial times, and, by and large, the social assets of that struggle have been worth the liabilities. Labor has learned that on occasion it must resort to economic force if it is to advance and preserve its economic interests and, likewise, employers have recognized the importance of preserving the right to use the weapons of economic force in their battles with labor. In view of the fact that the economic interests at stake are so great, it is probably true that any attempt to force upon either industry or labor the settlement of disputes by arbitration mandate is bound to break down.

However, unions cannot afford to ignore the agitation of certain pressure groups within the public for the adoption of a compulsory-arbitration system. It behooves labor to do a much better job than it has been doing in educating the public about its problems. The average layman is not familiar with the complex factors involved in maintaining harmonious labor relations in any of the large American industries, such as the maritime industry. The public is quick to resent any action on the part of employers or unions in a given dispute which interferes with the routine social and economic life of the community. Labor needs to give greater heed to the fact that, after all, the public is the final arbitrator in all labor disputes. Thus unions should pay attention not only to their industrial relations, but also to their public relations—and that goes for the employers too.

We hear a lot about the public's rights in labor disputes, and of the obligations of labor to the public and to the community in which a dispute occurs. However, we do not hear enough about the public's obligation in a labor dispute. The public should recognize to a greater degree that it has the obligation to keep itself informed on the merits or demerits of a particular labor dispute before passing judgment on that dispute. There is too great a tendency on the part of various public groups to be either prolabor or proemployer, to judge all labor disputes on the basis of a preconceived prejudice.

Returning now to the subject of voluntary arbitrations, the question is asked frequently: What power should be given to arbitrators to enforce their decisions? The most sound answer would seem to be that no power should be given to them. The only power which they need is inherent in their position itself.

The force of logic and the fairness and soundness of his decisions constitute all the power that an honest, impartial arbitrator needs. When he renders a decision of that type, then he is entitled to the good faith of the parties. However, if his decision is found to be partial, if it goes beyond the record of the case, if it gives evidence of blind prejudice, it is not entitled to be enforced, and the parties under such circumstances should proceed to get rid of the arbitrator. There is a great difference between a decision which is not fair, honest, and impartial, and one which is purely judicial in nature but which the losing party does not like. In the latter case the losing party has no right to refuse to be governed by the decision, and it weakens its own cause as well as the usefulness of arbitration whenever it fails to live up to the terms of an honest arbitration award, even though it may not like the results.

However, it should be remembered that arbitrators are human and, therefore, unions and employer groups should not agree to an arbitration clause in a labor contract which binds them to accept a given arbitrator for a long period of time, such as for the life of the labor agreement. They should agree to bind themselves to abide by the terms of the decision of an arbitrator in a given case, so long as it is an honest, impartial decision. But it is a mistake to agree to accept a certain arbitrator for a long period of time under a labor contract or to accept a given decision which gives evidence of being a prejudiced or corrupt decision. Hence it is desirable to agree to accept a certain arbitrator under a contract only for such time as he is satisfactory to both parties to the contract.

Thus the right to file an affidavit of prejudice against the arbitrator should be preserved. It is a procedural right which is guaranteed in many state jurisdictions, and a right which is vital to the best interests of both employers and unions. If one or both parties to an arbitration contract lose confidence in the arbitrator, if they decide he is not impartial, if they think that he is biased or that he cannot render a fair, honest decision, or if they feel that he is influenced by any factor or consideration other than a strictly judicial one, they should have the right to file an affidavit of prejudice against such an arbitrator and ask for the appointment of a new one. Such a provision exists in the longshore agreement whereby the Department of Labor is called upon to appoint another arbitrator, it being impliedly understood that he will serve so long as he is acceptable to the parties.

The affidavit-of-prejudice procedure is common in state courts, for example, in Oregon. If a judge is found to be prejudiced, or believed to be prejudiced, counsel may file an affidavit of prejudice and the state will send in another judge to preside over the case. A private judge, trying an arbitration case, should in this respect model arbitration procedure after good court procedure.

Furthermore, when a labor organization or an employer association submits an issue to arbitration in a given case, it should be understood by all that there is reserved to the parties the right, upon proof of corruption or violation of the judicial function, to request the appointment of a new arbitrator and have the case retried. However, in the absence of any such proof, the parties must consider themselves bound by the agreement and abide by the arbitration decision, even though they dislike very much the application of the particular award. Unless the union and the employers abide by the arbitrator's decision, they subject themselves to the criticism that they have not acted in good faith, and that they have not lived up to their agreement. Nevertheless, they should have the right to get rid of an arbitrator in whom they have lost confidence, and, therefore, procedural machinery should be provided in each arbitration agreement for the appointment of a new arbitrator after an affidavit of prejudice has been filed. At the same time they should remember that all they are entitled to is an honest and impartial arbitrator, possessing the professional ability to function as a private judge. It must be recognized that arbitrators will make honest mistakes; but, so long as they are honest mistakes of judgment, the parties must be willing to run the risks inherent in arbitration.

Remember, also, that arbitrators themselves grow with experience and are much better able to perform their functions after they have become fully familiar with arbitration procedure and arbitration law. Little is to be gained by frequent changes in arbitration personnel.

On the other hand, no fair-minded arbitrator wants to serve as an arbitrator in a labor case unless both parties sincerely want him to serve. It is a difficult assignment at best, and worthy arbitrators do not want to serve as arbitrators one second beyond the time that either or both parties have ceased to want their services.

Although up to this point this article has been somewhat critical of arbitration as a method of settling disputes, nevertheless, there are many types of issues which can be settled best by way of arbitration. For example, when the parties disagree regarding legal rights guaranteed to them under a contract, there is only one sensible place to go to determine those rights, and that is to contract law. A competent arbitrator can determine those rights just as soundly and effectively from the standpoint of the law as can a public judge. However, the use of arbitration in such a case, rather than the use of the courts, saves a great deal of time, which usually is of the essence in such disputes and, also, it has the advantage of economy. It should be remembered that many labor contracts are written under great pressure; the history of the longshore contract shows that many points of differences of opinion can develop over the meaning of a labor agreement. But the parties need to remember that, when they, through their representatives, have signed a contract and pledged themselves to live up to its terms, they are bound by it, even though they subsequently discover that, on the basis of the law, the agreement really means something different from what they thought it meant.

There is another type of arbitration which is growing in favor, and that is the arbitrating of the terms of labor agreements themselves. It is doubtful whether arbitration is the best process which could be used in settling such disputes. It is clear, though, that it should be resorted to if other peaceful and orderly methods fail. Arbitration of disputes over wages, hours, working conditions, and the other terms of a proposed labor agreement is usually conducted by a board of arbitrators, consisting of three or five persons. The union selects one or two representatives, and the employer one or two, and then an impartial person to serve as chairman is selected, either by the parties, or by some other agency such as the Department of Labor.

Of course, we should not assume that such a board is actually a board of arbitration. In reality there is only one arbitrator in that picture. The arbitrators on the right and on the left of the arbitrator in the middle are, in fact, partisan arbitrators. They each represent a partisan viewpoint. The chairman, in the middle, is the only impartial, neutral, completely judicial official on such a board. Nevertheless, there is much value in having the partisan arbitrators on the board as assistants to the chairman. The chairman has, in addition to the advantage of hearing the lawyers for the two sides present their cases in the formal hearing, the further advantage of hearing the partisan arbitrators present the arguments all over again in the executive meetings of the board. But there is one rule of procedure that should be strictly followed by the so-called middle arbitrator: he should never become a party to the debates and the discussions and the proposals which are presented in the executive meetings of the board of arbitration. If he does so, then he becomes a mediator and a conciliator rather than an arbitrator.

The best procedure in such a situation is for the partisan arbitrators to meet at the close of the hearing and see if they can agree on any of the issues which have been tried before the board. If the partisan arbitrators can reach a mutual agreement on any of the issues, then their agreement should be made a part of the final award of the board of arbitration, the decision making clear what sections of the award were written by the partisan arbitrators, and not by the impartial chairman. If the partisan arbitrators, after hearing all of the evidence, are not able to agree on some of the issues, they should so notify the chairman. It is then his duty, on the basis of the evidence presented in the record of the case, applying to that record the rule of the preponderance of the evidence, to write the decision on such issues as could not be decided by the partisan arbitrators. When the chairman has written the decision on the issues referred to him by the partisan arbitrators, he should call the entire board into conference and read to the board his tentative decision. The partisan arbitrators should then be given an opportunity to suggest corrections of fact, and to express in an orderly way any differences of opinion with the decision. The impartial chairman should then be allowed to reconsider the record of the case in light of the views expressed by the other members of the board and make such revisions in his decision as he thinks are justified by the record of the case. But, under no circumstances, should the impartial chairman adopt a compromise principle in the interests of unanimity in board action. In an arbitration of this type it is always wise to refuse to compromise any proposal that may be made by the partisan arbitrators.

Now what should be the procedure if the other two arbitrators refuse to sign the award as written by the impartial chairman? An arbitration agreement calling for this type of arbitration should provide that, if the partisan arbitrators cannot agree between themselves, then the decision of the impartial chairman should be final and binding in a given issue. However, most arbitration agreements of this type require that at least a majority of the board must sign the final arbitration award. The danger of such a provision is that some arbitrators serving as chairmen may be inclined to adopt a compromise in the interests of unanimity. However, that objection is not a serious one if the arbitrator fully understands the importance of always preserving arbitration as a judicial process. Such a provision in the contract does have a serious weakness when the three members of the board of arbitration all write different opinions and the representative of the union and the representative of the employer refuse to compromise and agree upon a provision which can be substituted for the decision of the impartial chairman. When such a situation arises, there is but one thing to do, in spite of the fact that it involves delay and expense, and that is to secure a new board of arbitration and start all over again. The best protection against such a possibility is to provide that the decision of the impartial arbitrator in such a situation will be final and binding.

The wage factor is perhaps the most difficult problem to settle by way of arbitration. However, when an arbitrator is asked to fix wages, then he should be guided by the preponderance-of-the-evidence rule applied to the record of the case. There does not exist any fixed scale of wage measurement or any "rule of thumb" set of wage criteria which can be applied automatically by an arbitrator in settling a wage dispute. It is generally recognized that employees are entitled to wages and salaries sufficient to enable them, through the exercise of thrift and reasonable economy, to maintain themselves and families in decency and comfort and to make reasonable provision for old age. Such a wage is generally referred to as a fair and living wage or an "American standard of living" wage.

However, there is no universal agreement among courts and arbitration boards concerning just what criteria should be applied in determining a so-called fair and living wage; in fact, there is such a great difference in evaluating the factors which should enter into the computing of a fair and living wage that research experts working in the field of wage economics seldom agree in their computations.

Nevertheless, there is general agreement that there are certain criteria which should be given weight by any court, arbitration board, agency, or group charged with the task of fixing a just and reasonable wage in a given dispute. They are as follows: (1) the scale of wages paid for similar kinds of work in other industries and by competitors; (2) the relation between wages and cost of living; (3) the hazards of employment; (4) the training and skill required; (5) the responsibility and authority entrusted to the employee; (6) the character and regularity of employment; (7) inequalities of wage rates within the industry; (8) opportunities for advancement within the industry; (9) the financial condition of the employer; and (10) the judgment and findings of other arbitrators, courts, and wage boards who have been called upon within recent periods of time to consider wage disputes in the same industry and in other industries within the same economic area.

When the disputants present a record of evidence and exhibits based upon the above-mentioned wage criteria, then an arbitrator has something definite and certain upon which to base his wage award. . . .

It is to be hoped that every employer and labor leader as well as the rank and file of the unions will recognize the fact that this is no time for the calling of strikes, if strikes can possibly be avoided. Every attempt should be made to settle labor disputes by use of such peaceful methods as collective bargaining, negotiation, mediation, and judicial arbitration.

IS NATION-WIDE BARGAINING AHEAD? [4]

During the First World War the labor unions of this country were chiefly concerned with recognition. At that time the unions were considered the underdogs in our social structure; they needed protection and special privileges as an aid in their efforts to secure recognition and the right to collective bargaining. The public, therefore, looked with favor upon the continuance of the prerogatives which union labor established during the war. The right of collective bargaining has since been guaranteed by the Wagner Act.

It is a far cry from the day when a sympathetic Congress passed the Wagner Act to the day when an angry Congress, alarmed by open defiance of government by a power-drunk labor leader, passed the Smith-Connally bill to curb labor's power. Now that the public has become apprehensive of the power of unionism to enforce its will upon government, it may be well to take stock of some of labor's current objectives and the gains which it hopes to make during the present emergency.

Most significant is labor's demand for a greater degree of active participation in government. In general, our American unions have followed the pattern of British unionism in this respect. Realizing that many of the so-called prerogatives of labor inevitably would be modified under the exigencies of war, the British unions offered to suspend these prerogatives in exchange for an increased class recognition on the councils and administrative boards of government. As a result, they are now represented in the Cabinet and in various administrative agencies which deal with the prosecution of the war.

While American unions have felt the same impulse as British labor, they have not been so successful in achieving their objective. In one instance only have they managed to secure any real governmental authority for their group: on the present

[4] By Almon E. Roth, First President of the San Francisco Employers' Council; Member of the War Labor Board. *Atlantic Monthly.* 172:70-4. August 1943.

National War Labor Board they have been given governmental authority on a tripartite basis with industry and representatives of the public.

Labor has also demanded and has finally secured representation on various committees connected with the War Production Board and the War Manpower Commission. Its function on these joint committees, however, is an advisory one. We may be sure that labor will continue its drive to secure the same degree of authority in relation to manpower, price control, and war production that it now enjoys as a tripartite member of the War Labor Board.

The War Labor Board was established by an executive order founded upon an informal agreement by individual leaders of labor and industry. None of the subscribing parties had any legal authority to bind individual unions or individual employers.

With us the representation of industry on governmental boards is quite different from that which prevails in England. We have no employer agency in this country comparable to the British Confederation of Employers, which can speak officially for organized employers. For instance, we find that many of our unions enjoy such a high degree of autonomy that the authority of international labor leaders to speak for them is questionable. It is therefore not surprising that we have some 250 wild-cat strikes each month in violation of the national no-strike pledge, and that individual employers have challenged the authority of the Board and questioned its representative character.

The greatest threat to the War Labor Board's continuance on a tripartite basis arises from the pressure of union politics upon its spokesmen and from inter-union rivalries.

It should be noted that the recognition and authority now accorded to labor on the War Labor Board extends only to the A.F. of L. and the C.I.O., and that many strong independent unions, including some of the oldest and most stable in this country, are not represented on the Board. Because of the various jurisdictional conflicts in our labor movement we find that, as a practical matter, the government must either hold to this formula or extend representation to such a large number of labor organizations that the War Labor Board and its various sub-sidiaries would become unwieldy. The inevitable result is that a very large segment of organized labor is excluded from parti-cipation in government, to say nothing of the complete exclusion of unorganized workers.

It also should be noted that the C.I.O. and the A.F. of L. organizations nominate their representatives on the War Labor Board.

Thoughtful labor leaders have stated that they consider that participation of labor on the War Labor Board is one of the most significant things that has ever happened in the history of the labor movement. Both the A.F. of L. and the C.I.O. were much upset when the President's stabilization directive gave to Administrator Byrnes the authority to determine a na-tional stabilization policy. The delegation of this authority to Director Byrnes was considered a curtailment of that power which labor had recently gained.

It was, therefore, only natural that when it became necessary to decentralize the functions of the War Labor Board on a regional basis, labor should insist that the tripartite principle of representation, coupled with actual authority to make decisions, be also extended on a regional basis. We thus find that on our Regional Boards we have representatives of the C.I.O. and the A.F. of L., but no representative of other labor organizations or unorganized workers.

The principle of tripartite representation is also applied to the panels which are to hear cases. Some concession has been made to other elements in our labor movement by providing that, where independent unions or unorganized workers are involved in a case, they shall be permitted to nominate the labor representatives on the panels. Inasmuch as the decisions of the panels are merely recommendations, the C.I.O. and A.F. of L. have not surrendered any real prerogative of representation by consenting to this arrangement.

A significant aspect of this new governmental institution (the tripartite War Labor Board) is its independence of the Department of Labor.

The authority of the Secretary of Labor, a Cabinet member, covers conciliation, which is a purely voluntary process, the interpretation of the President's directive on overtime payments, and the administration of such statutes as the Fair Labor Standards Act and the Walsh-Healey Act.

The average citizen probably has no conception of the significance of the departure from our pattern of government which is involved in the establishment of this tripartite War Labor Board. In every other instance of which I can think, the members of a governmental agency, whether it be the courts, the legislature, or administrative departments, are either elected by the public or appointed by their elected representatives. In the case of the War Labor Board, however, the labor representatives and the industry members have been nominated by two special interests—organized labor and industry—and act in their behalf.

I am not saying that this system of class representation is not the most satisfactory method by which to deal with our labor-relations problems. I am merely pointing out its significance as a departure from our fundamental system of government.

This class recognition in governmental matters in all probability will continue after the war. Labor is already looking ahead and talking of the necessity of perpetuating this type of tripartite machinery for the settlement of labor disputes. In any event, we are weaving a new pattern, and its significance should be evaluated.

The second important trend in our collective bargaining is the extension of the collective bargaining unit to an ever broadening base. Some exponents of the need of employer organization on a community-wide basis, in order to balance labor's power in the pressure game of collective bargaining, are becoming alarmed concerning the possible overextension of this principle.

The C.I.O. appears to be committed to the extension of collective bargaining on a national industry-wide basis. As an incident, it hopes to abolish community wage differentials and raise all wages throughout the country to the level of the highest paid in any particular area.

The C.I.O. at its recent convention endorsed the principle of industry-wide bargaining and urged its extension on a national basis. It did not go so far as to suggest that wages be standardized throughout the United States. Since the convention, however, prominent C.I.O. officials have stated frankly that it is the intention of their organization to abolish area and community wage differentials.

The A.F. of L. has not yet officially committed itself to such a program. One of the strongest of our independent groups of unions, the printing unions, has long adhered to a policy of establishing wages on a strictly local basis, with due regard for what the traffic can bear in the light of local conditions.

The implications of this new force in collective bargaining are startling. An examination of our present collective bargaining structure in this country indicates that we have already gone further along the road toward nationalization of collective bargaining, and toward the centralization of power in the hands of a few labor officials, than is generally recognized.

In the steel industry we find that, while the contract provisions have not yet been so fully standardized as they are in coal, we do have the Steel Workers of America, through their national officials, writing the ticket for all the steel workers of the country.

Incidentally, the C.I.O. has been greatly aided and abetted in its program by the National War Labor Board, which has extended the wage structure of the basic steel companies to many concerns which have not been commonly regarded as members of the basic steel industry.

In another vital industry, transportation, we find that we still have a much higher degree of local autonomy so far as both employers and unions are concerned. But here, also, the trend is evident. The tendency is very definitely toward the enlargement of collective bargaining units. We already have one such unit, which comprises the "over road" operators of eleven states.

The establishment of national and area commissions and panels by the War Labor Board will help to promote this movement. The following such commissions have been established:—

A Lumber Commission has been established to hear disputes and approve rates in the Pacific Coast lumber industry. Although it was the original intention that jurisdiction of this commission should be limited to the manufacture of raw-lumber products in the Pacific Northwest, it soon found itself involved in the fixing of rates in the retail lumber yards of Los Angeles, one thousand miles away.

The unions were quick to take advantage of this agency to urge that rates fixed in the retail yards be extended to the industries engaged in the fabrication of lumber products. So much confusion has resulted that the War Labor Board has now restricted the Lumber Commission to the limited jurisdiction originally intended.

A national tripartite commission has been established to deal with disputes and wage increases in the trucking industry. A national panel has been set up for the newspaper publishing industry. A commission administers standard wages and job classifications for the Pacific Coast airframe industry. Now it is suggested that this program be extended on a nation-wide basis.

A Copper Commission was recently appointed to deal with wage problems in the copper industry in the eleven Western states. Although it was distinctly understood that this commission should be limited in its geographical jurisdiction to the Western states, it had hardly been appointed when union representatives urged that it be given national jurisdiction.

There is nothing in these setups which requires national standardization of wages or working conditions. On the contrary, I think that the War Labor Board intends these commissions to have due regard for existing community and area wage differentials. But labor is already endeavoring to use this machinery to advance its program for common termination dates of contracts—this being a first step in the standardization of wages.

What are the far-reaching implications of this trend in our national labor relations? Perhaps the most significant result will be the centralization of tremendous power in the hands of a few national labor leaders, with a corresponding curtailment of local autonomy in collective bargaining.

The coal industry is a striking example of what may lie ahead. John L. Lewis has become so powerful as president of the United Mine Workers that he was able to destroy the National Defense Mediation Board. More recently, he has challenged the authority of the War Labor Board and defied the government of the United States.

Once a union obtains the closed shop on a national basis, the hierarchy of officials in charge of that union possesses the power to determine whether any individual citizen shall have the right to earn a livelihood in that industry in any part of this nation. This is now true in the coal industry; it may soon be true in many other industries.

Under decisions by our Supreme Court, labor unions are exempt from all provisions of our antitrust laws. As a result, they are permitted to exercise monopolies and to carry on malpractices in which no other citizen in this country can engage. It chills the mind to contemplate the combined power over the economic processes of this country which the nationalization of steel, trucking, and mining would place in the hands of a small group of union officials.

Mr. William Leiserson, in a recent article in the *United States News,* has discussed the concentration of power in union government and has pointed out that union conventions seem to be increasingly willing to amend their constitutions to grant unrestricted authority to their officials. One union has provided that its president "shall be vested with unlimited discretion in the application and administration of his powers and duties."

The constitution of another union expressly gives its president the power to "issue such orders or mandates as he may deem necessary or advisable."

The constitution of the American Federation of Musicians provides that its president "may (*a*) enforce the Constitution, By-laws, etc., or (*b*) may annul or set aside same or any portion thereof."

Unfortunately, possession of such concentrated power does not carry with it a corresponding control over the action of the local unions in so far as strikes and slowdowns are concerned. As evidence of this fact, I need only refer to the recent anthracite coal strike over the collection of increased union dues, where it was apparent that John L. Lewis either was powerless to prevent local miners from striking in violation of their contract, or was reluctant to exercise any such authority.

The constant alibi given by national labor leaders for strikes in violation of the national no-strike pledge is that these are wildcat strikes.

Many examples could be given to prove that the delegation of power and authority to central labor organizations does not necessarily result in greater union responsibility. On the contrary, centralization of authority can be used to carry on a widespread program of disruption. It fits readily into the communist pattern of using labor-union machinery to create industrial disorder as a means toward social revolution. We have had a bitter foretaste of this program in the maritime industry of this country and other nations.

When the condition exists that some of our national unions are not only organizing supervisory employees but are actually engaged in the unionization of small employers themselves, the centralization of authority in the hands of union executives should cause the public to sit up and take stock of what lies ahead if this process continues.

Both the rank and file of labor unions and individual employers have a very real stake in the development of a pattern of national collective bargaining. Such a system to a great extent will mean the end of local autonomy in labor relations. The delegation of the power to negotiate and to interpret labor contracts on a national basis to a few topside representatives on each side will place the balance of power in the hands of large locals and large employers. It will constitute a form of regimentation for both unions and employers which will in a large measure disregard local conditions and individual rights.

In a recent case before the National War Labor Board, the Bakery Wagon Drivers Union asked the Board to compel scores of individual employers throughout the New England states to execute a common master contract—despite the fact that heretofore contracts have been negotiated and administered on a community basis. At the hearing in this case the employers made the point that the establishment of collective bargaining on such a large area basis would mean the end of the small operator's independence and the curtailment of his right to negotiate a contract in the light of his individual needs and local conditions.

The coal industry is a striking example of the extent to which such regimentation can be carried, for in this industry the unions have finally succeeded in standardizing both wages and working conditions on a national basis without respect to capacity of the individual operator to pay, location of the mines, efficiency of labor, or any other factor normally receiving consideration in labor relations.

Many nation-wide industries and large utilities are wondering whether they shall standardize wages and working conditions throughout their systems or insist on local negotiations geared to community wages and working conditions.

The extension of high wages paid by concerns in high-wage areas to their plants in low-wage areas will unquestionably have an unstabilizing effect upon the wage structures of the low-wage communities and will be strongly resented by local employers.

If the War Labor Board were to adopt a theory that a company which operates on a national basis can equalize wages at the highest level paid at any of its plants, such a company would have a decided advantage over local concerns in the competition for manpower.

Such standardization of wages takes no account of many competitive factors, such as proximity to raw materials and to markets, and the efficiency of labor or management. Obviously, if wages are standardized, many industries will find it impossible to compete with those that enjoy more favorable conditions. Wage differentials have heretofore made possible the survival of many industries in competition with their more favored competitors. Standardization of wage structures on a national basis will put a premium on the use of laborsaving machinery, with a resulting decrease in the number of workers to be employed.

To those who would ask, What can and should employers do with regard to these trends in collective bargaining? I would offer the following suggestions:—

The trend toward nation-wide bargaining is so significant for the future of American business and our American system of free enterprise that it merits the attention of the best brains that industry can assign to the job. The danger is that labor, through its superior organization and its favored position with the government, will be able to develop this pattern of nation-wide bargaining before American business is fully aware of its significance and its implications.

I would not have you think from anything that I have said that I do not favor industry's bargaining through organization of employers. On the contrary, I think that it is only through employer organization that we can maintain a proper balance in collective bargaining and preserve a reasonable degree of local industrial autonomy. Where I differ from my labor friends is on the size of the unit. From the standpoint of effective employer organization and from the standpoint of competition, the bargaining unit should be limited to a community or area in which the fundamental conditions of operation, such as markets, materials, efficiency of labor, and cost of living, are fairly uniform.

ARBITRATION—AN ANALYSIS [5]

[5] By Willard E. Hotchkiss, Maurice Falk Chair of Social Relations, Carnegie Institute of Technology. Reprinted by permission. *Society for the Advancement of Management Journal.* 4:45-8. March 1939.

Arbitration is a genus of which there are many species, and the species occur in varied settings. Anyone, who has lived in a community in which a street railway, a taxi, or an elevator strike has tied up traffic, naturally thinks of arbitration as a means of escape when crises jeopardize public convenience or safety. When such crises are met through arbitration, opportunity is seldom offered for arbitrators to study thoroughly the background of issues which divide the parties, and the atmosphere of proceedings is likely to be charged with politics. Public officials, even judges, who become arbitrators under such circumstances, find it difficult not to respond to pressures which do not always reflect the merits of the case; and if pressures from the two sides are fairly even, effort is sometimes made to split the difference between their respective claims.

Many difficult issues have been settled, or at least postponed, by this type of arbitration, to the great relief of citizens who suffered from interruption of essential services. However, beyond confirming public assurance that industrial emergencies bring with them a means of escape, permanent benefits from such ad hoc adjustments are limited; they represent the most elementary phase of arbitration.

A more advanced phase is a situation in which employers and employees in an industry or trade recognize in advance the probability of conflicts which they will be unable to resolve and set up proceedings for handling them which include either designation of an arbitrator or board, or stipulation of methods to be followed in setting up impartial machinery. One form of constituting arbitration procedure in advance is embodied in provisions by which the parties each agree to designate one member of a board and delegate to the two persons so chosen, the task of selecting a third member. This procedure has two serious defects. The first lies in the fact that selection of the man who has the deciding vote is left to be performed in the stress of conflict. The second defect is that, although the three persons nominally constitute a board, each of the members designated by the parties usually votes in favor of his own side, with the result that the so-called board breaks down into two advocates and one arbitrator. In most circumstances, better results are secured by having the persons who act as advocates, so designated. Selection of arbitrators in advance is susceptible of infinite variation but seldom occurs except in connection with trade agreements in which the jurisdiction of the arbitrator or board is specifically limited.

Whatever the jurisdiction of impartial machinery, its value depends largely upon the attitude of the parties, the extent to which their representatives can speak for the rank and file, and the circumstances which either help or hinder arbitrators in making thorough inquiry into the issues involved. A major source of usefulness lies in the aid which arbitrators may give the parties in narrowing the area of their disagreements. It is notable that in those industries in which voluntary arbitration has functioned most successfully and over the longest periods of time, the volume of business transacted by arbitrators tends to diminish as procedures mature, and as representatives of the parties become more familiar with their rights and obligations under agreements. On the other hand, when once the arbitration principle finds permanent embodiment in the labor agreements of an industry, trade, or concern, arbitrators participate in many conferences through which the number and magnitude of issues which go to arbitration may be greatly reduced.

Regular contacts which arbitrators who serve continuously have with employers and employees, put them in position to render service which, if wisely performed, tends to check extreme action. Basic conditions, such as wages, hours, and working conditions, are seldom left to the determination of third parties, except by specific mutual consent. However, availability of persons to whom both employers and employees have agreed in advance to refer particular issues is frequently helpful in respect to more basic issues. The same persons who serve as arbitrators with limited jurisdiction under an agreement may become mediators in respect to issues which lie beyond their jurisdiction as arbitrators.

Arbitration has been referred to as constituting a type of industrial judiciary. Careful scrutiny of the actual work performed by arbitration boards, whatever their degree of permanence, reveals that their work is frequently more administrative than judicial. It is not permissible for arbitrators to change the terms of agreements under which they operate, nor to go beyond their scope. However, labor agreements, like statutes, are at many points susceptible of differing interpretations; and when dispute concerning the meaning of particular language in an agreement arises, it is essential to combine wisdom with correct principles of interpretation in resolving the issue. Such a combination may easily lead to one kind of decision at a given time and under given circumstances, and to another kind under different circumstances. In other words, arbitrators look both to the agreements under which they function and to the probable consequences of decisions which they may make. Legalistic interpretations are sadly out of place in labor issues. This point appears sufficiently obvious, but specific examples will clarify it.

Collective bargaining agreements properly aim to safeguard the position of union representatives in the discharge of their duties, but no agreement can cover in specific terms all of the mutual rights and obligations of union representatives and the supervisory personnel of the shops to which they are assigned. Disputes which arise under such provisions raise questions such as these: (1) Has the union representative exceeded his authority and acted in such a way as to destroy the necessary discipline of the shop? (2) Have members of the supervisory personnel been antagonistic and tried to prevent representatives from performing proper union duties?

In a recent decision, discharge of a union representative was upheld substantially on the following grounds: While the subordinate representatives of management may have been unduly officious and regarded proper union activity as an intrusion, responsible officers of the company had never countenanced restraints upon union representatives, and a commendable spirit of cooperation was evidenced by officials, both of the corporation and of the union. The ground for sustaining the discharge in this case was repeated infraction of rules, improper language, and a failure to utilize the initial adjustment processes in handling cases. This particular decision was coupled with notice that discharge of union representatives would be sustained only in clear cases, and a warning that no attempt to embarrass such representatives in the performance of their duties could be tolerated under the agreement.

In contrast to this type of case, one which involves merely review of discipline administered to a regular employee usually hinges on questions of fact which give a basis of judgment, (1) concerning the acts which occasioned the discipline, (2) concerning the appropriateness of the particular discipline. In other words, such cases become much more matters of judgment than of legal interpretation.

A type of case which is of peculiar importance in times of inadequate employment has to do with layoff. It is customary for agreements to contain some sort of seniority provision which guarantees to the employer the right to administer layoff so as to retain properly qualified personnel for doing the work of the plant, and to insure that qualified employees shall be given preference both in layoff and in recall over employees whose seniority is less.

Cases under such provisions often involve question concerning the departments to which seniority rosters apply, and in some cases the meaning of the word "department" as found in a specific agreement. About the only useful function which an arbitrator can perform in this kind of case is to lay down general principles of interpretation as a guide in administering seniority. It would be extremely difficult for a plant to function properly if routine seniority provisions had to be administered by an outsider.

Another type of case links the question of employment to technology. Practically all of the agreements in mass production industries, which have recently become unionized, recognize the right of the employer to make technical improvements. On the other hand, the rights of the workers who may be affected by such improvements are safeguarded to the extent that the adjustments to technical change become subjects of conference and cooperation. In other words, the employer's freedom of action is somewhat tempered by the union's right to conference and the obligation of both parties to cooperate in working out a satisfactory solution of problems.

Although issues of this kind may not be specifically subjects of arbitration, agreements frequently contain provisions under which workers' representatives may bring them to arbitration if they believe that the employer is proceeding more drastically than the agreement contemplated. In disputes that have to do with administrative aspects of agreements, such as layoff and technical changes, an arbitrator sometimes occupies a sort of "no man's land" on the fringes of the agreement, and his usefulness then depends upon the contribution he can make to the tolerance and good temper with which the parties meet the issue.

Use of impartial machinery under collective bargaining agreements has perhaps its most comprehensive embodiment in the railroads. Under federal legislation, culminating in the Railway Labor Act of 1934 which was passed with the approval of railway unions, arbitration in respect to application and interpretation of agreements is in force on all the railroads of the country. The compulsory features of this act do not cover making new agreements. However, parallel with arbitration machinery for settling issues under agreements already in force, the National Mediation Board was created to serve as a channel of communication between the carriers and the railway unions and to assist them in making and changing their agreements. The availability of a disinterested agency which maintains contacts with both sides minimizes the danger of crises in negotiations and aids in meeting these crises when they occur. The National Mediation Board is appointed by the President of the the United States and sits permanently in Washington.

In case the carriers and the unions cannot agree upon a basic issue, and mediation does not succeed in bringing them together, the Railway Labor Act provides that service shall not be interrupted pending full consideration and report on the issues by a special board appointed by the President of the United States. No strike can legally occur in respect to such issues until after the President's board has published its findings. An example of the operation of this provision occurred in respect to the recent demand of the carriers for a 15 per cent reduction in wages. This issue was carried through mediation without the parties being able to agree; whereupon the President appointed a special board to study and report upon the issue. After this board had found that the requested reduction in wages was ill-advised, the carriers withdrew the demand.

The body to which are referred railroad issues that arise under agreements already in force is known as the National Railroad Adjustment Board. Its several divisions, each covering a group of railway services, are made up respectively of an equal number of carrier and labor members. The labor members represent those railway services which are covered by the particular division. The National Railroad Adjustment Board sits continuously in Chicago and hears cases from all of the railroads of the country.

The regular members of the Board, equally representative of carriers and labor, settle as many issues as possible without intervention of an outside person. However, the Railway Labor Act provides that when cases arise which the labor members and the carrier members of a division cannot settle, the National Mediation Board shall appoint an impartial referee to sit as a member of the division and that a majority vote of the Board thus constituted shall decide the issue. Since the Railway Labor Act of 1934 was enacted, hundreds of cases have been disposed of by agreement between the carrier members and the labor members of the several divisions, and other hundreds have been decided by majority vote of the Board with a referee sitting as a member.

Ability of carrier and labor members to agree without the aid of a referee has varied considerably between the several divisions of the Board. The theory of the act is that, although carrier members and labor members are respectively representatives of opposing sides, their detachment from local conditions enables them to view controversies more objectively than is possible for men on the particular property. As was expected, this has resulted in many decisions without the aid of a referee.

Cases decided by referees have served to clarify numerous provisions of railway labor agreements under which they arose. Most of the issues are sharply fought, and decisions are freely criticized and sometimes openly challenged. In exceptional cases, one party or the other may ask for a re-hearing or for clarification of some particular point in a decision, but when decisions are promulgated they are final and conclusive as between the parties, subject only to appeal to the courts.

The Railway Labor Act has been held up as a model for other industries, especially for the maritime industry, the presumption being that the success which it has achieved in forestalling interruption of service on the railways could be carried over to another industry. Such an assumption has merit, but it should be recognized that the Railway Labor Act of 1934 is an evolution from previous laws and is predicated upon a long history of orderly relations under collective bargaining agreements. Arbitration machinery on the railroads is largely a result of self-discipline by the carriers and the workers. As an instrument of adjustment, it is rather an expression of this discipline than a cause of it.

The sharp distinction in the Railway Labor Act between procedures for making agreements on the one hand, and for applying and interpreting them on the other, reflects the strong opposition which until recently labor has shown for compulsory arbitration. The willingness of railway labor to grant compulsory powers to the National Railroad Adjustment Board is predicated upon the definite exclusion from arbitration of basic issues which have to be met when agreements are made or changed.

Although there have been strong advocates of compulsory arbitration in enterprises which are affected with the public interest, unions and, to a large extent, employers have been traditionally opposed to it. There has never been any widespread public sentiment in favor of making arbitration an instrument of general application for fixing wages, hours, and working conditions.

In the years following the World War, when industrial conditions were disturbed and basic industries were interrupted, the idea of limited compulsory arbitration appeared to some persons as a necessary escape from what they considered intolerable conditions. This view was expressed in the industrial commissions appointed by President Wilson in 1919 and in the deliberations of the United States Coal Commissions in 1923. However, even the most conservative opinion recognizes the right to strike which to a man without property is fundamental. Abridgment of that right, except by the voluntary act of the worker himself, results in forced labor. Moreover, when once a strike has been made illegal, the joining of two or more persons to promote a strike becomes conspiracy—in other words a crime. Such a situation would be obviously incompatible with free institutions, however unfortunately the right to strike may at times be exercised. In these circumstances, provision for compulsory procedures, for impartial study and for complete publicity concerning issues involved in industrial conflicts is about as far as compulsory adjustment machinery can safely go.

Voluntary arbitration, on the other hand, is eminently a democratic process which, under one form or another, has for many years been utilized in several industries, but it has not in any sense become standard practice under collective bargaining agreements. In competent hands it serves as an effective supplement to day-to-day relationships under such agreements and performs a highly constructive function.

INDUSTRIAL LAW UNDER THE NEW CONSTITUTIONALISM [6]

In 1930 union membership was approximately three million in the United States. Today it is eleven million. One out of

[6] From article by Edward F. Albertsworth, Northwestern University Law School. *American Bar Association Journal.* 28:106-12. February 1942.

every five persons gainfully employed is a member of some kind of a labor union. These are about evenly divided between the American Federation of Labor and the Committee for Industrial Organization, with a million in independent or non-affiliated unions. The last great stalwarts of industry—the Ford Motor Company and the United States Steel Corporation—have now become unionized.

Assuming union dues to average $2 weekly, plus initiation fees and special assessments, collections from eleven million persons would be approximately between one and two billion dollars annually. What happens to these funds thus collected? Enlightened union leadership has here a problem of labor statesmanship, and unless business-like methods of accounting for these vast sums are practiced, regulatory governmental controls will result. I think they are certain to result, inasmuch as there are but few unions who do present to their membership regular and reliable stewardship of the moneys collected. There are today in the United States as a general rule no laws compelling accounting by union officials of the sums collected from their membership nor their expenditure. Banks, insurance companies, and even political parties must publish their incomes and expenditures, but not labor unions. The British law so requires, and goes further in providing that consent of the union dues payer to expenditure of his dues for political purposes must be obtained. With the great growth of unionism during the past decade in the United States, the question arises, Is there legal responsibility commensurate with this growth?

The victories of organized labor in legislation and judicial decisions should also, in my judgment, increase its responsibilities, and if these are not voluntarily executed will lead to increasing governmental control. Growth of great economic power in the United States has been one factor in the equally great growth of the Corporate State because of popular demand for regulatory devices. This will be equally true of the increasing might of labor unionism. During the past year, the Supreme Court has held that no criminal indictment under the Sherman Act will lie against a labor union or a collection of laborers. Last year the Court held that no treble damages in tort would lie under the Sherman Act against unionists or workers in the so-called Apex Case. Again last year, it held that the United States Government was not a juristic person within the meaning of the treble damages provision of the Sherman Act. Again, the Court held that no injunction will lie against workers in the Federal courts even though the Sherman Act was violated and acts of violence were perpetrated by them, provided only that the dispute was one in the same industry, trade, craft or occupation with that of the complainant employer or in which the men had a direct or indirect interest.

Under the National Labor Relations Act the organized workers won other victories in the Supreme Court. In the Phelps Dodge Case the Court determined that in hiring workers, the employer must not discriminate against them on the basis of union affiliation, so that if they had been [discriminated against because of union affiliation] the offending employer must offer to them employment with pay retroactive to the time of the commission of the "unfair labor practice." The Court also held in the Heinz Case that once collective bargaining has resulted in an agreement, the employer can be forced to put the agreement into written form. Finally, in Olson v. Nebraska, the Court held that the state power was ample to regulate the maximum fees of employment agencies, and practically overturned all prior legal learning on the subject.

Apparently the only set-back for organized labor during the past year is the decision by the Court in the Meadowmoor Dairies Case. There the holding was that if the litigation arises in the state courts, injunction under state law may issue against violence and other unlawful acts of all the strike participants because of the unlawful acts of a few members of the union under the doctrine of "respondeat superior." The other decision coming up from the state courts was favorable to the workers, in the Swing Case. There the Court held that neither peaceful picketing nor peaceful persuasion could be enjoined by the employer even though no employer-employee relationship existed between them. The Court predicated its holding strongly upon the social interest in free speech, as it had done the year previously in the Senn Case.

A crumb of comfort was given the employers in the Republic Steel Case during the year when the Court held that the employer guilty of an unfair labor practice under the Wagner Act need not reimburse the W.P.A. for maintenance of men on strike by that governmental agency.

Today in the United States, as a result of these numerous victories in the Court by organized labor, there is left to the employer as a protective device against unlawful acts of workers only the general tort law of the several states and the criminal law. The first remedy may be illusory in that the workers are financially irresponsible; and the second results in no reparation for losses sustained by him.

The present setting of great power in organized labor in the United States is a reproduction of similar development in Great Britain a generation ago. After the Parliament in 1825 repealed the Combination Laws, the nineteenth century witnessed a gradual but persistent increase in the strength of labor unionism facilitated by various Parliamentary enactments. In 1871 the workers were expressly held immune from restraint of trade statutes, and in 1875 Parliament immunized them from criminal conspiracy doctrines. In 1906 unions were removed by statute from all tort liability, and also individual members if engaged in the "furtherance of a trades dispute." The theory in England was that trade union dues and other funds collected from union members were held in trust for the purposes of legitimate unionism, and should not therefore be attachable by way of judgment in tort. By 1926 the strength of organized labor in England was so great that a general strike was called by it to intimidate the government itself, to compel it to effectuate the objectives of trade unionists in disputes with employers in the coal mines. The British public then awoke to the great powers that had been granted to unions, and in the next year Parliament withdrew some of them by making illegal any strike if it had any object other than or in addition to the furtherance of a trades dispute within the trade or industry in which the strikers and employers were engaged, and was designed or calculated to coerce the Government either directly or by inflicting hardship upon the community. In similar terms, strikes of a sympathetic character outside of a certain industry were illegal. Thus in England, after a long period of trade union growth through statutory and judicial encouragement, a set-back occurred in juristic treatment of the activities of unionists. In other words, excessive powers conferred upon and acts perpetrated by unionists brought governmental regulation.

Legislation in the United States has often followed the pattern in Great Britain in social and economic fields. Will this be the case also with respect to the future of organized labor despite its present apparent great powers?

It may be said by some that organized labor has nothing to fear from the increasing might of the Corporate State in the United States in that the Thirteenth Amendment is its great Magna Charta, particularly with respect to the simultaneous cessation of labor or strikes. However, I invite attention to the wording of that amendment, namely: "Neither slavery nor involuntary servitude, *except as punishment for a crime,* shall exist anywhere in the United States." The power is expressly given to define a crime and to punish for its commission. The state, then, has authority under the Constitution to make the withholding of labor a criminal act. This is true even in periods of so-called normalcy; it is all the more true in times of crisis or emergency. In public service callings, and in service for the government—such as that rendered by postal employees, firemen, and police—legal opinion and precedent in the United States support the view that strikes may be by law prohibited without infringement of the provisions of the Constitution. In times of war, or preparation for war, I have no doubt that statutes of Congress preventing strikes entirely would be constitutionally valid.

By virtue of recent Supreme Court decisions, there are now in existence in the Federal Government various potential regulatory devices of organized labor in practically all phases of its activities. With the decisions of the Court under the Wagner Act, the sphere of federal cognizance was greatly enlarged in the field of labor disputes. While no new constitutional doctrines were there created, the existing formula of "obstructions upon interstate commerce" was given new application in labor disputes by large numbers of workers in interstate businesses. The Darby Lumber Company Case has emphasized this trend by applying it to the *individual* worker in such businesses so far as wage claims are concerned. The Appalachian Electric Power Company Case this year extended the federal power still further acting under "admiralty and maritime" authority. The Electric Bond & Share Company Case in the previous year, sustaining the registration phases of the Public Utility Holding Company Act, likewise drew to the Federal Government power over various phases of corporate activity and control. As a condition of user of interstate commerce and the mails, broad powers are now judicially declared to reside in the Federal Government over an increasing number of aspects of industrial and business life. The stage, then, is set for adequate federal control over unions and their activities, and the decisions which were victories at the time for organized workers have implicit in them numerous potentially restrictive techniques. Supervision of elections in labor unions, disclosure of officers' names and accounting of funds of members paying dues and other assessments, regulation of strikes in certain types of industries—all these may now constitutionally be required by the Federal Government.

Inasmuch as today organized labor in the United States has become all powerful "within the law," will there come into juristic science a legal formula by which justification for regulation of unions in numerous of their phases can be found? Labor unions "affected with a public interest" would seem to be the formula. Great powers conferred by law, or which have been gained in fact, carry with them commensurate responsibilities to the labor membership and the public. The American public is already familiar with the fact that labor unions in certain trades and industries are virtual "bottlenecks" where either obstruction or furtherance of trade is made possible. And this formula has been applied often and effectively in American industrial life to situations other than labor relations. The State of Kansas in 1920 attained national recognition when its legislature sought to "affect with a public interest" certain types of *business* not theretofore regarded as "public businesses. But the United States Supreme Court in review of the legislation gradually made the Kansas Industrial "Court" Act a dead letter. However, the formula "affected with a public interest" is a flexible one and has, since the decisions in the Kansas cases, been amplified to various new situations. With a new majority personnel upon the Supreme Court of the United States, there is sound justification for the belief that, as the American public may become convinced of regulation of unions of workers both in its interest and that of the union membership, the Court will sustain the reasonable statutory regulations of labor unionism now impending.

MAINTAINING INDUSTRIAL PEACE [7]

Strikes are costly: *To workers*, in loss of wages. In 1936, 776,081 workers were involved in 2,089 strikes which resulted in 13,763,206 man-days of idleness during that year. Wage losses due to strikes in 1936 must therefore be measured in tens of millions of dollars.

To workers, in terms of special assessments and contributions to strike funds.

To industry, in terms of orders that have been delayed or lost entirely. A. P. Sloan, president of General Motors, estimated the loss to the national income from the General Motors strike in the hundreds of millions.

To capital, in expenditures for espionage, strike breakers, tear gas, etc. The gross income of the Pinkerton Detective Agency from "industrial service" was $900,000 in 1934, $1,-000,000 in 1935, and $440,000 during the first seven months of 1936. Pinkerton's is only one of approximately 200 detective agencies which have specialized in industrial service of this type. One Pittsburgh contracting company spent $289,452 in 1931 and 1932 for such services in order to avoid payment of a union wage scale which would have cost $51,849 on that particular project.

To local merchants, who suffer from loss of income by a large proportion of their customers. As an example of what this can mean in a particular city, the weekly wage loss in Saginaw, Michigan, during the recent General Motors strike amounted to approximately $250,000.

[7] By Lyman S. Moore, Assistant Director, Institute for Training in Municipal Administration; Author of *The Merit System in Illinois. Public Management*. 19: 103-7. April 1937.

To local government, in loss of time of municipal officials and police departments. The time of mayors, managers, councilmen, and other officials is often completely monopolized at the expense of regular city business, while special police can be detailed only by causing other police activities to suffer.

To local government, for tear and nauseating gas and other equipment which have been purchased to handle strikes and violence. During the first nine months of 1936, local governments spent at least $50,000 for gas and gas equipment alone. It is reported that the sheriff of Lake County, Illinois, spent at least $3,000 for the gas used in one attack on strikers in the Fansteel strike at Waukegan, Illinois.

To governments, in loss of public revenues. The state of Michigan is reported to have estimated its loss in sales tax revenues during the first two months of 1937 at $500,000 as a direct result of the widespread strikes in that state.

To the entire community, when the result of a strike is the permanent discontinuance of an industry. Two such cases have already occurred, in Joliet, Illinois, and Wilmington, Delaware. Such results may spring from an arbitrary attitude on the part of either labor or capital, or both. In such cases the costs in terms of unproductive capital and the readjustment of idle labor are difficult to determine but are certainly high.

Of even more importance than the money cost of strikes is the cost to the nation as a whole as a result of lowered morale, the bitter feeling which results from violence, and strained relations between capital and labor as partners in industrial enterprise. This leads to the statement of a proposition with which few can disagree: namely, that government in the United States has the responsibility for so determining the conditions of a labor dispute that violence and strikes are unnecessary factors in the negotiations. Government must take the lead in discovering alternative, less costly, and more peaceful methods of discussion between capital and labor as they negotiate their fair shares of industrial income.

What role should local government play in the exercise of this responsibility? The part that a city manager can play in the peaceful settlement of a labor dispute is demonstrated in the article by Henry Traxler in this issue of *Public Manage-*

ment. But the chief administrator of a city is not always so fortunate in his relationships with capital, labor, and the community at large; and the part that he personally can play in settling disputes must necessarily be limited by the size and nature of the community and by his own status in the community. It is probable that only in smaller cities where industries are few and where the chief administrator has the complete confidence of all community groups can the city rely on the city manager's or mayor's own acts to achieve peaceful settlement of such disputes.

At least two of the larger cities in the country, Philadelphia and Toledo, have recognized the desirability of providing a local labor relations board to which capital and labor can turn for conciliatory service in negotiating a dispute. Mayor La Guardia has just announced the appointment of a similar board in New York City. A brief description of the nature and activities of the Toledo Peace Board may be of value to other cities considering a similar agency.

The Toledo Peace Board was initiated in the summer of 1935 at the suggestion of Edward F. McGrady, assistant secretary of the United States Department of Labor. The membership consisted of 18 citizens, 5 nominated by the central labor union, 5 named by the local chamber of commerce, and 8 selected at large by Mr. McGrady. The representatives at large included two judges, two attorneys, a Catholic monsignor, a Jewish rabbi, a merchant, and the county relief director.

During the first eight months of its existence, the Board was entirely a voluntary agency and had no relation to the municipal government. On March 30, 1936, however, the city of Toledo assumed responsibility for the financing of the Board under an ordinance which permitted the mayor to fill any vacancies. Members of the Board serve without compensation, but a full-time director is employed. The Board was authorized to expend not more than $5,625 during the last nine months of 1936.

The principles governing the action of the Toledo Peace Board as suggested by Mr. McGrady are as follows: "(1) Members of the Board should never vote on the question of an issue being right or wrong but should strive to find that which is fair and suggest it to the parties in dispute; they may accept or reject. (2) Members cannot and should not order anyone to do anything. The mere fact that a union or employer can lose nothing through dealing with the Board will make for greater confidence in and cooperation with the Board. (3) Services of the Board are always conciliatory, and arbitration never should be undertaken by any member or the director, even though both parties may agree to it. Even if the Board should arbitrate fairly at all times, confidence in it would be lost in some quarters. (4) The Board cannot promote organization of employees, nor can it interfere with such organization activities. During its brief history, then, the Board has served merely as a conciliatory agency and has been the means of bringing about peaceful negotiation through the efforts of its director and its members. In July, 1936, it was reported that "since the Peace Board became effective no labor situation has developed to anything like the extent of ugliness which characterized its earlier labor troubles in the Toledo area. Only one difficulty has developed into a strike of any stubbornness. In that case, while both parties were somewhat reluctant at first to throw their cards on the table before Peace Board representatives, those representatives had a major part in the settlement."

It appears that the Toledo Peace Board has secured prestige and position for itself in the community as far as the public, newspapers, labor, and management are concerned. In no case has it attempted to coerce either party to a dispute, but its position is such that when it publicizes its willingness to serve as negotiator this constitutes legitimate pressure on the parties because of public feeling on the question.

There are certain basic questions which must be answered by any city which wishes to set up a similar conciliation agency. Some of these questions can be answered on the basis of Toledo's experience and some will have to be decided anew.

Representation. The method of appointing board members must be chosen with care. Representatives of capital and labor should be selected by local organizations which best represent the two groups—chambers of commerce, central labor unions, etc. Even if public officials were completely objective in these appointments, to deny each group the opportunity to name its own representatives would permit them to challenge the representativeness of the appointments and might jeopardize the whole experiment.

It goes without saying that labor and capital should be represented equally on the board. From the viewpoint of labor, this may create some difficulty in a community where the conflict between C.I.O. and A.F. of L. labor groups is acute. It should be recognized that the national conflict between these two organizations is not always carried down to the local communities. Where the two organizations exist side by side in bitter struggle, however, some answer will have to be found to the problem of giving both groups a hearing and at the same time giving labor no more than an equal voice with capital on the board. On the basis of Toledo's experience, it is probably desirable to give representatives of the public a more numerous voice than either labor or capital, but not as great a voice as both combined. For example, on a board of seven this might mean two representatives of capital, two of labor, and three of the public.

Appointment of public representatives on the board should be made by some public official. The choice probably narrows down to the chief administrative officer or the legislative body. Inasmuch as the board is dealing primarily with questions of public policy the council may properly be given final authority over the appointments. The chief administrator, however, will have frequent contacts with the board and may, therefore, be authorized to make the initial appointments. This suggests that the mayor in mayor-council cities or the manager in council-manager cities might nominate a list from whom the council would appoint, or might appoint with confirmation by the council. In council-manager cities, the mayor might be considered as the initial appointing authority. Toledo was unusually successful in securing public representatives who demonstrated their capacity for impartial and objective consideration of questions brought before them. The appointing authority who is responsible for selecting these impartial representatives of that broad group called "the public" will have to exercise this responsibility with the utmost caution. Obviously, impartiality cannot be secured simply by requiring it in the ordinance or other provision setting up the board.

2. *Finance.* Even though the members of the board are not compensated for their services, there will be certain necessary expenses. In any community which is undergoing a series of labor disputes, a full-time director or secretary will probably be found necessary. The Toledo experience indicates that the activities of the director in making direct contacts with parties of the dispute were invaluable in persuading these parties to bring questions before the board. The principle of public responsibility for all expenses incurred is a valid one to follow and it would be unwise to secure contributions from any private groups in the community because of unwanted obligations that this might entail.

3. *Rules of Procedure.* These should apply to the acts of the board as a whole and of the individual members. Here the principles suggested by Mr. McGrady for the Toledo Board may serve as a guide, as they seem to have been successful in Toledo in insuring confidence in the activities of the Board. The fact that neither party to a dispute had anything to lose by asking the good offices of the Board appears to have been significant in Toledo.

It will have to be decided whether the board should act as a whole or by panels appointed for each dispute. The first chairman of the National Labor Relations Board discovered that success was often achieved by appointing a panel of two, one representing capital and the other labor (but neither having any personal connection with the case) to investigate and advise on particular disputes. "When you bring together an experienced labor leader and a fair-minded industrialist and say to them, 'Here is a controversy; work it out together,' you have given them a challenge and a responsibility which they will do their level best to meet. They realize that it is up to them; there is no neutral or public representative present before whom they might be tempted to serve merely as advocates for the respective disputants. The job is theirs, and theirs alone. And so they sit down and hear both sides and thresh the matter out between themselves. Experience has shown that they will nearly always agree that one side is wrong and that it should recede from its position, or that there is a measure of right on both sides, in which event they will agree upon some reasonable middle ground for disposing of the issue. The parties themselves will be prone to accept the recommendations, because the employer will be greatly influenced by the view of his fellow-employer on the committee, and the union will be greatly influenced by the views of the labor member of the committee." The psychology of this method of conciliation may operate to minimize the controversy and emphasize the conciliatory aspects of the problem. The two-man panel has been used with success by the Mayor's Labor Board in Philadelphia.

The panel method is desirable because it gets the working group down to an effective size. However, the panel might properly be required to report frequently to the full board during the negotiations, because the more people who are informed on the real issues, the better.

4. *Jurisdiction.* Here is involved the vital problem of the relationship of a local labor relations board with agencies established by state and national government to deal with similar problems. It is rather obvious that a local labor relations board should not be asked or expected to deal with a labor dispute which is national in scope. No local labor relations board could have been successful in dealing with the General Motors strike, which had to be handled by negotiation between an industry with plants in many states and a nation-wide labor organization. It required both national and state authorities to deal with these conflicting interests, and any local labor relations board should be expected to deal only with labor disputes which are local in nature.

The jurisdiction of the board may properly be limited in another direction. The board should not be expected to consider individual grievances of a petty nature, unless these affect the labor relations and personnel policy of the entire plant. Industrial management should be held responsible for establishing a constructive personnel policy and orderly machinery for handling such grievances, and unions should forego the use of the strike or other coercion to compel the settlement of individual cases one way or the other. Only where the frequency of grievances indicates the lack of effective machinery within the plant, should such cases be considered of sufficient importance to come to the attention of the board.

It is probable also that at this stage in their development, local labor relations boards should not be authorized to exercise coercive authority in any labor situation. Governments in this country are just feeling their way as far as arbitration and conciliation are concerned. The Wagner Act, which establishes a national labor relations board with full authority to investigate any labor dispute, to make certain findings with respect to the facts of the dispute, and to issue orders to either or both parties leading to collective bargaining on the issues involved, was held valid by the Supreme Court on April 12. Bills have been introduced into several state legislatures which provide for miniature labor relations boards patterned after the national board, and a "baby Wagner Act" has just been passed in Wisconsin. It should therefore be recognized that governmental machinery in the field of labor relations is still in a trial and error stage.

Until some stability has been achieved on national and state lines, local communities must proceed slowly in vesting extensive authority in local boards. However, limited experience indicates that local boards whose authority is purely conciliatory can be of exceptional value in supplementing state and national activities and in dealing with local disputes which cannot compete in importance with larger scale disputes which must necessarily take first place as far as national and state authorities are concerned. Also, as labor dispute machinery develops, some communities may wish to experiment with voluntary arbitration, which the Toledo board has refused to undertake.

No matter whether city manager, mayor, or peace board undertakes the arduous task of conciliator, the central problem is one of diplomacy, tact, and enduring patience. Varying degrees of reasonableness in either or both parties will make each dispute peculiar in itself. In some cases when all facts are made known to both parties in an impartial hearing the dispute will dissolve.

"Sweet reasonableness" in labor disputes may be a mirage which cannot be hoped for. However, public administration, like scientific management in private industry, has always set its goal as finding "the one best way." Public administrators may legitimately persuade parties to labor disputes that intelligent decisions based on the known facts will produce better results for both sides than bird-shot settlements compelled by violence and grounded on partial ignorance of the situation.

WANTED: A NATIONAL LABOR POLICY FOR INDUSTRY AND LABOR [8]

Few problems which confront the country after the war will be more important than the development of good relations between business and trade unions. At present trade-union membership is about twelve million, or well over one third of all non-supervisory employees outside of agriculture. No one knows whether after the war unions will make large additional gains, as they did in the first year and a half after November, 1918, or whether the demobilization of war industries will cause a large drop in membership. One thing, however, is certain— the union movement will be larger and more powerful than it was before the war. Furthermore, over the course of years trade unions will gain in numbers and strength.

During the nineteenth century large and powerful trade-union movements developed in Europe. These movements recognized little or no stake in existing economic institutions; in fact, most European labor movements were more interested in overthrowing existing economic institutions than in making them work better. We cannot afford in the United States to have a labor movement which is devoted to overthrowing our institutions rather than to improving their operation. Hence, twentieth century America has the problem of developing the labor movement into an integral part of the industrial community—

[8] From article by Sumner H. Slichter, Lamont University Professor of Economics at Harvard University. *Public Opinion Quarterly.* 8, no. 3:407-15. Fall 1944.

a movement sharing with business management the responsibility for the general level of employment and size of the nation's payrolls.

To the problem of the relationship of trade unions to industry there are three principal approaches. One is what I have called the "arm's-length" policy—the policy of keeping unions at a distance and having as little as possible to do with them. Perhaps the most prevalent policy in industry today, it is quite understandable. The employer who used to fight unions and who now recognizes that such a course is futile, is likely, as the next step, to have as little to do with them as possible. I do not believe that the "arm's-length" policy will long remain the most prevalent one in industry, for it is really based upon the tacit assumption that the economy is self-adjusting and that the total volume of employment can be left to take care of itself. That this assumption is not true is now fairly plain. Under twentieth century conditions, the volume of employment depends upon the nature of business and governmental policies. A high and stable level of employment will not just happen. It must be created by human thought and ingenuity. A large and powerful labor movement cannot escape responsibility for the kind of policies which are selected and, therefore, for the level of employment. If that is correct and if the nature of the policies will depend in large measure upon the information which organized labor has about the problems of business and upon the attitudes of leaders of unions toward these problems, business management cannot afford to maintain an "arm's-length" policy toward unions

A second approach may be called the "legalistic" one. Many people seem to think that most of the problems of union-community and union-business relationships can be handled by laws regulating labor organizations and their activities. Few persons, even within the ranks of labor, would deny that organizations as large and powerful as trade unions are affected with a public interest. Consequently, they are bound sooner or later to be regulated in certain respects.

1. Unions are likely to be forbidden to exclude persons because of race, color, or creed. Several states have taken this step.

2. To an increasing extent the right of unions to expel members or to fine or suspend members is likely to be made subject to review.

3. Just as corporations are steadily being required to give more complete reports to their stockholders, so unions will be required to give more information to their members.

4. The terms of trade agreements may in some respects be subjected to public scrutiny, and the right of employers and labor organizations to impose restrictions on progress may be limited.

5. Both employers and unions may have imposed on them greater obligations to endeavor to avert lockouts or strikes. For example, the legality of certain types of strike activities, such as picketing, may depend upon whether the union has in good faith accepted mediation and made an honest effort to avert a rupture. Similar obligations may be imposed upon employers.

6. Support of certain types of strikes, such as strikes to compel an employer to violate the Wagner Act by dealing with minority groups, may be prohibited.

Regulations of the sort that I have indicated will tend to strengthen trade unions and help them to gain members. They will not, however, reach to the heart of the problem of developing a satisfactory relationship between unions and the community or between unions and business. It is unnecessary to tell a group of business men that legislation cannot give men knowledge of industry or wisdom in analyzing economic and business facts. It cannot give them foresight or breadth of view. The responsibility for developing a satisfactory relationship between unions and the community and between unions and business must rest in the main upon the leaders of business and the leaders of labor themselves. This I call the "administrative" approach.

The foundation for a satisfactory relationship between unions and industry must be made in tens of thousands of plants throughout the country. It must be based upon an interest on the part of employers in the problems of unions and on the part of unions in the problems of employers. This is important for two reasons: (1) it enables each side to avoid policies which aggravate the problems of the other side; and (2) it gives both sides a clear understanding of the problems which they have in common.

Few business men, I venture to suggest, have taken much trouble to acquaint themselves with the problems of the unions in their plants and with the effect of managerial policies upon those problems. A plant with a force of a thousand men does not simply have a thousand individuals. A thousand men constitute a little society. This little society contains a wide variety of people who are usually grouped into small clusters with leaders for each group. These little societies are being played upon constantly by a wide variety of influences—just as is the larger community in which we live. Some of these plant societies are orderly and well adjusted; others are chaotic and full of maladjustments. The policies of management are bound to be an important influence in the lives of these societies. Sometimes managerial policy produces adjustment and order; sometimes it produces maladjustment and chaos. A common situation is for an articulate radical fringe to demand that their leaders "deliver" the impossible. The leaders may be struggling to build up among their constituents a common sense view of what working conditions or wages are within reason and what are beyond the safe limits for the company to pay. The management which pursues an "arm's-length" policy plays into the hands of the radical minority. The "arm's-length" policy tends not only to keep the workers ignorant of facts about the business but to diminish the prestige of the union leaders.

One of the greatest difficulties of unions is to get their best people to serve as shop stewards. Unions do, of course, succeed in inducing a considerable proportion of able workers to become shop stewards. Nevertheless, the job of shop steward is a thankless one. A good shop steward has the responsibility of telling some workers that their grievances do not represent valid claims. He is bound to fail to win cases which the workers think that he ought to win. Sometimes the men may wonder whether he tries as hard as he should have tried. Management has many opportunities to reduce the unpleasant aspects of the job of shop steward and, thus, to affect the kind of men who are willing to take the job.

Not only have most employers given little attention to the problems of the unions with which they deal, but they have made little effort to inform the union leaders concerning the problems of their enterprise—the efforts of the management to win larger markets by reducing prices and improving products, the production problems which management faces. The biggest single mistake in industrial relations, in my judgment, is failure of management to tell the men what it is doing and why. Managers do not always realize how their prestige may suffer when they withhold information. A short time ago there came to my attention a small strike in a shipbuilding company. It occurred over a cause which was not too important in itself. The real condition which made the strike possible was the low morale of the men which, in turn, was the result of their belief that their bosses were no good and that there was not much use in trying to make a good production record for such poor bosses. Twice, after installing the radio equipment on a vessel, the men were told to tear it out and put it back in a different way. The men thought that their bosses could not read specifications and blueprints. One of them said, "It would drive you crazy the way we work. We can have no confidence in our foremen." The real reason why the work was twice torn out was that Washington had changed the plans—probably with good reason. The management, however, did not bother to explain to the men the reasons behind its orders to tear out the work. One of the supervisors, when asked whether management had give the men an explanation, replied: "No, why should we?"

Let me give you a different kind of example—a small manufacturer in the Middle West who several years ago was confronted with the demand by a union that he consent to a system of shop stewards. The manager agreed on one condition—namely, that the shop stewards agree to meet with management once a month. The manager said very sensibly that he did not wish shop stewards attempting to represent the men unless the stewards were well informed concerning the operations of his business, its competition, and its problems. At these monthly meetings the prospects of the business are discussed and information is given to the shop stewards on questions which they raise.

The shop stewards are kept abreast of the efforts of the enterprise to get its product into new markets. Just before the new line each year is displayed to the trade, it is shown to the shop stewards and other union officers. The changes in the product are pointed out and the reasons for the changes are given. At these monthly meetings the union representatives may raise almost any questions. On one occasion they asked why the company did not charge more for its product, an inquiry which gave an opportunity for a well-rounded discussion of costs and competition. On another occasion the stewards asked why the company part of the time bought first-grade lumber and part of the time second-grade lumber. The policy was explained. On still another occasion they asked why the company did not do its own trucking instead of hiring a contract trucker. There followed a comparison of trucking costs under the two methods.

No one should expect that the interest of unions in the problems of employers or of employers in the problems of unions will eliminate all conflicting interests. Just as purchasing agents and salesmen will always argue over prices of materials, so unions and employers will always differ over the price of labor. The extent of the common interest of employers and unions, however, is much broader than appears on the surface. Hence, the mutual exploration of each other's problems is almost certain to broaden the area that each side recognizes as one of common interest with the other side.

HOW TO SELECT AN ARBITRATOR [9]

The one thing you're sure to encounter when dealing with human relations is a lot of human nature. Labor disputes seem to carry an especially heavy burden of heat and emotion. This makes the process of voluntary arbitration particularly valuable in the labor field, both now and in the future when war controls are lessened or abrogated.

But voluntary arbitration has its problems, too, and selecting the impartial arbitrator is the crux of the most important phase of it.

[9] By Paul Fitzpatrick. *Arbitration Magazine.* 2:5-11. September 1944.

When management and labor agree to enter into voluntary arbitration, they invoke, as a fundamental right, the process of selecting, by mutual choice, the arbitrator who is to hear and decide their differences.

What provision, then, should parties make, in their collective bargaining agreement or in their submission to arbitration, in order to insure the services of an impartial, unbiased arbitrator in whose qualifications they will have justifiable confidence?

First, the parties to an agreement should decide upon the number of arbitrators desired to determine the issues between them—whether it shall be a single arbitrator, or a board of three, or five, or more.

Then, there are numerous ways in which provision is made for the appointment of an impartial arbitrator. Under those most commonly used, the parties may—

1. Agree upon a single arbitrator, and name him (and perhaps an alternate) in the contract;

2. Provide for naming a single arbitrator, by mutual agreement, when and if disputes or grievances arise;

3. Leave to an outside agency, or to an individual, the naming of the impartial arbitrator;

4. Provide that each party will name one arbitrator (or more), and leave selection of the impartial arbitrator to the agreement of the two so chosen, or to the mutual choice of the parties;

5. Agree upon a board composed of an equal number of arbitrators appointed by each party;

6. Agree to have a single impartial arbitrator, appointed under the rules of such an agency as the American Arbitration Association.

None of these methods is fool-proof; none perfect. Some are risky or dangerous or unwise. Others have proved by experience and trial-and-error tests that they are as nearly sure-fire as they can be made. It might be well to examine them briefly.

1. The naming of the single arbitrator in the agreement is the simplest form of selection and, except for the usual vicissitudes of death, illness, or inability to serve at a given time and place, is not infrequently satisfactory. But there is also the risk

that hindsight may prove better than foresight, and the parties may find they have made a bad bargain if the contract has a long period to run, for the named individual's viewpoint, or philosophy, or self-interest, or position, may change during the time his services are under contract.

It is also possible that the permanent arbitrator may become by gradual degrees an auxiliary arm of management authority without corresponding responsibility. There is sometimes developed a tendency for employees to run to him for settlements that should, if possible, be reached direct with the supervisory and administrative staffs of management.

2. Under this arrangement the parties "agree to agree" upon an arbitrator when and if a dispute arises. This method assumes the permanent continuance of the parties' ability to agree, which was manifest when they entered into their contract. If that should turn out in fact to be the case, there should not be too great difficulty in reaching agreement upon an arbitrator. Labor-management relations often improve under a collective bargaining agreement. But should there be unsettled grievances, they can also worsen rapidly, and to a point where neither party will accept the suggestion of the other. The rendering of an agreement into writing is a tacit admission of the possibility of dispute. The inclusion of grievance machinery, with arbitration as a "terminal point," is a frank acknowledgment of that possibility. Dispute over one subject has never yet predisposed parties to agreement over another. So it is the better part of wisdom that provision should be made against a deadlock in the choice of arbitrator in the event inability to agree occurs when the dispute emerges.

3. If the parties want to take the easy course, and leave to an outside individual or a Federal or state agency the selection of the arbitrator, it is a simple matter to name an individual of known integrity—a judge, a clergyman or a citizen of standing in the community—who is given power to appoint the impartial arbitrator if, as, and when a dispute arises. In this form of selection it is to be noted that not alone do the ordinary vicissitudes apply to the appointing individual, but in the event selection is made according to plan, the arbitrator may easily be

entirely unknown, or quite unsatisfactory, to one or both of the parties; he may be selected from a limited group of acquaintances, none of whom possesses all the qualities necessary to the labor arbitrator. He may have had no experience with job analyses, wage stabilization schedules, or the myriad complications with which the labor arbitrator is confronted today.

In one case under this type of clause, power to name the arbitrator was vested in the president of an organization. When the arbitrator was needed, the president had entered military service and the organization was temporarily without a president. One of the parties refused to delegate authority to another officer of the organization, arbitration was frustrated, the grievances multiplied, and a strike ensued.

In another case, the individual named demurred at being drawn into the controversy between the parties and refused to name the arbitrator. There was considerable delay before the parties reached an agreement to select the arbitrator under the procedure of the American Arbitration Association.

If power to appoint the impartial arbitrator is delegated to an outside governmental or state agency, such as the War Labor Board, United States Conciliation Service, or a State Mediation Board, certain elements of chance are reduced, but certain others are increased. The element of "Hobson's choice" remains in full force. The parties should be well acquainted with the *modus operandi* of the agency named. . . .

4. The provision whereby each side will select an arbitrator, the two so appointed to agree upon a third, is one of the most common, and one of the most trouble-making of arbitration clauses. What isn't provided is a means of breaking the deadlock if the two partisans cannot (or will not) agree on an impartial third. If, however, the parties go further and agree that within a specified, limited time the "named" arbitrators' power to appoint lapses and is automatically transferred to an outside agency, the procedural defect is thus cured, but the parties may be deprived of an effective voice in the choice of their "judge," contrary to the original intention.

Perhaps more basic than the procedural defect is the fact that two of the three arbitrators are presumptively partisan advocates of the parties appointing them. Thus, the arbitration board is composed of one impartial arbitrator and an advocate for each of the opposing parties. A board so constituted would seem to be less efficient (to put it mildly) than a board appointed by a method which assures the impartiality of the arbitrators.

The composition of such a board also presents the following questions for determination by the parties:

a. Shall the award be by majority or unanimous vote?

b. Should the impartial arbitrator cast his vote on equal parity with his colleagues?

c. Should the impartial arbitrator, or umpire, take no direct part in the proceeding except when called upon to decide a deadlock, and then cast the deciding vote?

d. If the other arbitrators are partisans, should the impartial umpire make a sole award, subject to such influence and persuasion as the partisan arbitrators may bring to bear?

As an example of the defects of the log-jam type of clause, take the agreement between the coal operators and mine workers, which expired last year. It provided:

> Should the Board [two miners and two operators] be unable to agree on the selection of an umpire, he shall be designated by the International President of the United Mine Workers of America and the President of the Operators' Association affected. The decision of the umpire in the event shall be final.

Unfortunately, there was no "decision of the umpire" for the simple and almost inevitable reason that the two persons upon whom the ultimate choice rested never reached agreement. Result: The most disturbing and costly wartime strike.

Or, to see "human nature" at work, notice this from a recent letter:

> During our attempt to agree on a man the union first stated that they would take "Professor Blank" and no one else. We do not know Professor Blank and had no objections to his service, but believed we should not agree with them on their choice stated in that manner. We offered four names, stating that we would accept any man they might choose from those four. They refused to do that also and left only the alternative of taking "Professor Blank" or no one. Our answer to that, of course, was "no one."

5. Perhaps the height of deliberate frustration is the provision that empowers each party to name an arbitrator (so-called) "the two to decide the issue." One wonders why two presumably intelligent men would sign such an agreement. They divest themselves of the right to negotiate, and pass it on to two outsiders—who must proceed to negotiate in their stead. This is certainly a "process"—but it lacks every one of the basic requirements of arbitration. A variation came recently to light where a so-called labor arbitration board was composed of 9 of the union's members and 9 members of the employers' association—and no impartial chairman!

6. When the parties provide for selection of an impartial arbitrator, or board of arbitrators, from a panel such as that maintained, for example, by the American Arbitration Association, both the agency and the parties have certain obligations laid upon them. The Association does not, except upon the mutual, express demand of the parties, arbitrarily name an arbitrator without their joint concurrence.

Instead, when the agreement calls for arbitration under the Association's Rules, or it is designated to name the sole arbitrator, or the impartial chairman of a board of arbitrators, it submits simultaneously to each party identical lists of arbitrators having the qualifications demanded by the type of controversy to be determined, which qualifications are made known to the parties. Independently *and without consultation with the other*, each party strikes from this list the names of any individuals he might wish to veto for any reason whatsoever, thus leaving on the list only arbitrators satisfactory to him. He is instructed to number these in the order of preference. When the lists are returned the Association makes the choice of an impartial arbitrator, or board, as the case may be, from among those men whose names remain on both lists. The individual who stands highest in the preference of both parties is tendered the office of arbitrator. If he is unable to serve at the time designated, the office is tendered to the one having the next highest preference rating.

Perhaps the greatest single contribution the Arbitration Association has made to the cause of voluntary arbitration is its invention of a method by which two parties who are not "on speaking terms" can come to a satisfactory mutual choice of an impartial arbitrator without a single word of direct communication between each other.

Couple this with the availability of most of the best arbitrators in America who are members of its panels and one understands why there has been such a phenomenal growth during the war of the use of the Association's arbitration clauses and tribunals.

Mention might be made here of a new type of arbitration provision that might be called the *Last Man Up* method. Among those who, through prior experience, have seen demonstrated the high quality of competence and the impartiality of the Association's Panel of Arbitrators, a modification of the standard practice is growing rapidly. This calls for the submission of, say, seven names. Each party may "veto" three. At least one name is thus left on both lists and is the mutual choice of the parties. The same principle can apply with lists of nine or eleven, or any odd number.

It will be noted that man's ingenuity in inventing many ways to do the same thing has led to some queer results. Proponents of one or the other will heatedly support their own pet recipes. And perhaps no one method will ever satisfy all of the requirements.

But there are four tests to which every method should be subjected: Will it produce a sole arbitrator or a board—

1. That is impartial and competent;

2. That represents a high degree of mutual choice;

3. That can arrive at a fair decision without compromise; and

4. That can be appointed in spite of any neglect or refusal on the part of a recalcitrant party to the contract?

With this "yardstick" in mind, those responsible for drafting provisions for arbitration into collective bargaining agreements should give consideration to this—the *Four Square* method.

A tripartite board, with representatives of management and labor, and an impartial chairman, has much to commend it, in theory—and in practice, provided certain safeguards are established.

The first of such safeguards would seem to be that neither the management nor the labor arbitrator should have a direct interest in the particular case. Each should be chosen by some method which assumes that they are not the special advocates of the particular parties involved in the dispute. They should be good representatives, however, of the respective viewpoints. The impartial chairman of such a board must, of course, be completely neutral.

Perhaps the most effective method of selecting such a board, so as to secure the highest degree of attainable impartiality, is by the parties calling for tripartite, odd-number lists of names from a responsible nominating agency. They then would each have the privilege of vetoing a minority of the names from each group. If five names from each group were submitted, each party might veto two, and number the remaining names in their order of preference. Failure to veto any would be automatic approval of all. The arbitrator to be selected from each group would be the man of highest mutual preference.

In this way a high degree of choice is preserved and a board is created which reflects a true cross-section of viewpoint. Both labor and management could profitably develop this method into wider practice. It offers security against "deadlock" in the selection, gives a higher dignity to the labor and management representatives, and enlists a greater degree of effort on the part of all the members to find the true and just settlement.

Whatever method of selecting impartial arbitrators the parties elect to use, they should examine and study it carefully for any preventable loopholes, or weaknesses, or insufficient coverage.

Does it provide alternate methods, whereby deadlocks may be prevented if one method fails? Does it employ time limits to prevent lag in naming the arbitrator and getting the proceeding under way? Does it enlist the machinery of the best available sources for supplying arbitrators?

If the clause itself does not so provide in detail, does it invoke adequate rules of procedure that provide a method that safeguards the rights of both parties?

And does the clause preserve, to the fullest possible extent, the principle of voluntary arbitration which assures both parties the greatest possible opportunity to exercise *mutual choice* in their selection of the arbitrator and yet avoids the possibility of "log-jam" frustration of the agreement to arbitrate?

When an arbitrator is conscientious, painstaking, and fair in arriving at his decision, and bases that decision upon the proofs submitted, when he brings his competence, experience, and commonsense to bear impartially upon the issues before him; when he follows the procedure laid down in the parties' agreement, or in whatever rules of procedure they have adopted, so that each party knows he has had a fair trial—then arbitration commands confidence, and the award will be one that satisfies justice.

This is the simplest and best formula to follow: "Get a good arbitrator, and you will have a good arbitration."

COMPULSION UNDER THE NAME OF ARBITRATION [10]

Labor troubles have moved to a crescendo during the past several months. John L. Lewis, whose advocacy of arbitration is in reverse, faced down the mine owners, the War Labor Board, and the President. Under a thin transparency of conformance with stabilization standards, the miners received, substantially, the increase Lewis had promised.

This touched off a train of events in which, under the name of arbitration, a number of actions were taken which only faintly resemble arbitration, either in principle or practice.

The railroad labor dispute had been gathering momentum for months. A modified form of compulsory arbitration is provided for the settlement of such disputes in the Railway Labor Act. An emergency board proceeding under the act recommended, in May, a wage increase of 8 cents to conform to their understanding of wage stabilization requirements, instead of the 20 cents the non-operating unions were asking. Administrator Vinson

[10] *Arbitration Magazine.* 2:7-8. January-February 1944.

vetoed the 8-cent increase. The President urged that the unions and the railroad executives try to arrive at an agreement. They accepted the suggestion and agreed, again, on 8 cents.

The President intervened again, asking the non-operating unions to wait until the operating unions' case came up for settlement. The latter had been in process under the compulsory arbitration provision of the law since January, 1942. The National (Railway) Mediation Board awarded the operating unions an increase of 4 cents but indicated in its report that it would have allowed 8 cents but had been "authoritatively informed" that 4 cents was the maximum.

The President then appointed another emergency board to redetermine the non-operating unions' case and its recommendation was for a sliding scale of increase ranging from 4 cents to 10 cents.

At this point, both groups—the operating and non-operating unions—took a strike vote. The National Mediation Board, acting under the law, called the parties to appear before it on December 20th. Perhaps it would have awarded the, by now, famous 8-cent increase, and perhaps not. Perhaps the unions would have accepted it. Perhaps not. But even this delayed and trouble-frayed "arbitration" was not allowed to proceed. In lieu thereof, the President offered himself as arbitrator. Two operating unions accepted him. Three declined. The non-operating unions jockeyed for an advance commitment, and finally accepted him as arbitrator one hour before he took over the railroads and ordered all workers to stay on their jobs.

As this is written, announcement is made that the fifteen non-operating brotherhoods have accepted, and Stabilization Director Vinson has approved, a sliding scale increase of 9 to 11 cents. As the operating brotherhoods and the railroads had previously reached an agreement on a flat 5-cent hourly increase, the danger of a railroad strike faded, and control of the railroads was turned back to their owners at midnight on January 18th.

The point to emphasize here, however, is that in all these gyrations and delays, and in the frustrations to union members which led to the strike vote and seizure of the railroads, real arbitration has had no part.

There is much that masquerades under the name of arbitration. But the long train of failures in this situation must be charged to other factors.

True arbitration is a speedy process. The railroad-labor crisis has been developing for two years.

True arbitration is economical. The direct cost, and the indirect economic loss caused by the delay in meeting the railroad situation four-square, are incalculable, but enormous.

True arbitration is essential justice. The real merits of the railroad case have not as yet been decided by an impartial tribunal free from interference or administrative direction.

Therefore, it should be realized by all thinking men that wherever the blame may lie in respect of the mishandling of the railroad case, it does not lie on the doorstep of real voluntary arbitration—the only procedure apparently that has *not yet been used*.

That arbitration, of all methods of settling disputes, has the highest batting average of success, makes it only the more regrettable when it is not assigned the job of settling disputes when the disputes first arise.

No dispute or controversy is really settled until both parties to the dispute or controversy are convinced in their own minds of the absolute fairness of the decision or the award. And that is arbitration's great and lasting value. It appeals to the fair minded before the dispute is submitted. It appeals to them equally strongly afterward, because in a well-run voluntary arbitration proceeding there is nothing but fairness, equitability, speed, and justice.

OPPRESSION OF LABOR [11]

For four years a subcommittee of the Senate Committee on Education and Labor conducted an intensive investigation of violations of civil liberties and undue interference with the rights of labor to organize and bargain collectively throughout the United States.

[11] By Robert M. La Follette, United States Senator from Wisconsin. *American Federationist.* 51:27-8. August 1944.

As chairman of the subcommittee I had the active and energetic help of Senator Elbert D. Thomas of Utah in its work. He and I conducted extensive hearings dealing with numerous instances of the violation of free speech and free assembly, and all types of anti-labor practices.

The subcommittee's record and its reports constitute one of the most complete and thorough analyses of anti-labor practices and their underlying causes ever made. Many recent books on labor relations contain references to our work.

The committee proposed legislative remedies for the evils which it uncovered. The Oppressive Labor Practices Act was passed by the Senate in 1941, but failed in the House. It would have banned the use of the labor spy, the professional strike guard and strikebreaker, and the use of industrial munitions in labor disputes. Reintroduced in 1942, the bill contained amendments which would have made illegal the more flagrant practices of anti-union employers' associations.

The revelations made by the committee often seemed shocking and sensational to the general public. But to working men and to members of unions, particularly American Federation of Labor unions, who had suffered from the use of labor spies, professional thugs and strike guards for years, there was nothing so unusual in the facts which we disclosed. Nevertheless, the disclosure of these evils in our industrial life raised a storm of public indignation and created an appreciation in the public mind of the difficulties which union organization faced. Today I believe that it would be very difficult for an employer to justify the use of such oppressive labor practices or for the so-called detective agencies to engage openly in purveying such services as labor espionage or strikebreaking.

The committee's investigations started with detective agencies engaged in selling anti-labor devices. The most "respectable" of these agencies, Pinkerton's, with offices in downtown New York, as well as the least reputable, such as E. L. McGuffin's National Corporation Service of Youngstown, Ohio, engaged in the dirty business of sending paid spies and informers into labor unions. It was the job of such spies to expose workers to threats and discrimination, to foment labor disorder, to create a distrust of organized unionism, and in many cases to create as well as to break strikes. All this was done cold-bloodedly, with prices quoted at so much per spy report or so much per day for the services of skilled union wreckers.

Next, the committee took up strikebreaking services, which were purveyed on the same commercial basis. Some of the detective agencies specialized in providing professional strike guards and in recruiting members of the underworld to pose as "loyal workers" or replacements in labor disputes. Many of the strike guards had criminal records. Some of these men confessed in public hearings that they customarily created disturbances among pickets and stimulated violent incidents. Their purpose was to "heat up the job," precipitating such disorder and rancor or so prolonging the strike that the employer would believe that he should extend their employment or hire additional strike guards and strikebreakers.

The committee also investigated the industrial munitions companies selling tear and sickening gas and gas guns and projectors. Their chief customers were the so-called detective agencies and employers. Because these weapons, while dangerous enough and sometimes deadly, were not ordinarily as lethal in their effect as firearms, they afforded greater license to the professional strike guards or to aggressive company police or disorderly deputies to break up peaceful picketing or lawful assemblages of workers.

The committee also investigated oppressive company police systems which had been used by some employers to repress and destroy union organizations. These systems were in vogue among some of the steel and coal companies. In such company police systems, rabid anti-union employers combined all the vices and terrors of the detective labor spy agencies, the strikebreaking system and the use of industrial munitions.

These oppressive labor practices have had a long history in the United States. For decades the unions of the American Federation of Labor had struggled against them. Most of the data which the committee extracted by its subpoenas from the files of the detective agencies, the tear gas companies and anti-union employer groups had to do with the use of these practices against member unions of the American Federation of Labor. In the metal trades, the building trades, the service trades and in transportation, the story was the same. As an example, the committee's hearings laid bare the story of paid spies who had been operating in the International Association of Machinists for years, seeking to wreck one local after another, sometimes absconding with union funds, or breaking up negotiations with employers. When the A.F. of L. began to create federal unions in organized industry under Section 7a of the N.I.R.A. in 1933 and 1934, the detective agencies recruited new swarms of spies to destroy them.

The committee also made an intensive examination of another phase of anti-unionism. This was the anti-union, or as we call it, the "belligerent" employers' association. This was not the type of association with which some unions of the A.F. of L. for many years have had fruitful collective bargaining relationships. It was the type of association which was unequivocally committed to the proposition that there should be no genuine collective bargaining with labor. In some of these associations the employer members even pledged themselves under penalty of forfeiting considerable sums of money not to enter into contracts with organized labor. One of the most prominent of the associations of this type was the National Metal Trades Association, which for almost two decades had been waging relentless war on the International Association of Machinists and kindred unions. It provided its members with a complete line of oppressive labor practice services.

While some of these associations were built on trade lines, others followed a local or regional pattern. One of the latter was the Associated Industries of Cleveland, founded shortly after the last war, which at length, at about the time of the committee's investigation, bowed to the law of the land and public opinion and gave at least lip service to the practice of collective bargaining.

In California the committee uncovered a state-wide network of local anti-union employer associations. The most prominent among them were the Industrial Association of San Francisco and the Merchants' and Manufacturers' Association of Los Angeles.

The committee made an elaborate examination of the work of the latter of these associations. It was powerful, inclusive, well financed and implacable in its determination to weaken the unions in Los Angeles and to prevent new labor organization there. It summoned all its energy to frustrate the efforts of the International Brotherhood of Teamsters to organize the trucking industry in Los Angeles in 1936 and 1937. It sought to unify not only the trucking companies but all the shippers of Los Angeles against the legitimate efforts of this affiliate of the American Federation of Labor. It had the backing of the Los Angeles Chamber of Commerce, leading businessmen and various spurious citizens' associations, women's groups, such as The Neutral Thousands, and other "fronts."

This association sought to create a public attitude of fear and hostility with respect to the Teamsters Union and to create a picture in the public mind of the leaders of the Teamsters Union as lawbreakers and racketeers. So great was the popular pressure created by this anti-union association of employers that one trucking company, which finally decided to obey the law of the land and to recognize the organization of its employees, was compelled to keep secret the fact that it had signed a closed-shop contract with the union.

The machinations of the Merchants' and Manufacturers' Association of Los Angeles, and its affiliated anti-union organizations, extended to a host of other A.F. of L. unions besides the Teamsters. They affected among others the culinary workers, the dairy workers, the streetcar workers, the cabinet workers, the produce workers, the lumberyard workers, as well as C.I.O. unions. Originally the Merchants' and Manufacturers' Association had even been opposed to company unions, but finally in 1936 and 1937 a "new spirit" prevailed in its councils and it tolerated their creation.

The study of this and similar anti-union employers' associations on the West Coast and in the East and Middle West furnished the committee with the whole story of the anti-union employers' movement in this country since World War I. It is an interesting and shocking story not found in the ordinary textbook.

During World War I membership in the American Federation of Labor grew tremendously. The government agencies concerned with labor relations took the position that collective bargaining between employers and unions of employees was the only alternative to industrial strife and actively encouraged the formation of unions and the practice of collective bargaining.

After the war this protection was swept away and various active elements among the ranks of anti-union employers set out in a businesslike way to destroy, insofar as they could, the labor union movement in America. Local anti-union associations of employers sprang up all over the country in the years 1920 and 1921. These local associations combined with industry or trade associations of an anti-union character, such as the National Metal Trades Association, in nation-wide groups such as the American Plan Open Shop Conference or the National Association of Manufacturers.

The local and trade associations of this character had two faces—the one they showed to the public and the other which they showed to the employee. They spread public propaganda to the effect that union organization was a bad thing and that they themselves were acting in behalf of the workers' rights to employment.

With this campaign as a background, many of them launched a fight on genuine labor organizations, using labor spies, disrupting unions, coercing employers into breaking contracts, blacklisting union members, furnishing strikebreakers and otherwise harassing union organizations. The first assault of the local associations was against the building trades and from there they spread out to other unions.

The effects of this concerted anti-union drive, which extended from 1920 down through the early thirties, were notable. Union membership in general declined almost steadily as a result of the onslaught. Collective bargaining was weakened or eliminated in a number of industries.

With the passage of the N.I.R.A. and later the Wagner Act, and with the tremendous upsurge in union organization which began in 1933 and which has continued to date, the struggle entered another phase. Today, I believe, there is far less anti-union sentiment among employers than there was when these anti-union associations were in their heyday and were able to trample upon the rights of workers unhampered by either public opinion or the government.

However, there remains a powerful minority of employers who are only awaiting economic and political conditions which will enable them to renew their drive to smash trade unionism in the United States.

RAILROADS VIEWED AS FACTOR IN MANPOWER PROBLEM [12]

We are in the midst of the gravest crisis in our history. Our country and our lives are at stake. We need all available man-power and we need it now.

The government is trying to use the nation's manpower to the full. But its task is not being faced candidly. The shortage in manpower is not due solely to the lack of available workers. Indeed, that shortage is due in part to the deliberate effort of labor unions, by rules and devices, to prevent men from working full time. Thus surplus employees, unnecessary in their jobs, become unavailable for work. This is a new form of hoarding; of keeping idle and unused services badly needed elsewhere.

How absurd to talk about total mobilization, compulsory service, shifting labor to distant cities, while men on the job all over the United States are wasting time under union orders. Such policies do not help to win a war. The war will be won in spite of such policies, not because of them.

However, the crisis is compelling a more realistic approach. Public opinion is becoming aroused. The union leaders who put country above union are increasing in power.

The railroads suffer from unique devices to make work. These devices hamper wartime transportation. These devices also reveal a basic defect in the manpower policy of the government. The government listed the shortages of railroad labor as of Sept. 15, 1942. Otto S. Beyer, director of the Division of

[12] By Elisha M. Friedman, Consulting Economist, New York; Author of Economic works. *New York Times.* p. 8E. February 21, 1943.

Transportation personnel of the Office of Defense Transportation, stated: "Considerable numbers of vacancies were reported in junior train and engine service positions, including 2,565 vacancies for brakemen and 827 for firemen. Only thirty vacancies were reported for conductors and 116 for engineers."

Mr. Beyer talks about "increased railroad traffic" and "need for increasing the number of workers" but he says nothing about increased use of the hours of idleness enforced by "featherbed rules" and other fake-work devices.

This writer attempted to get an estimate of the manpower waste on the railroads and the annual cost. He directed his inquiry to an important source of railroad information and the reply was: "The subject of labor waste is closely connected with the manpower problem but this body avoids controversial matters of this nature."

What do the official figures show? Form M-300 (1941) of the Interstate Commerce Commission shows "Straight Time Actually Worked" and "Straight Time Paid For." The difference is time paid for and not worked. Mr. Beyer's shortages are as follows: 0.1 per cent for conductors, 0.3 per cent for engineers, 2.4 per cent for firemen and 4.3 per cent for brakemen.

But Form M-300 shows that these approximately 250,000 men in Group VIb, train and engine service, were idle about 22 per cent of the time and were paid for idling. It shows a surplus or waste of over 100,000,000 man-hours, or 50,000 man-years, for 1941 in one sector alone due to one cause. These men could, if they worked full time, easily make good the shortage that Mr. Beyer cites. Nay, more, thousands of these trained men could be released to make ships, tanks, planes and guns.

Exact figures are not available, but on a rough guess it is probable that in all labor sectors and due to all causes there is a total waste of railroad labor of about 200,000,00 man-hours a year or about 100,000 men a year. In wartime such waste of precious manpower is really sabotage.

Not a single word has been uttered by any government official on this subject. These union restrictions persist not only with their connivance, but with their approval.

The Director of Manpower is seeking to conserve manpower. But the government referees dealing with railroad labor squander manpower. The make-work rules on the railroads have become increasingly onerous. In fact, in the last decade government referees have invented curious "principles" which extend and multiply such rules. These have become known as "featherbed rules" or the equivalent of a soft snap in ward politics. The railroad workers who benefit most from these rules are those in the train and engine services who operate the trains.

A fertile source of wasted manpower is the "dual basis of pay." The engine and train service employes are paid on this basis. Under the rules, the employes may be paid either on the basis of piece-work—miles, or on the basis of time—hours worked. They are paid by the method which produces the higher result. A day's work is 100 miles for all freight train service crews. Often a crew can do 100 miles in four hours. But the wage therefor is a full day of eight hours. However, if the 100 miles requires ten hours, the crew receives overtime rates of time-and-a-half after the eighth hour. This is like a game of "heads I win, tails you lose." On a fast train workers figure their wages by miles and on a slow train by hours.

As train speeds increased, the crews can often earn three or four days' pay in one day of work. If these men worked every day, the annual salary of some of them would be equal to that of a member of the Interstate Commerce Commission, or $12,000 per annum. The rate is $24,000 a year on the Union Pacific's Streamliner, the Santa Fe's Super Chief and the Milwaukee's Hiawatha.

Such annual wages would become a public scandal. Therefore, the operating brotherhoods introduced limitations on mileage or output. In other industries, such limitation is termed "soldiering" or "ca'canny." For example, on the run from New York to Washington, passenger engineers are limited to ten days a month, and firemen to nine days. During the rest of the month they are idle. Three times the number of men must be employed. What a waste of manpower in a war crisis!

Suppose the chauffeurs on city buses or the motormen on subways were paid by the mile at the rate set in 1880 for drivers on horsecars.

Another fertile source of wasted manpower are the "featherbed rules" which distinguish between work on the road and work in the yards. The basic idea is that each group of workers has a monopoly of a small section of the job. Therefore, the crews of road trains may not perform any switching work whatever.

With the rapid changes in our dynamic economy, traffic may shrink at one point. Switching crews then become unnecessary. However, under the "featherbed rules" the railroads may not discontinue the switching crew. If a road crew should do any switching, its members are paid a full day for a few minutes of switching work. But in addition the yard or switching crews who are not present must also be paid another day's pay for "not going" this few minutes of work. Railroads in order to avoid paying double wages must therefore maintain switching crews in idleness all day waiting for a few minutes of switching work. What an artificial separation of duties!

Manpower is also wasted through the "starting time rules." The regular yard crews must start at strictly limited hours. For instance, on three shifts, the first crew must begin at 8 A. M., the second at 4 P. M. and the third crew at midnight. There is a 90-minute leeway before these times. But, if the traffic requires that a switching crew be on hand 30 minutes before the limit some absurd results follow. The crew is paid one day at regular rates for the early half-hour, plus one day at overtime rates of time-and-a-half. Thus for one additional half-hour of work, the additional wage paid would cover 12 hours.

These "featherbed rules" for starting time do not apply to the railroads' competitors—buses, trucks and ships, which operate more efficiently and cheaply. Therefore, traffic leaves the rails. Therefore, there is less work for the railroad crews. This is a crazy form of hara-kiri for the railroad workers. Imagine a department store operating on the same absurd system! Department stores are free to call their employees to begin to work at any time. Stores arrange to have the peak of employment at the hour of peak buying by customers. If the department stores were limited by "featherbed rules" as to starting time, either they would have to charge more for their merchandise or the stores would go broke.

What was the origin of these absurd rules? During World War I, the United States Railroad Administration encouraged rules which required each operation to be broken down into monopolistic categories, the exclusive property of one craft. When the railroads were returned to private ownership after the war, the managements tried to modify these restrictive rules. In this controversy over the "national agreements" the then existing United States Labor Board decided against the railroads and in favor of the unions. Therefore, today, in World War II, during a crisis and a serious shortage of manpower, these cock-eyed rules still persist.

How did these rules become so pervasive and pernicious? In recent years the situation has been rendered infinitely worse. The reason was the 1934 amendment to the 1926 Railway Labor Act. The instrument was the National Railroad Adjustment Board. This board interprets existing agreements on the complaint of the employees. These interpretations are strained. They rest on strange principles. They require that unnecessary workers be employed. In numerous cases it has granted awards or heavy penalties against railroads for not employing such unnecessary workers. The board's fantastic interpretations often go far beyond the intent of the working rules as originally written. Nor could such interpretations possibly be accepted in new negotiations or contracts between men and management.

Thus, in distinguishing between road work and yard work, the board has established the principle that where a yard crew was discontinued, because little work was left, a member of the yard crew may claim back pay for many years equal to the amount he would have earned if the work had continued. In one of these cases, the members of the yard crew, on whose behalf the union had filed claims, could not be found without great difficulty. On search, one was found to be a farmer, another had become a postmaster, and a third was in jail. In another case, where even after search the men could not be found, the railroad, in order to comply with the order of the adjustment board, told the local chairman of the union, "Here, take the money, and divide it as you like."

In another case, a decision of the board produced the following absurd result: A fireman made a round trip totaling fifty miles, outbound with passenger cars and returning with freight cars. The board awarded the fireman three days' pay; one day's pay for the twenty-five miles outbound in the passenger service, one day's pay for backing the engine to the turntable, and a third day's pay for bringing a freight train home over the same twenty-five miles. The entire trip took much less than eight hours. After the board made this award, every other fireman on that run was granted the same "gravy," retroactive for three years.

In the National Railroad Adjustment Board, the railroad labor unions have a new kind of supreme court—a court of last resort. But it does not function under standards of American judicial procedure. The railroads are not permitted to see the employe's claim before they answer. No evidence is taken. There is no cross-examination. The parties to the dispute may not appear before the referees who decide the case. Nor may their lawyers. No transcript of the proceedings is permitted. No stenographer may be brought in. The atmosphere is secret. The public is not admitted. The press is rigidly excluded. The proceedings are similar to the seventeenth century star chamber. The procedure of the Adjustment Board has thrown court processes back three centuries. Is this a court or an instrument of coercion?

An important case is now pending in the United States Supreme Court to determine whether railroads may have legal relief in the regularly constituted courts, whether they can arrest the proliferation of further rank "featherbed rules," and whether a drumhead court-martial—the Adjustment Board—will replace our legal procedure.

A lower court has held that the railroads cannot appeal from the decision of that board. Thus they may not have relief. Thus the board has absolute power to require the employment of all the additional and unnecessary employees that the unions may choose to demand. Thus the board becomes the court of final appeal—the highest in the land.

Why should the railroads be subjected to such methods? Why tolerate and encourage such an indefensible waste of man-power in this acute crisis of manpower, to say nothing of injuring investors and consumers, who must foot the bill? Has not the time come for sober labor leadership? Should not labor's statesmen heed the admonition forty years ago of Louis D. Brandeis? He said:

"Their action (of labor unions) is frequently arbitrary, the natural result of the possession of great power by persons not accustomed to its use. They need something to protect them from their own arbitrariness. The employer and the community also require this protection. The success of labor unions as well as their usefulness to the community, would be much advanced by measures which tend to make them more deliberate and less arbitrary, and more patient with the trammels of a civilized community. The unions should show that they are in full sympathy with the spirit of our people whose political system rests upon the proposition that this is a government of law and not of men."

Is not this the hour to give effect to this prophetic utterance? Have not all three branches of our government, legislative, judicial and executive, a duty in this crisis? Courage is the essence of statesmanship. Expediency merely defers dangers. Often compromise courts ultimate disaster.

STRIKES, PROFITS, AND DEFENSE [13]

The protagonists in the labor-capital conflict conduct their struggles through two mediums, strikes and legislation. These are the immediate focal points of the propagandas.

A strike is labor's strongest weapon. The union says it is defensive; the employer says it is offensive. In any event, if it is successful it stops the work of the plant until the company negotiates a satisfactory agreement. On such victories the unions

[13] From article in *Propaganda Analysis*. 4:7-14. April 28, 1941. Copyright by the Institute for Propaganda Analysis, Inc. New York.

live and flourish. If the strike fails, the union is usually set back; it may die altogether. And success or failure depends on two cardinal factors of opinion: the convictions of the employes themselves as to their cause, and the convictions of the public. On the latter depend usually the actions of the public officials involved. If the public favors the strikers, the officials give the employer little or no aid; when it is hostile, they give much aid.

So an intense propaganda conflict is waged. It is conducted on the one hand by persons who have criticisms of the unions' actions or proposals for restrictive measures, and on the other hand by the defenders of the unions. Today it centers mainly around the strikes in defense industries. The strikes, say the critics of the unions, are jeopardizing the national rearmament effort by delays. Said Walter D. Fuller, president of the National Association of Manufacturers and of the Curtis Publishing Company (publishers of the *Saturday Evening Post*), "It is alarming for fathers of draftees in this country to find out that enough time has already been lost through strikes to build 480 destroyers and half a million modern Garand rifles for their boys to carry."

President Roosevelt, Sidney Hillman, Associate Director of the Office of Production Management, the *Wall Street Journal* and *Business Week* made reassuring statements. President Roosevelt said that only one four-hundredth of the defense industries had been affected by strikes at the same time. The O.P.M. made public a list of strikes on March 27 showing 40,000 workers out in important defense industries on that date. This is about one tenth of 1 per cent of the total workers in the country. The *Wall Street Journal* reported its own survey in eight key industrial areas on March 12, under the headline, "No Serious Strike Damage to Armament Output Yet; Trouble Looms; Wages Rise." *Business Week* on March 1, 1941, said:

Actually, in the first six months of the defense program there have been fewer man-days lost in strikes than in any other comparable period since the passage of the Wagner Act, and labor disputes have not been nearly as serious as they were in 1917. . . .

But headlines make better reading than historical facts. And headlines have created a steadily mounting concern about labor difficulties in defense industries.

Prolabor publications pointed out that many of the strikes were caused by efforts of the companies to thwart the Wagner Act.

Said Rose M. Stein in the *Nation*:

Labor is unquestionably trying to advance its position by seeking union recognition from recalcitrant employers. There can be no question about the validity of this endeavor, since it merely aims to effectuate what is already public policy. Neither can there be any doubt that the employers who are refusing to deal with unions are defying public policy.

Other writers maintained that some old enemies of unionism were provoking strikes in order to brand the unions as interfering with national defense—and thus break the strikes, and the unions. The Senate majority leader, Mr. Barkley, pointed to the bad labor records of some of the big companies involved. He mentioned Ford, Allis-Chalmers and Bethlehem Steel particularly. It was entirely possible, he stated—speaking in the Senate on April 2, 1941—that a good case could be built up against most of the larger industries "which have been defying the laws of the United States." He did not believe, he asserted, that labor's side had been properly presented.

His reference to companies "defying the laws" harked back to labor's efforts to have defense contracts withheld from violators of the Wagner Act. A ruling withholding all government contracts from such violators was long demanded. A ruling to this effect was announced by Sidney Hillman, labor member of the National Defense Advisory Committee. The ruling was based on an opinion by Attorney General Robert H. Jackson. Under a Congressional attack it was quickly dropped however.

In answer to efforts to minimize the extent of defense strikes many papers and commentators like the Springfield (Mass.) *Republican* and Scripps-Howard Columnists General Hugh S. Johnson and Raymond Clapper, who criticised the unions, pointed out that a small strike at one plant might delay vital parts that would hold up a whole section of the arms program.

But, say union officials, other bottlenecks over which labor has no control have caused more delays than strikes. They cite the delay in getting defense production started, a delay that the Temporary National Economic Committee monograph blamed on business.

> In the 1940 national defense crisis [the monograph said], business displayed much the same attitude that it had shown 23 years earlier. Business would help the government and the people, but the basis of payment therefor would have to be fixed before the wheels would begin to turn. Profits, taxes, loans, and so forth, appeared more important to business than getting guns, tanks, and airplane motors into production. . . .

> It developed that business did not want to work for the country on the basis of a 7 or 8 per cent profit limitation written into the Vinson-Trammell Naval Expansion Act in 1935, so these provisions were repealed. Thus, the whole cost-plus basis of defense contracts which industry liked so well during the last war when it had practically a free hand in determining costs, went by the board in 1940 when the allowable items of cost were determined by the Treasury Department. . . .

> Business . . . controls the natural resources, the liquid assets, the strategic position in the country's economic structure, and its technical equipment and knowledge of processes. . . . Business is apparently not unwilling to threaten the very foundations of government in fixing the terms on which it will work.

Walter Reuther, director of the General Motors Department of the United Automobile Workers, pointed out in a public debate on March 20, 1941, that some of the most serious hindrances to armament production in America were the agreements some American companies had with German companies whereby our plants were seriously limited in the production of certain military necessities. Mr. Reuther cited specifically the agreement between the Aluminum Company of America and the I. G. Farbenindustrie of Germany whereby American production of magnesium, a highly important mineral for airplane parts and some kinds of bombs, was kept low. Magnesium is a third lighter than aluminum.

A report on this and similar agreements in other industries was made to the Patent Committee of the House of Representatives on March 11, 1941 by Assistant Attorney General Francis M. Shea. His statement was made in support of legislation to free companies from the operation of the patent monopoly in the production of goods needed for national defense.

The Aluminum Company agreement has allowed only one company to produce magnesium in this country, Mr. Shea said. This is the Dow Chemical Company. Its production was limited in 1940 to 6,000, while German production was 25,000 tons, and possibly double that figure. One of the great needs of the British today is for magnesium, Mr. Shea said, but the Dow Company was by express agreement limited to shipping them 300 tons per year. The restrictions on the manufacture of magnesium in this country, Mr. Shea said, have resulted in a serious shortage of suitable foundry facilities. The Department of Justice in January secured indictments against six corporations and nine individuals in the magnesium industry for violation of the anti-trust laws.

Mr. Shea also told of similar German-controlled restrictions on the American production of tungsten carbide, the hardest substance known next to diamond, used for the cutting edges of machine tools; and on berylium, an exceedingly valuable metal that gives great durability to copper and other metals even when used in small quantities, in demand for airplane parts. Even Bausch and Lomb Company, the dominant American manufacturer of optical equipment needed for range finders, periscopes, altimeters, torpedo directors, gun sights, telescopes and bore sights, has an agreement with Carl Zeiss of Germany which has seriously limited the development of facilities for manufacturing these articles in the United States. Mr. Shea claimed that this agreement, formed in 1921, has required the Bausch and Lomb military department to be supervised by persons acceptable to the Zeiss company. The agreement concealed the German ownership of patents held in the United States.

An additional factor in delaying American defense production, union men say, is the failure to use available facilities. Mr. Reuther of the C.I.O. Automobile Workers declared in his debate that not more than 10 per cent of the potential output of the gigantic American automobile industry had been producing defense materials; the rest, he said, was "doing business as usual" in commercial automobiles.

A cut of 20 per cent in the commercial production has just been agreed to by the automobile industry, Mr. Knudsen announced on April 17, 1941. It will take effect in the production year starting August 1, he said.

C.I.O. President Philip Murray has proposed the setting up of joint industry-labor councils to speed production, but his proposal has not been taken up. He reported in the *New York Times* of January 29, 1941, after a detailed study of the steel industry, that the total employment of workers and salaried employes in the steel industry was still 26,106 below the peak of 603,106 reached in August, 1937.

Large steel firms are overloaded with orders [he said]; backlogs of orders are running from two to four months, while smaller steel firms are operating their open-hearth departments as little as 45 per cent of capacity. . . . One steel firm has such a disproportionate amount of the steel armaments contracts that it presents a bottleneck to the defense program all by itself.

Mr. Murray's formula, which he sent to President Roosevelt, the cabinet, and the O.P.M., was for the organization of the entire iron, steel and tin producing industry into one great production unit.

Next to the question of whether defense production has been seriously delayed by strikes, the biggest point of critics of the unions has been that the strikes have been manipulated by Communists to delay production. Many prominent persons have declared this to be the case. O.P.M. Director William S. Knudsen in his Army Day speech on April 5, 1941, made a brief reference to "radicals" in Milwaukee in connection with the Allis-Chalmers strike. This was the strike in which Mr. Knudsen joined with Secretary Knox in asking the union and the plant to resume work without a peace formula after a specific formula had earlier been submitted by the O.P.M. and had been accepted by the union but rejected by the company. Mr. Knudsen said:

The important part was that the radical leaders with the help of other unions in Milwaukee and vicinity could show the state and the nation where to get off—and both our friends and their foes across the water have this wonderful piece of morale builder served with their next morning's breakfast.

Chairman Dies of the House Committee on un-American Activities made specific charges in connection with several strikes.

One of his attacks was on the Steel Workers Organizing Committee. He said on March 24, 1941, that his Committee had "indisputable evidence" that the Communist party was working toward a complete tie-up in the steel industry, which has billions of dollars worth of defense contracts.

He told the House of Representatives that he had a record of active Communists who had penetrated the steel industry through the S.W.O.C.:

Our committee [he continued] is in possession of indisputable evidence that that Communist party, through its members and organizers in the S.W.O.C., are working toward a complete tie-up in the steel industry, an industry which has billions of dollars in defense contracts.

Our committee is in possession of evidence which shows that hundreds of employees in steel mills have recently signed the Communist party's election petitions.

It is an indictment of this labor organization that it ever allowed so many Communists of public record to infiltrate into its organizing work.

Mr. Dies later named 27 Communists who, he said, were on the S.W.O.C. payroll. C.I.O. President Philip Murray, chairman of the S.W.O.C., replied equally specifically. Eleven of the persons named had never been employed by the S.W.O.C., Mr. Murray reported; fifteen of the others had not been with the S.W.O.C. for the past three to five years. In any case, he said, he had no knowledge that any of the individuals named was a Communist.

Time, while holding that events demonstrated the presence of at least some Communists in the strikes, remarked that Mr. Dies "blazed away every time a bush shook."

Mr. Reuther of the Automobile Workers insisted that the "red scare" was essentially a new anti-union device developed by employers to keep the workers from forming strong unions. He said:

Many years ago . . . they started scares of various kinds. One scare the bosses raised was the Catholics against the Protestants. Another scare they used very successfully was the American-born against the foreign-born. Then they placed one foreign-born group against another, like the Poles against the Germans, and so on.

All that is played out now. It has been worked too often. So now the bosses are raising a new scare: the red scare.

What the bosses really mean, however, is not that a leader is red. They mean they don't like him because he is a loyal, dependable union man, a fighter who helps his union brothers and sisters and is not afraid of the boss.

Secretary Knox pointed out that the number of strikes in 1940 was only half as great as in 1917 when the country was at war. The Communist movement had not started in the United States at that time and the trade union membership was about a third what it is today. The Springfield *Republican* pointed out on March 13, 1941, also, that the duration of strikes in January was 9.6 man-days per strike as against an average of 16.6 man-days per strike in January in the five years 1935-39.

Many critics of the unions have made much of jurisdictional strikes. The critics say that in these the employer is the innocent victim and that there should be a legal barrier to such strikes. President William Green of the A.F.L. has made repeated statements of plans by which the A.F.L., which has many such strikes between its own unions, is attempting to eliminate them. The C.I.O. industrial union plan, the C.I.O. officials say, minimizes such strikes, since their unions cover a whole industry.

In the fights between the A.F.L., and the C.I.O., the Labor Board has said in some instances the employer was not the victim but was conniving with one of the unions. It has voided a number of contracts on this ground. The United States Supreme Court on November 12, 1940 upheld the Board's voiding of a contract of a local of the International Association of Machinists, A.F.L.; it supported the view that the company had discharged and otherwise intimidated its workers to induce them to favor the A.F.L. union over a C.I.O. local.

Should there be restrictive legal measures on strikes? One of the hottest debates of recent years has centered on this operation. Numerous speakers, including Secretary Knox and O.P.M. Director Knudsen, have advocated labor restrictions of various kinds, and their proposals have been given prominence in press and radio reports.

A Gallup poll released on March 28, 1941 showed 72 per cent of the public think strikes should not be allowed in defense industries. An earlier poll, however, showed that 61 per cent believe that workers on defense projects should have the right to protest if they believe themselves underpaid.

A 30-day "cooling-off period" has been the main theme of proponents of new governmental measures. The National Association of Manufacturers, in sponsoring this idea (it suggested a 40-day period) described the period as one in which mediation could take place. Advocates of this plan suggest that strikes are voted in the heat of fights over terms and that if a delaying period were required mediators could often effect a settlement. . . .

Labor thinks the proposal is a veiled weapon intended to give an employer time to disrupt a strike during the time between the vote and the effective date. Actually, said Mr. Reuther of the Automobile Workers in debating with Governor Stassen, it ignores the long periods already consumed in negotiations before a strike vote is taken. In the Allis-Chalmers strike, he said, the union negotiated for five weeks first; with International Harvester, the negotiations had gone on for more than six months; with Ford the union had been "cooling off for the past two years."

Representative Dies proposed a bill to make it illegal for employers to hire Communists or "fellow-travelers." Representative Hatton W. Sumners, another Texan, and chairman of the House Judiciary Committee, stated in Congress that "if the American people knew the truth there would be no more strikes"; he suggested the possibility of sending to the "electric chair" "enemies of the nation in the factory or elsewhere." He later said he was not thinking of rank and file union members. The Federal-State Conference on Law Enforcement Problems of National Defense on December 14, 1940, put forward four proposed state acts. One, called the Model Sabotage Prevention Act, is now pending in a number of states. A committee appointed by Secretary Perkins to study it said it "would seriously curtail or prohibit the rights of labor to strike." The Texas legislature passed an act submitted by Governor O'Daniel providing two years imprisonment for "any person acting in concert with one or more other persons to assemble at or near any place where a 'labor dispute' exists and by force or violance attempt to prevent any person from engaging in any lawful vocation."

In Georgia a bill was introduced to forbid the collection of union dues among defense workers; it was amended to permit "voluntary contributions" and then passed.

These state measures were listed by the New York *World Telegram* in a story by Thomas L. Stokes on March 21, 1941, headed: "Rash of Labor Curbs Breaks Out in States. Reflects Public Alarm and Desire of Interests to Throttle Unions."

Various research bodies threw doubt on the effectiveness of restrictive measures. Said a study on "Labor and National Defense" issued in early 1941 by the Twentieth Century Fund:

> In no democratic country has it proven possible to prevent strikes simply by legislation. Under an authoritarian regime disturbances may be minimized, though never entirely prevented, by the constant threat of imprisonment and death. In a country unwilling to resort to such methods there is no way by which a thousand workers who quit work in a body can be prevented from doing so."

Australia, the Twentieth Century Fund study reported, "has had a compulsory arbitration statute since 1904. . . . Yet during the past twenty-five years Australia has had far more strikes relative to her population than either the United States or Great Britain."

According to *Time* magazine of April 21, 1941, William Hammatt Davis, vice chairman of the National Defense Mediation Board, told the House Military Affairs Commitee:

> When you pass compulsory legislation, you make the working man a slave, and there is no use producing defense materials for a nation of slaves, because if there is anything certain in history, it is that a national establishment which has to depend on slaves to produce its materials is inevitably destroyed.

President Roosevelt in his April 1 press conference argued against restrictive measures. Pleased with the progress of the National Defense Mediation Board, he wanted to give conciliation plans a fair trial.

In opposing measures other than mediation, President Roosevelt was following in the footsteps of President Wilson. In the first World War numerous demands were made for restrictive measures. Many of these demands, made by business groups and individuals, appear in the files of the Creel Committee—the

Committee on Public Information of the first World War. That Committee knew it had to "keep labor in line if the war was to be won," said Messrs. Mock and Larson in their study of the Committee's work. They added:

That was perhaps the biggest of all the big jobs assigned to the C.P.I. and the formal record does not even suggest the careful attention with which the campaign was followed.

But Creel declared:

The most important task we have before us today in the fight for unity is that of convincing the great mass of workers that our interest in democracy and justice begins at home.

The editor of the then [1917] popular *McClure's Magazine* wrote proposing a campaign utilizing a newspaper cartoon that showed Doughboys fighting in France with "no question of hours and overtime." The editor asked Creel:

Do you want us to build a sentiment for the conscription of labor or do you want to prevent the necessity of conscripting labor by wide circulation to such sentiment, as are in the . . . cartoon?

Creel replied:

I have reason to know that the workers of the United States are bitterly resentful of this sort of thing. They feel that if they are to surrender their demands in the matter of hours and overtime, that employers, manufacturers, wholesalers, retailers, and others, should make like concessions in the matter of profits. . . . This Committee cannot take part in the industrial dispute.

That was the national policy for the first World War. The propaganda struggle to decide the policy for this war is now at its height.

EXCERPTS

Strikes and lockouts (these miniature civil wars) are like wars between nations, both in their motives and in their consequences, a fact that shows more than all else how deep-seated a lack of equilibrium exists in democratic societies. The problem of the settlement of industrial disputes is at bottom the same as that of wars between nations. As the example of Great Britain has shown, it can be solved only by the collaboration of all parties which are engaged jointly in the production and distribution of goods.—*I. Bessling, on staff of International Labour Organisation, Montreal. Arbitration Journal. Ap. '41. p. 177.*

[The probabilities are that] public demand for a Federal agency to preserve the function of preventing strikes will remain. As soon as Germany is beaten, and war production begins to fall, labor will have incentive to strike to protect wage levels. To minimize strikes in vital industries, revamping of the War Labor Board or setting up a substitute as a permanent agency, probably outside the Department of Labor, is being proposed. Restraint on the strike weapon would be exercised through establishment of procedure calling for steps to assure full use of arbitration before resort to a strike. This subject is likely to be the hottest issue in the coming fights over labor policy.—*United States News. D. 1, '44. p. 16.*

In the more controversial field of disputes, two things seem to me to stand out. One is the spread of the idea that arbitration should be the final step in the grievance procedure—a view which the industry as well as the labor and public members of the War Labor Board have been consistently supporting. The more I see of modern industrial plants, the more they seem to me to be communities of people; and as every community needs a system of discipline—and a system of impartial justice to administer it—so the addition of arbitration to the grievance procedure is simply the bringing in, as it were, of the judge without whom no community can really get along.—*Lloyd K. Garrison, Executive Director and General Counsel, National War Labor Board. "Toward a National Labor Policy." p. 15. American Management Association. New York. 1943.*

A prime difficulty in the situation lies in the fact that neither the public nor labor nor employers have been told frankly that the War Labor Board is a compulsory arbitration tribunal. It has been admitted by some board officials that it is "virtually" a compulsory arbitration body, but this has not been "spelled out" clearly enough it is felt.

The nearest machinery for compulsory arbitration is the Railway Labor Act whose emergency fact-finding board's recommendations, until the last year or two, were invariably accepted by the parties. This machinery has been impaired lately since emergency board findings have been appealed by the unions to the President and subsequently adjusted.—*Louis Stark, Newspaper Correspondent; Specialist in Labor News. New York Times. Je. 27, '43. p. 3E.*

The [Smith-Connally] bill is designed to make striking illegal in wartime. This is a corollary of the compulsory arbitration provided by the War Labor Board. If the government determines what the terms and conditions of work shall be, the excuse for a strike is removed. On this reasoning it would seem sufficient to forbid strikes in wartime on the ground that the merits of a case would be decided by government adjudication rather than by the strike weapon. The need for government seizure of a plant would arise only in cases where there was good reason to suppose that the management was failing or would fail to abide by a government decision on wages, hours or working conditions.

But the Smith-Connally bill provides for seizure of a plant in which a strike occurs whether or not the employer shares responsibility for the strike. The strike does not become illegal until the plant seizure has taken place. The implication of this is that a strike cannot be made illegal merely on the ground that a union has struck against the order of a government agency. You are not "striking against the government," according to the theory of the bill, unless in addition still another government agency announces that it has seized and is operating the plant. The effect of this step, which would otherwise be unnecessary or irrelevant, will be in many cases to confuse the issue. The employer will often be in appearance and in effect punished for conditions beyond his control. Workers may sometimes strike for the very purpose of forcing government seizure of the employer's plant.—*Editorial. New York Times. Je. 14, '43. p. 16.*

There were 3,752 strikes during the year 1943, in which 1,981,279 workers were involved. Idleness during these strikes amounted to 13,500,529 man-days, which was equivalent to fifteen one-hundredths of 1 per cent of the available working time. About 69 workers in each 1,000 employed wage earners were involved in strikes during the year.

A large share of the 1943 strike activity occurred in the coal-mining industry, over 69 per cent of the total strike idleness resulting from coal-mining stoppages. Excluding all coal strikes, there were 3,322 strikes in other industries, involving 1,376,182 workers and 4,153,646 man-days of idleness.

Most of the strikes in 1943 were of short duration, and a large majority were spontaneous stoppages of employees that were unauthorized by unions. Considerably more than half of the strikes were over wages issues and registered the dissatisfaction of the workers with the wartime wage-stabilization policy.

In June 1943 when the large coal strikes seriously threatened to interfere with production of war materials, Congress passed the War Labor Disputes Act (over the President's veto) making illegal any strikes that would interfere with war work, until 30 days after a notice had been filed and a formal strike vote had been taken under Government supervision. This law was in effect during the last 6 months of the year, but only 34 of the 1,919 strikes occurring during this period took place after strike votes were taken under its provisions.

The National War Labor Board was concerned with approximately 39 per cent of the total strikes during 1943. In 674 cases the strikes took place before the issues were submitted to the Board; 565 strikes occurred while the disputes were under Board consideration; and 200 took place after the Board rendered its decisions. Some of the last group represented workers' protests against Board awards, while others were called to obtain compliance by employers. In at least 300 of the strikes that took place while the issues were pending before the Board, delay in Board decisions was cited as a major factor in causing the stoppage.—*Summary of article by Don Q. Crowther and Ruth S. Cole, Industrial Relations Division, Bureau of Labor Statistics. Monthly Labor Review. My. '44. p. 927.*

Compulsory investigation not involving the prohibition of strikes and lockouts pending award does not interfere with property rights or with liberty of contract, and hence is always due process of law. Compulsory investigation involving the prohibition of strikes and lockouts pending award does interfere with liberty of contract, but is justified under the police power as applied to the public utility industries, to essential industries where the units of operation are large, and to essential industries where there is nation-wide labor organization. It is probably due process of law in all cases when applied to essential industries. Compulsory arbitration is due process of law when applied to public utility industries or to essential industries which are organized in large units of production or which have national labor organization, so that the result of a labor dispute is likely to be a national stoppage of operation which will be disastrous to the public. It is not due process as applied to ordinary competitive industry where the units are small, where there is no national labor organization, and where an interruption of operation through labor disputes will not have serious consequences to the public.

Compulsory investigation not involving prohibition of strikes pending award clearly does not involve involuntary servitude in violation of the Thirteenth Amendment. Neither does compulsory investigation where there is a prohibition of strikes pending award. The individual workman may quit. It is not involuntary servitude to forbid him to quit temporarily in concert with his fellows, when he intends to return to the employment and to secure concessions from his employer. The same principle applies to compulsory arbitration.

The Federal Government may enact compulsory investigation or arbitration statutes applying to interstate railroads or to industries where labor disturbances are apt to result in serious and direct interference with interstate commerce. This will be the case with basic industries which operate in very large units or which have national labor organization. In all other cases the power to pass compulsory investigation or compulsory arbitration statutes, provided it exists at all, inheres in the states.—*Lieutenant-Colonel Sidney Post Simpson. Harvard Law Review. Ap. '25. p. 791-2.*

The definitions of conciliation, mediation, arbitration, and compulsory investigation here set forth are those which are generally accepted by labor relations students. It should be pointed out, however, that the terms conciliation and mediation are frequently used as being synonymous. Where this is true, the term conciliation will typically be used to mean what is defined below as "mediation."

Conciliation means nothing more than direct negotiations between the parties immediately involved in the dispute without the intervention of a third party. Where the firm is unionized, "collective bargaining" would be conciliation, though conciliation also would embrace the negotiations concerning individual grievances.

Mediation involves the intervention of a third party *who has no compulsory powers* but who merely attempts to *persuade* the parties to reach a settlement. The mediator may act merely as a "go-between" in the negotiations between the parties, or he may make definite suggestions as to the terms of settlement.

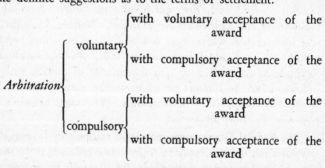

Arbitration involves the intervention of a third party for the express purpose of making a decision or an award with respect to the points at issue. Where the parties are not required to submit the dispute to arbitration, we have voluntary arbitration. Voluntary arbitration is usually accompanied by a previous agreement to abide by the award, i.e., by "compulsory" acceptance of the award but this is not necessarily so. Likewise the term "compulsory arbitration" as generally used means compulsory submission of the dispute to arbitration together with compulsory acceptance of the award, but technically we have compulsory arbitration wherever the submission of the dispute is compulsory regardless of whether the acceptance of the award is voluntary or compulsory.

Compulsory investigation involves the intervention of a state authority with the power to summon witnesses, take testimony, and make recommendations as to desirable terms of settlement even where either or both disputants are opposed to this process. Provision is usually made for publication of the recommendations in the hope that the pressure of public opinion will help compel the disputants to comply with the recommendations. Compulsory investigation is generally understood to involve the prohibition of strikes or lockouts pending the completion of the investigation and the publication of recommendations, but we may have (and do have in a number of laws) compulsory investigation without the prohibition of strikes or lockouts.—*Howard S. Kaltenborn, University of Nebraska; Chief Wage Analyst, Regional War Labor Board, Detroit, Michigan. In his "Governmental Adjustment of Labor Disputes." Foundation Press, Inc. Chicago. '43. Footnote, p. 2-3.*

When a man bites his wife, it's news. But when he brings home the groceries regularly, not even the neighbors know it. Strikes make headlines. What lies back of them rarely does. And industrial peace goes on month after month without benefit of printer's ink. Every student of labor relations takes this for granted. And so do most union leaders—although with occasional traces of asperity.

But to the average newspaper reader, it rarely occurs that the primary function of a union is to establish conditions under which it is possible to maintain industrial peace by the application to industry of democratic processes. These processes are generally dull and uninteresting. They consist of giving to workers a voice in determining the conditions under which they work and providing them with a right to appeal from the decisions of their immediate economic superiors.

Essentially, trade unionism in modern industry is the substitution of the ballot box for revolt, and judicial appeal for trial by ordeal. Collective bargaining rests upon the ballot box, and standard trade union grievance adjustment procedure boils down to the right of appeal. Both of them are substitutes for violence. When they break down, resort is had to economic or physical forces. Consequently, the answer to strikes in defense industries is not the abolition of trade unionism but more and better trade unionism.

Decent and law-abiding workers rarely go on strike for whimsical reasons. Back of most strikes lie grievances which are either real or *seem* very real to those who experience them. The problem is to adjust these complaints quickly or to show, by investigation, that they are imaginary. To suppress the overt evidence of unrest does not and will not solve the problem. The unrest will inevitably make itself felt in forms other than strike. Slowdowns on the job, excessive rates of labor turn-over, difficulties in securing adequate supplies of labor are the familiar results of accumulated and unrelieved unrest. Every one of these sources of inefficiency can be illustrated by reference to the past year of the defense effort in areas in which unionism is still fighting for recognition, or in which for various reasons it is not effectively operating. These losses in production do not get into the headlines. Yet they are quite as important as the losses which result from strikes. The answer in both cases is to extend and improve the machinery for investigation, adjustment, appeal, compromise, and the enforcement of agreements reached.

The function of trade unions in enforcing agreements is, I think, not generally understood. Few agreements are universally acceptable to everyone throughout the entire period in which the agreement applies. But unless an agreement can be enforced it has little meaning. Trade union officers spend a large part of their time, energy and prestige in persuading their constitutencies to abide by agreement which they have ratified. No sober citizen, concerned with the defense of his country, should permit that fact to be dislodged from his mind by scare headlines about strikes, racketeering or communism.

In summary of this point, I think it may be said that in countries, like those embraced in the British Commonwealth of Nations and in the United States, in which the traditions of individual freedom are generations or centuries old, the enthusiastic and efficient cooperation of their millions of workers can be achieved only by permitting them a voice in determining the conditions under which they work. This means not merely that legislative efforts to repress or restrict the growth and operation of the labor movement must be opposed, nor merely that the existence of organized labor must be tolerated, but that its growth and the development of its democratic procedure must be encouraged by every means available to the government.—*R. R. R. Brooks, Special Labor Consultant, Office of Production Management, Washington, D.C. Address at Annual Conference of the Canadian Institute of Public Affairs. Labour Gazette (Ottawa). O. '41. p. 1273.*

When compulsory arbitration was established in Australia, it was hoped that the existence of the [Commonwealth Arbitration] Court would promote more friendly relations between capital and labor and eliminate strikes. But labor in Australia has continued to show a strong sense of class solidarity, and strikes have persisted, although perhaps with lessened intensity. Yet both labor and capital are opposed to the abolition of the system and there is now very little open criticism of the Court except among the extreme sections on both sides. Some of the more radical element in the Australian labor movement feel that more could be accomplished for the workers by unrestricted collective bargaining. But most of the leaders in the labor movement believe that the arbitration system makes possible a higher general level of wages and better working conditions. Their opposition has taken the form of agitation for a change in the personnel of the federal court and for legislative amendments which would provide emphasis on conciliation and reduce legalism rather than for any drastic change in the system as such. And while there are employers here and there who have felt hampered by the arbitration system in the depression because it has restricted their power to cut wages, the majority of employers are grateful for the protection which the system affords against competitive wage cutting.

Most employers in Australia apparently prefer to have minimum wage rates fixed and to feel free to concentrate their attention on other items of cost.

It is open to question whether the Australian arbitration system has made for a reduction in industrial disputes. In their awards affecting working conditions, the arbitration courts have provided protection and fair treatment to the workers and removed some of the causes of industrial friction without seriously hampering the operating efficiency of private enterprise. Against this is the probability that the system, if it has not actually heightened the cleavage between capital and labor, has not served to bring them closer together. Thus, the early development of compulsory arbitration in Australia has, to some extent at least, kept Australia from pursuing the American experiments in employee representation plans and union-management cooperation. While there can be no doubt that in many cases the existence of the arbitration system has prevented strikes, it is uncertain whether the same result could not have been accomplished more effectively by some voluntary system of arbitration set up within each industry as a result of a mutual agreement between employers and the unions in that industry.

The cumbersome and overlapping system of arbitration tribunals has inevitably proved a handicap in adjusting industrial disputes. Wherever it is possible to prove the existence of an interstate dispute, litigants dissatisfied with a state award have transferred their claims to the federal court, thus adding greatly to the complication and expense of arbitration. Yet, legislative attempts, first in 1926, to extend the powers of the Commonwealth Court and later, in 1929, to turn over arbitration largely to the state courts, both failed. Attempts at unification are necessarily extremely difficult to accomplish in a federal system where state rights are zealously guarded. However, the gradual extension of the jurisdiction of the Commonwealth Court and its increased prestige have tended to reduce overlapping in recent years.

If a unified system of arbitration were adopted in Australia under the general jurisdiction of the Commonwealth Court but granting considerable local autonomy to regional tribunals, it would be possible to test the potentialities of compulsory arbitration. If conciliation committees were appointed for the industries of each of the states, under the chairmanship of a commissioner, and given full power to settle all industrial disputes except those which concerned wages and hours, with no appeal from their decisions, the process of arbitration would be expedited and freed from much of its present legalism. If suitable commissioners could be found, such a system might show a distinctly better record in eliminating industrial disputes.

In wage determinations the Australian arbitration courts have succeeded in eliminating excessively low wages and in maintaining a considerable degree of wage flexibility in the face of a strong and articulate trade-union movement. Although the labor movement has not accepted the Court's arguments in favor of wage reductions in the depression as valid, the discussion by the Court in 1931 of the necessity for wage reductions in view of the fall in the national income appears to have been of very considerable value in promoting an understanding of the economic situation of the country among a large section of the electorate. From the beginning of the depression the Court has taken more notice of fluctuations in economic conditions than almost any other official or semi-official body in the country. . . .

The record of experience with compulsory arbitration in Australia is not sufficiently satisfactory to lend great encouragement to those who believe that the United States should undertake a similar experiment. If it has proved difficult to administer a system of compulsory arbitration for 7,000,000 people, the problem would be vastly magnified in the United States. It appears desirable, therefore, for us to experiment further with voluntary arbitration methods before committing ourselves to any such system. Once adopted, compulsory arbitration is likely to interfere with the development of the best spirit of coöperation between capital and labor. Yet, we in this country may eventually have to accept it unless we can find a workable compromise between the extreme positions adopted by both labor and capital in some of the recent industrial disputes.—*W. Rupert Maclaurin, Massachusetts Institute of Technology. "Recent Experience with Compulsory Arbitration in Australia." American Economic Review. March* 1938. *p.* 77-9, 81.

CASE FOR VOLUNTARY ARBITRATION

SHOULD COMPULSORY ARBITRATION OF
LABOR DISPUTES BE INSTITUTED
IN THE DEFENSE INDUSTRIES? [1]

Virtually all attempts at compulsory arbitration legislation to end strikes in democratic countries have failed to achieve practtical success.

In the United States, Kansas tried it in 1920, but Kansas no longer has a compulsory arbitration law because it failed to end strikes. Workers went on strike despite the law, with the result that jails filled with skilled and semi-skilled workers who would have been far more valuable on the production line. The situation was much the same in Australia and New Zealand, when these countries tried compulsory arbitration.

On the basis of historical precedent, therefore, it has become clear that force and pacific settlement through a willingness to "talk things over" are incompatible and cannot be hitched together—with or without a national defense program.

If you accept the premise that a law forcing arbitration in all labor disputes will not necessarily halt strikes, then the legislation automatically becomes useless as a guarantee of greater production and more industrial peace. In addition, such a law, if passed, might increase the possibility of violence arising out of labor disputes since these would bring heavily armed officers into action immediately to put down the lockout or strike unsettled by enforced arbitration. Would it not be better for the United States to use voluntary arbitration, conciliation, and mediation than to bring into existence a law loaded with possibilities of widespread bloodshed?

But there are even more basic reasons why compulsory arbitration should not be instituted in labor disputes:

[1] By C. V. Whitney, Chairman, Board of Directors of Pan American Airways; President, American Arbitration Association. *Modern Industry.* 1:56, 60. February 15, 1941.

1. *The Democratic Reason.* Voluntary settlement of grievances or disputes is one of the highest expressions of civilization. To the rights of free speech, free assemblage, a free press and freedom of worship is added the right of individuals to settle their own controversies. This has become one of the highest forms of self-regulation—infinitely precious in a democracy and a bulwark against regimentation. Once compulsion enters, freedom is lost. If freedom disappears, democracy as we know it also vanishes.

2. *The Legal Reason.* The Kansas experiment in compulsory arbitration was held unconstitutional by the United States Supreme Court in the case of the Wolff Packing Co. against the Court of Industrial Relations of Kansas. It is reasonable, therefore, to assume that a federal experiment in compulsory arbitration would also be discarded eventually as unconstitutional.

3. *The Psychological Reason.* This is one of the strongest arguments against the proponents of a compulsory arbitration law—if the major premise in favor of such legislation is that it would increase production. All men and women, whether they work on an assembly line or behind a desk, will work harder and find more satisfaction in their jobs if they know their labor is not forced on them, not compelled by a law which says they cannot quit if they have a serious grievance. In the same way, the employer loses his "freedom of action," a psychological blow at his enterprise.

4. *The Enforcement Reason.* A compulsory arbitration law, if heavily opposed by labor in the form of many "test strikes" all over the country, might be very difficult to enforce. In the case of Kansas, as well as Australia and New Zealand, authorities found it virtually impossible to handle thousands of workers in strike outbreaks and deputies frequently refused to make mass arrests necessary under the law.

The newspapers and radio, especially in these days of intensified national defense efforts, have given great prominence to lockouts, strikes, and jurisdictional disputes by labor unions of all kinds. Very little notice is taken of the thousands of disputes settled peacefully and voluntarily without the waste of a single man-hour of work. If more prominence were given to the negotiated or voluntarily arbitrated controversies occurring almost daily in the United States, the public would get a truer picture of the sincerity and democracy of American industry.

The trend of American thought is away from compulsion. In 800 labor disputes filed last year with the Department of Labor in Washington, 62 per cent contained provisions for pacific settlement of all future disputes without any form of compulsion leading toward their use. Many of these agreements were between large unions and the management of industries vital to national defense. In literally thousands of instances, management and men are entering into labor agreements with arbitration provisions under their own steam, proving again and again that compulsion is not necessary and that only education is a primary necessity.

For twenty centuries of known history, through mighty battles and changing empires, the principle of conciliation and arbitration has survived unchanged and today flourishes in all of its simplicity and flexibility throughout this nation and the western hemisphere. In this form it is written into treaties and international trade pacts; it is written into labor and commercial contracts. It is embodied in the by-laws and regulations of trade associations. And it is imperishably written into American arbitration law and upheld by hundreds of American court decisions. It is today expressive of a great American freedom—the right to settle voluntarily a dispute by the two parties to it, by a judge of their own choice whom they clothe with the power to make a final judgment as to them.

The American Arbitration Association, which has organized civil, commercial, and industrial arbitration on the western hemisphere, not only has carried this tradition inviolate, but also is unalterably opposed to the slightest infringement upon that right either in times of peace or war; for once it is justified by war, it changes its inherited quality and arbitration itself will be destroyed.

There are three types of pacific settlement of disputes. One is by conciliation, which is a process of changing viewpoints so the parties themselves will settle their own differences. Obviously, no element of force can or should be applied where persuasion is the method.

There is a second type of pacific settlement called mediation. This is a process of bargaining, first by the representatives of each side; they too invite an outsider when their own efforts fail. Obviously, any element of compulsion will destroy free bargaining power.

Arbitration is the third type of pacific settlement. Here the parties, unable to arrive at a settlement by conciliation or mediation, and believing their own resources exhausted or their arguments futile, mutually agree to refer the matter to an impartial outsider. Only at this point does the controversy pass beyond the control of the parties.

How is voluntary arbitration made effective? If the dispute is already in existence, the parties sign a written submission, which sets forth the issue and refers it to an impartial person named by them, or according to a method they agree upon. In that written agreement they promise to abide by the award. No party may compel another to sign that submission and no arbitration can be had without it; and if it is sought to enforce it against a non-signatory, the court says *no*—it was obtained under duress. So, also, if fraud is used to obtain it.

But suppose the parties to a contract want to insure themselves against future litigation or labor stoppages at the time they enter into business or industrial relations? Then they put an arbitration provision in a contract providing that any dispute arising under or in connection with that contract shall be submitted to arbitration.

No person entering into such a contract is compelled to accept such a clause or abide by it if there is the slightest evidence of coercion, for the courts have repeatedly held such contracts to be void and unenforceable. No law requires a party in dispute to give up his right of litigation and make such an agreement. No one can compel him to forgo his right to a jury trial except by his own volition.

All an agreement to arbitrate a future dispute does and all any arbitration law does is to say that when two persons have voluntarily and willingly and without coercion made such a contract, they shall observe it in the same way as any other contract.

Should the exigencies of war and the program for defense change this essential quality and practice of arbitration? Emphatically no.

Any process of justice which imposes inequality—as between parties in dispute—destroys itself, for the elements of good faith and goodwill are not present, but have been driven away by force. There is then no disposition to obey the award. In the Voluntary Industrial Arbitration Tribunal, conducted by the American Arbitration Association, more than 400 decisions have been made under voluntary agreements to arbitrate and every one has been honored in good spirit by both parties. This is not the history of compulsory litigation, as appeal after appeal testifies.

Were arbitration to be made compulsory, it would not be long until it would become as arbitrary and inflexible as legal processes and all of its self-regulatory benefits would be lost. In place of voluntary attendance and cooperation, the summons and the subpoena and the marshal would appear. In other words, force would rear its ugly head and destroy the friendly elements of the arbitration process by gradually usurping the powers of persuasion.

One of the most successful organizations in this country is the National Mediation Board, which deals with controversies in the transportation industry. All of its processes are pacificatory. It investigates and mediates. If mediation fails, the Board is directed by law to endeavor to have the parties arbitrate. If that fails, the President is empowered to appoint a special emergency board to investigate and report its findings to the President. These successive processes have kept peace within industry for many years. They prove that force is unnecessary and that persuasive processes achieve the end more certainly and permanently.

Can stoppages of deliveries of war materials so vital to our national defense be avoided without compulsory arbitration? Emphatically, yes. First, by giving priority in the granting of those contracts to concerns that have conciliation, mediation, or arbitration arrangements with their men, voluntarily entered into by mutual agreement. Second, by having a model provision for arbitration in all labor contracts, which allows a cooling-off period before a strike can be called without denying the right, and which provides for arbitration when this fails. And lastly, by having impartial and competent facilities and machinery so there need be no delay in invoking these provisions the moment the grievance or dispute raises its head.

Whatever legislation may be found necessary to end strikes as a measure of national defense, it should not be in the direction of destroying the voluntary principle of arbitration, now being so generally used in labor contracts.

HOW TO INSURE INDUSTRIAL PEACE [2]

Strikes and work stoppages in defense industries make front-page news today. Everyone is concerned to know how we can secure industrial peace.

In some quarters the strikes in defense industries have led to demands for laws to prohibit such strikes or to enforce compulsory arbitration.

Those most closely in touch with the problem have not, however, given such demands any considerable backing. Leaders among employers and labor alike have opposed them. William S. Knudsen and Sidney Hillman, of the Office of Production Management, have testified against them. The Committee on Manufacture of the Chamber of Commerce of the United States has gone on record against compulsion in labor disputes. The National Association of Manufacturers has resolved that "Compulsory governmental arbitration of labor disputes is contrary to American principles."

How, then, are we to deal with the emergencies that do arise? The President, by his appointment of the National Defense Mediation Board, has indicated the Federal Government's confidence in mediation as the proper approach to the orderly handling of situations of which strikes and lockouts are the acute symptoms. The National Defense Mediation Board is an eleven-man body, consisting of three representatives of the public; four representatives of labor—two from the American Federation of Labor and two from the Congress of Industrial Organizations; and four representatives of employers. Cases are referred to the

[2] By William H. Davis, Vice Chairman, National Defense Mediation Board. From a five-way symposium. *Rotarian.* 58:27-9. June 1941.

Mediation Board only after the regular processes of conciliation have been unable to effect a settlement. When a dispute is certified to the Board by the Secretary of Labor, the Board names a panel of at least three persons, representing the public, labor, and employers, to deal with the case.

This panel is authorized, according to the executive order establishing the Board, to make every effort at adjustment by assisting the parties to negotiate arrangements and to afford them means for voluntary arbitration. The panel may designate arbitrators when requested by both sides. It may assist in seeking methods to avoid or resolve future controversies. It is empowered to conduct hearings, take testimony, and make findings of fact and formulate recommendations for settlements of disputes, and to make these findings public.

Thus the Government seeks to provide some concrete machinery by which the parties to an industrial dispute may reach a voluntary settlement of their grievances. An essential factor in effective mediation is that neither side is forced to accept a recommendation with which it does not agree, and neither side surrenders any of its fundamental rights. This contrasts, of course, with any sort of arrangement for compulsory arbitration, whereby the parties to the dispute are bound to accept an award, no matter what it may turn out to be.

Since there is in certain quarters a persistent sentiment for the imposition of some kind of compulsory control over labor disputes, it is worth while to examine how such controls have worked out in actual practice when other democratic countries have tried them. Here I refer to the findings of fact brought in by the research staff for a recent survey, *Labor and National Defense,* made by The Twentieth Century Fund. The Fund is an impartial agency for research in current economic problems. I am familiar with the findings for I serve as chairman of the special committee appointed by the Fund to review the factual report and make recommendations, based on the facts.

On the subject of compulsory arbitration, perhaps the most illuminating figures assembled by the research staff have to do with the experience of Great Britain during the World War in 1914-1918. During this conflict, Great Britain introduced compulsory arbitration of disputes in the war industries. The Munitions of War Act of July 1915, made strikes and lockouts illegal, imposed heavy penalties for violations, and provided that all disputes must be referred to the Board of Trade for settlement. During the next 33 months, however, more than $1\frac{1}{2}$ million munitions workers took part in illegal strikes and made themselves liable to potential fines. Only about one fifth of one per cent of all the workers in the illegal strikes were actually prosecuted. Voluntary methods proved much more effective in settling disputes than the use of force.

During the present war, strikes in war industries have once more been banned by an order-in-council, but this was agreed to by both labor and employers and the order contains no penalty provisions against strikers. The Government has relied on the influence of labor members of the Cabinet and on the long history of cordial relations between unions and employers. The regular machinery of collective bargaining has been effective in adjusting disputes even in a severe emergency, and relatively few strikes have occurred.

Another country whose experience may be cited is Australia. The Fund research staff reported that Australia has had a compulsory arbitration statute since 1904, "yet during the past 25 years Australia has had far more strikes relative to her population than either the United States or Great Britain. While many of these strikes were clearly illegal, penalties have seldom been imposed on the strikers."

Another example cited is Canada, which has had a law since 1908 requiring a period of delay and investigation before strikes may be called in the mining and public-utility industries. During the period 1908-1925, the staff reports, "there were 425 unlawful strikes in which requirements of the act were simply ignored. . . . Any attempt to enforce this section would have alienated all union support and would probably have brought a quick repeal of the act."

The United States got through the first World War without any law prohibiting strikes. The tremendous pressure of the wartime demand for continuous production was made effective through governmental agencies operating on the basis of voluntary agreement.

It was on the basis of such findings as these that the Fund Committee came to the conclusion that "world experience has demonstrated that the cooperation of labor cannot be gained by compulsion. Strikes in democratic countries can be prevented only by agreement between employers and workers—not by law. Opposition to compulsion in the settlement of labor disputes is one subject on which there seems to be agreement in all divisions of the labor movement and in the ranks of management."

It may be well now to examine some figures on how mediation has worked. Research has shown that the proportion of mediation cases successfully adjusted usually runs above 90 per cent. The United Conciliation Service was able to adjust all but 146 of the 1,678 disputes in which it intervened during 1938-1939. The New York State Mediation Board adjusted all but 30 of 310 cases during 1939. Many of these disputes would have been settled without mediation, but they probably would have been settled more slowly and with much greater loss of working time.

Because of the great variety of situations which arise it is hard to generalize about the actual technique of mediation. Since the mediator can intervene only by consent of both parties and has no coercive power, his first task is to create confidence by showing a grasp of the problem and a non-partisan attitude. The next step is usually to define the area of controversy by discovering on what points the parties are already in substantial agreement. Beyond this the method followed varies from case to case. The mediator may hold joint conferences to debate the issues and explore possible bases of settlement. He may confer with each side separately, and serve as a medium for the transmission of proposals. If these methods do not work, he may have to improvise a plan of settlement and urge both parties to accept it. The force of public opinion provides a sanction for his proposals, particularly during a period of great national effort, such as the current defense program.

The processes of conciliation require more than mere withholding of a strike or lockout; they demand that existing conditions be maintained, that labor's pledge "to take no action which may in any way impede production" during the conciliation period be matched by a pledge on the part of management to make no changes in working conditions during that period. These basic requirements need to be supplemented by established procedures to which the parties are more or less accustomed or to which they have expressly agreed. The strikes which have occurred in the defense industries are evidence that, despite the purpose and determination of the national leaders of management and labor, these essentials of effective conciliation have not been brought home to the parties concerned in many specific cases.

In view of the desirability of voluntary mediation, the Fund Committee made a specific recommendation toward the encouragement of such procedure by voluntary agreement between the parties concerned. The Committee recommended:

> That there be initiated a concerted effort to incorporate by voluntary action in all existing collective agreements affecting plants engaged in defense production (a) a specific covenant not to strike or lockout during the term of the agreement and to set up grievance machinery to settle disputes arising under the agreement, in all cases where the collective agreement does not already contain such a covenant, and (b) a further covenant that the working conditions established by the agreement shall be maintained without change and that there shall be no interruption of work during negotiations for renewal of the agreement.

This proposal offers some concrete suggestions for extending the basic principle that, in my opinion, points a way toward industrial peace—namely, the principle of voluntary mediation.

COMPULSORY ARBITRATION [3]

Compulsory arbitration means compulsory labor. Compulsory labor means involuntary servitude, which is forbidden by the Thirteenth Amendment to the Constitution of the United States. It is also in conflict with the Fourteenth Amendment to the Constitution which assures freedom of contract.

Compulsory arbitration would mean that some public official would appoint members of an arbitration board without consultation with either the employers or employees. Therefore, the representatives of the employers and employees would appear before

[3] American Federation of Labor. Washington, D.C. 6p. mimeo.

the board in the guise of litigants. They would argue to the bitter end for the most extreme demands. Whatever the decision reached it would be unsatisfactory to one side or the other or both.

Compulsory arbitration implies compulsory compliance with the award made. This would compel the employes to work against their will. If they rebelled they would be fined, sent to prison or both. Such a law would be repugnant to all justice-loving and freedom-loving Americans.

But the United States Supreme Court has declared that the price of a product or the wages of workers in private employment cannot be fixed by legislation. June 11, 1923, it declared the provision of the Kansas Court of Industrial Relations Act, which provided that the Industrial Court should fix through compulsory arbitration the wages of employees in certain industries, was unconstitutional. The Court said:

> It has never been supposed, since the adoption of the Constitution, that the business of the butcher, or the baker, the tailor, the woodchopper, the mining operator or the miner was clothed with such a public interest that the price of his product or his wages could be fixed by state regulation. It is true that in the days of the early common law an omnipotent parliament did regulate prices and wages as it chose, and occasionally a colonial legislature sought to exercise the same power; but nowadays one does not devote one's property or business to the public use or clothe it with a public interest merely because one makes commodities for, and sells to, the public in the common callings of which those above mentioned are instances.

> If, as in effect contended by counsel for the state, the common callings are clothed with a public interest by a mere legislative declaration, which necessarily authorizes full and comprehensive regulation within legislative discretion, there must be a revolution in the relation of government to general business. This will be running the public interest argument into the ground, to use a phrase of Mr. Justice Bradley when characterizing a similarly extreme contention. It will be impossible to reconcile such results with the freedom of contract and of labor secured by the Fourteenth Amendment.

In declaring that law unconstitutional the Court said:

> We think the Industrial Court Act, insofar as it permits fixing of wages in plaintiff-in-error's packing house, is in conflict with the Fourteenth Amendment and deprives it of its property and liberty of contract without due process of law.

The Kansas Act also provided that the Industrial Court should fix the number of hours in a workday. An appeal was made to the United States Supreme Court and on April 13, 1925, it repeated its former decision declaring the law unconstitutional and "violative of the rights of freedom of contract and property guaranteed by the Constitution." In its decision the Court said:

On three occasions when the Act was before us we referred to it as undertaking to establish a system of "compulsory arbitration." *Howat* v. *Kansas,* 258 U.S. 181, 184; *Wolff Packing Company* v. *Court of Industrial Relations,* 262 U.S. 522, 542; *Dorchy* v. *Kansas* 264 U.S. 286, 288. The Supreme Court of the state in a recent opinion criticizes this use of the term "arbitration." *State* v. *Howat,* 116 Kan. 412, 415. We recognize that in its usual acceptation the term indicates a proceeding based entirely on the consent of the parties. And we recognize also that this Act dispenses with their consent. Under it they have no voice in selecting the determining agency or in defining what that agency is to investigate and determine. And yet the determination is to bind them even to the point of preventing them from agreeing on any change in the terms fixed therein, unless the agency approves. To speak of a proceeding with such attributes merely as an arbitration might be subject to criticism, but we think its nature is fairly reflected when it is spoken of as a compulsory arbitration.

The Court added:

When the case was first here the question chiefly agitated, and therefore discussed and decided, was whether the authority to fix wages as an incident of the compulsory arbitration could be applied to a business like that of the Wolff Company consistently with the protection which the due process of law clause of the Fourteenth Amendment affords to the liberty of contract and rights of property. The question was answered in the negative and the act was held invalid insofar as it gives that authority. The subject was much considered and the principles which were recognized and applied were distinctly stated.

In summing up the principles upon which the Court based its decision it said:

The authority which the Act gives respecting the fixing of hours of labor is merely a feature of the system of compulsory arbitration and has no separate purpose. It was exerted by the state agency as a part of that system and the state court sustained its exertion as such. As a part of the system it shares the invalidity of the whole.

January 27, 1908, the Supreme Court in its decision in the Adair case, sometimes referred to as the "blacklist" case, said:

The right of a person to sell his labor upon such terms as he deems proper is in its essence the same as the right of the purchaser of labor to prescribe the conditions upon which he will accept such labor from the persons offering to sell. . . . In all such particulars the employer and employe have equality of right, and any legislation that disturbs that equality is an arbitrary interference with the liberty of contract which no government can legally justify in a free land.

In the Coppage case the Supreme Court said:

Included in the right of personal liberty and the right of private property—partaking of the nature of each—is the right to make contracts for the acquisition of property. Chief among such contracts is that of personal employment, by which labor and other services are exchanged for money or other forms of property. If this right be struck down or arbitrarily interfered with, there is a substantial impairment of liberty in the long-established constitutional sense. The right is as essential to the laborer as to the capitalist, to the poor as to the rich; for the vast majority of persons have no other honest way to begin to acquire property save by working for money.

The Court then quotes from certain laws that had been held constitutional, such as a state statute requiring coal to be mined for payment of miners' wages before screening, requiring the redemption in cash of store orders issued in payment of wages, regulating the time within which wages shall be paid to employees in certain specified industries and other cases of like import and effect, but adds:

In none of the statutes thus sustained, was the liberty of employer or employees to fix the amount of wages the one was willing to pay and the other willing to receive interfered with. Their tendency and purpose was to prevent unfair and perhaps fraudulent methods in the payment of wages and in no sense can they be said to be, or to furnish a precedent for, wage-fixing statutes.

With the decisions of the Supreme Court before us it would seem a waste of effort on the part of those who favor compulsory labor to persistently urge such legislation. Apparently continual harping on the subject is for propaganda purposes.

Labor favors arbitration, but it must be voluntary. In any controversy labor should select one arbiter and the employers should select another, and the two should agree upon an umpire. Even voluntary arbitration should not be resorted to until after the employers and employees had endeavored by around the table talk to come to an agreement. In these conferences it has always been found that much bitterness disappears and each side endeavors to the best of its ability to protect its interests without doing serious injury to the other. If finally the employer and the employees cannot agree then labor believes they should resort to voluntary arbitration. Whatever decision is reached by a voluntary arbitration board will, in nine cases out of ten, be satisfactory to both sides, but if not satisfactory, it will not create bitterness, causing relations between the two to become more strained.

Propaganda has been spread in regard to compulsory arbitration laws in Australia. The following is an extract from a speech made in the Federal Parliament of Australia by Prime Minister Hughes in March 1920:

The industrial question, looked at from one point of view is the result of eternal conflict between the classes. Looked at from another point of view—and I believe, the right one—it is the inevitable consequence of modern civilization and modern methods of production and distribution.

I confess that I have no remedy at hand. This House has been a laboratory of industrial experiments. I listened to Alfred Deakin introduce the arbitration and conciliation bill in a most glowing speech, and I feel now as I felt then that along the lines then outlined mankind ought to walk, abandoning the crude barbaric methods of industrial warfare. Years have passed and this perfect piece of legislation has turned out to be, despite every kind of minister in office, the most inefficient and hopelessly futile effort to solve the industrial question that ever came out of the laboratory of any industrial shop. Even the president of the court from time to time indulged in gloomy jeremiads and had been torn with pangs of despair.

It is a court the approach to which is marked by barbed-wire entanglements. At the very threshold of its portals there is an almost bottomless pit, and those who by happy chance found their way into the court wander aimlessly about, and at last come out almost without knowing it and saying, "Where are we?" or "What has happened?" It has frequently been necessary to strike in order to get into the court, which was designed to prevent industrial strife! Law abiding unions which had been waiting patiently have then been pushed aside, and the others have gone in and come out full to repletion. The jurisdiction of the court has been riddled again and again by High Court judgment.

Among the associations that have persistently fought the trade unions with every step in their progress and which has never made a secret of its antipathy to the trade unions and the principles for which they contend is the Illinois Manufacturers' Association. Nevertheless Mr. Dorr E. Felt, who was its president, in December 1920 delivered a speech before the National Association of Employment Managers in which he said:

In studying the industrial history of England, I am rather discouraged respecting much that is being advocated; for instance, compulsory arbitration.

I am very well acquainted with Mr. George S. Beeby, Minister of Labor for New South Wales, Australia, where labor legislation has been carried further than in any other place in the world, involving a complete system of Wage Boards and Courts for the settlement of industrial strife instituted and now in operation since 1901. Mr. Beeby is the author of the present law. He tells me that, instead of reducing industrial strife, under laws which forbid strikes, industrial strife and strikes have increased. In fact, the time lost on account of industrial disputes in New South Wales was six times as great in 1917 as in 1913.

In one of our recent bills in Congress there was a proposition to forbid strikes on the part of public employees, in this case railroad employees. I am not in favor of that, because the experience with such laws in Europe has been a failure. It is a good deal like plugging up a volcano, sooner or later you have an explosion that is greater than anything that would have happened had the vent been open all the time.

After the Black Death—The Great Plague—I think that was in 1347 —there was a great scarcity of labor, something similar to the present. Laws were passed forbidding labor organizations and strikes. The first one was passed in 1351. It didn't do the work, so from time to time more severe laws and penalties were enacted, until they finally got to the point where those that struck were worked in chain gangs, and some were branded with hot irons.

I have never found a case where laws forbidding strikes were effective. In the early middle ages under conditions of extreme ignorance and serfdom, it seemed to work for a time, but in the end it always failed.

It will thus be seen that the men best informed as to the working of compulsory arbitration laws in Australia and the president of an anti-labor association of manufacturers in the United States are all of the same opinion as to its impracticability.

THE RIGHT TO STRIKE AND COMPULSORY ARBITRATION [4]

The offensive against labor now going on in Congress and in the commercial press is reaching new heights of fury and vindictiveness expressed primarily in the Vinson bill and the Ball bill, secondarily in a host of legislative and administrative acts and proposals aimed at one purpose—to smash the trade union movement.

The Vinson and Ball bills are the two main weapons being employed in this all-out anti-labor drive. Together, they would destroy the right to strike, freeze wages and conditions at present levels by outlawing union shop contracts and sanctifying the open shop, would declare an open season on union leaders and active members by permitting employers to fire them on suspicion of being subversive, and would prohibit normal union activities by outlawing so-called "coercive methods."

The Federal Anti-Sabotage Act and the Model State Sabotage Act already enacted in a few states implement the attack on labor unions.

It is not necessary to go into detail on these prohibitions. Any person who has had experience with the courts knows precisely how such sections of the bills would be used against labor. They have been so used in the past, and there is nothing in the record to convince us that they would not be so used again. There is nothing in the record of the men who are pushing these bills to convince us that they have any other purpose in mind other than the single purpose of smashing organized labor.

What is more interesting, though, is the campaign behind these bills, the steady work of anti-labor agitation in Congress, in the press, on the radio, in numerous government agencies, that has led up to their presentation to Congress and to the present drive to rush them through before the country becomes aware of the serious threat to the whole fabric of democracy which they contain.

[4] By Lee Pressman, General Counsel, Congress of Industrial Organizations. Address before the National Lawyers Guild Convention, May 31, 1941. *Lawyers Guild Review.* 1:40-5. June 1941.

Frequently this campaign is laid to war hysteria. The present emergency, it is argued, makes Congressmen lose their heads, makes it possible for reactionary forces to seize on a period of confusion and fear to push through a program they would not dare undertake otherwise, makes former friends of labor fall away and even makes labor itself hesitant in defending its rights and its existence.

This is only part of the origin of the drive to take away labor's right to strike and to impose compulsory settlement of disputes, as provided in the Vinson and Ball bills. The hysteria exists, it is true, and it has been deliberately whipped up for the purpose of getting such strait-jacket measures across. But the campaign to put these restrictions on labor began a long time ago, both in Congress and in the press. The present hysteria is not the source of these proposed restrictions. It is only the mask under which they are proposed.

To accept war hysteria as the cause of these anti-labor plans is to fall into a trap prepared by the enemies of labor and of progress. It is an illusion that can lead, and has already led, many well-meaning people into believing that the hysteria itself is the disease, rather than a symptom, and that once the hysteria passes, all will be well again.

The real source of this anti-labor offensive lies much further back than the present emergency period, further back than 1940 or even 1939. It lies in a long-range plan to destroy labor's organized strength in order to guarantee monopoly profits to the employers, profits that can only be secured at the expense of labor, the farmers and the common people generally. The destruction of labor's rights and labor's gains is absolutely necessary to carrying out this long range plan, because organized labor is today the only force standing in the way of its realization.

Another half truth that tends to prevent clear thinking about this anti-labor drive is the argument that it is the product of a period of inflated war profits, drawn from the present arms program. Of course employers are getting inflated profits today. You have only to look at corporation statements published over recent months to see the fantastic sums they are drawing in. And of course they are very happy to be doing so—but they are after more than even the huge amounts they are making under the present programs.

The profit records of major corporations in 1940 and the records for the first three months of 1941 indicate that this year will be one of fantastic profit levels in spite of some increases in taxation. For example, the United States Steel Corporation has reported a profit of $102,000,000 for 1940—100 per cent higher than in 1939. The General Motors Corporation announces a profit of $195,500,000 for 1940 after deducting $125,000,000 for taxes. The Company employs on an average of some 220,000 employees. At the rate of profit announced, each worker earned for the company an average profit of $890 in 1940.

These corporations are interested in making these profits permanent, in making sure that they will enjoy them beyond the present emergency. Employers are realistic, up to a point, and they realize that even this war and the armament program must come to an end sometime. To prepare for that event, they must again see to it that labor's opposition is effectively silenced.

The proof of this long range plan is evident, as a brief study of the record will show. It began long before the present emergency. It began even in the golden days of social legislation, when the labor movement was able to do more than simply defend its gains, when it was able to secure new protective laws.

You have only to look at the record of labor's fight to secure passage of the Wage-Hour Act, its fight to secure enforcement of the Wagner Act, its fight to make the Walsh-Healey Act proof against law violators, to make the government live up to its own obligations in enforcing these protective laws it was sworn to enforce.

The Wage-Hour Act was held up two years before its passage in 1938, held up in the same House Rules Committee that rushes anti-labor bills through in a week or less. The same men now pushing the Vinson bill were dominant in the House Rules Committee then—the same group of poll-tax Congressmen who act as monopoly's front in pushing the drive against the right to organize and the right to strike today. Almost as soon as it was passed, the Wage-Hour Act was subjected to a ferocious drive to amend it out of existence—a drive that was stopped as we remember, only by labor, led off with a few blunt and very telling phrases by John L. Lewis.

The story of labor's struggle to put teeth in the Walsh-Healey Act, by requiring government contractors to obey the laws of the United States, is an even longer history of struggle against the reactionary control in Congress. This fight began in 1937, in the salad days of progress, and it is still unfinished. Three times the C.I.O. bill—a very simple measure, merely requiring government contractors to obey the Wagner Act—passed the Senate, and three times it was killed in the House, by the same group now pressing the Vinson bill. And finally in 1940, when high government officials issued a mild statement to the general effect that government contracts should not go to lawbreakers, a blast from the Smith Committee (the same Vinson bill group again) sent them crawling for cover in a flurry of denials and apologies for even having thought of such a thing.

The history of the Wagner Act is even more familiar, with the beginning of the reactionary plot to scuttle it going back to 1937. Here again the attack on labor was led by the forces that now talk loudest about the national emergency, that are now most vocal in calling for anti-strike laws, for compulsory mediation, for forced labor.

These people—the poll-taxers who front for big business—were in positions of power in Congress then. They are still in the same strategic places. They are more vocal now, perhaps, and they get more attention in the press. But they were doing the same dirty work as of three and four and even five years ago. They didn't wait behind the walls for this period of war hysteria. They've been out in front all along.

These three measures, of major importance to labor, have been under attack since their passage, since they were first proposed. There are dozens of other legislative fronts of this anti-labor campaign with an equally long history. The cuts in W.P.A. starting in 1937, cuts in housing, the refusal to adopt a national health bill, the anti-alien and other anti-minority acts, the drive to legalize wire tapping, the plot to exile Harry Bridges

for the crime of organizing workers, the flat refusal to adopt
an anti-lynching bill, to do anything about the poll tax, to stop
the use of labor spies and employer violence against workers, are
only a few of the anti-labor attacks that have taken place in
Congress over the past several years.

This is only a brief review of recent anti-labor congressional
history. It is useful, however, in a clearer understanding of
the present situation, because there we find its real roots. The
Congressmen that led the attack then are leading it today. They
represent the same reactionary forces. The difference is that
they are moving nearer to success today than they were a few
years ago, that they are able to use a carefully whipped-up war
hysteria as a cover for their conspiracy that they did not possess
then.

This is not the only difference, of course. Looking back
on earlier fights for labor's rights in Congress, we must recognize
that we face an even more serious situation today than we did
when defending the Wagner Act or the Wage-Hour Act and
attempting to secure their enforcement. We are facing the
all-out stage of the war against the labor movement today. And
if we lose at this stage, we will have lost a major engagement,
one that will set back the clock of progress for a period of years
—as it is meant to do.

The Vinson bill is perhaps the most menacing of these
current threats to progress in our country. Let us look briefly
at the effect it is intended to have, and at the results its sponsors
hope to achieve.

Its most important section is the enforced "cooling-off"
period, during which workers cannot go on strike without facing
severe criminal penalties, and during which they must submit
their dispute to enforced mediation.

The effect of this section is clear. It would destroy the
right to strike. While this right is destroyed, the employers are
perfectly free to assemble every weapon in the arsenal against the
workers, are free to work with government to prepare for the
destruction of the union. Nothing is said in the Vinson bill
about the settlement of the grievance that caused the strike vote
to be taken. All that is provided is enforced mediation, with
no guarantees to protect the workers' rights during that period.

The grievance is left untouched. The workers are forced to stay at work without a settlement, while the cumulative effect of the grievance piles up.

This enforced "cooling-off" is described by its backers as a method of bringing workers back to earth after they have decided to go on strike. The implication here is clear; workers are to blame for every strike that takes place. The employer, of course, is blameless. Therefore, all the workers need is some sort of cold shower to cool off the hotheads, and all will be well.

If this were true, labor relations would be a simple problem. All you would need to do is to apply an enforced cooling-off period and disputes would simply disappear. Of course it isn't true—and what is more important, the authors and backers of the Vinson bill know that this isn't true.

They know, as well as the workers know, that the right to strike is basic to all labor rights. Without it, labor loses its bargaining power. Organization for better wages and working conditions becomes meaningless. Labor cannot bargain with both hands tied behind its back. To ask it to bargain without the right to strike is a contradiction in terms.

President Murray of the C.I.O., expressing the opposition of 5,000,000 workers to the Vinson bill, put it very succinctly when he said:

> The imposition of cooling-off restraints would be a negation of collective bargaining, rather than its encouragement. The voluntary system of collective bargaining is essential to afford the greatest assurance of peaceful industrial relations.

Parallel with the cooling-off idea in both the Vinson and Ball bills, is the proposal for enforced mediation of labor-capital disputes. Under these proposals, a strike will be taken from the hands of labor and employers and placed with a Board for imposition of a settlement. The procedure is not detailed in either of the bills, but presumably this board will make findings of facts, and on that basis, issue a decision which both sides will be required to observe.

On the surface, it looks good. Mediation is frequently a desirable process; it can be useful in settling strikes. Labor has no opposition to mediation as such, in fact has accepted it for many years. But labor has every opposition to enforced mediation and to its twin, compulsory arbitration.

This opposition is well founded. The record of compulsory mediation and compulsory arbitration is full of cases where labor has been forced to accept settlement on the employers' terms, rather than on terms that meet labor's needs. The record is also filled with cases where labor's grievances have been put through a process of stalling and delay that has weakened the unions to the point where they can no longer hope to enforce their demands.

In the face of the widespread hysterical condemnation of all stoppages which we are now witnessing, certainly there should be a more realistic appreciation of the factors which cause the strikes. The workers in a typical plant do not consent to strike with relish or advance enjoyment. They do so most hesitatingly and with considerable reluctance. The workers through bitter experience have learned that strikes bring in their wake, to them and to the members of their families, considerable hardship, and require many sacrifices. During the strike period, they, of course, receive no wages, and their obligations continue. They are not financed by any benevolent institution. They must suffer the rigors which pursue workers who are unemployed—evictions, loss of their chattel goods, and lack of food for their wives and children. In addition, through the use of local and state police forces added to the thugs and strike breakers that may be hired by the employer, they will suffer severe physical injuries including loss of life.

In the face of these facts, one should, in all fairness, be extremely reluctant before condemning workers who have been compelled to go on strike as the result of the arrogant and arbitrary attitude of the employer. To the contrary, it should be accepted that only the strongest reasons could have led the workers to go on strike—that only because of the infinite patience of the workers in tolerating unadjusted grievances over a long period of time has earlier action been avoided.

Further let us examine for a moment what are the customary demands of the workers; recognition of their union as a collective bargaining agency, more decent wages, and improved working conditions.

The law of the land says that workers should be protected in their right to organize and to choose a union which may bargain for them, but several large corporations have ignored this law and have refused to abide by this law. Where the workers of such an employer are denied this right guaranteed to them by the federal law, what are they to do? Bear in mind that these employers to whom I refer, are in no way condemned by government, but, to the contrary, receive the benefits of huge profitable government contracts while they are violating the law of the land.

At the present time, corporations are earning tremendous profits. Technological improvements have resulted in a terrific speed up of workers who are operating the machines. We also know that two thirds of the workers employed in industry today receive less than a thousand dollars per year. They ask for wage increases and improved working conditions.

The coal miners, engaged in the most hazardous industry in the world asked for a wage increase of one dollar per day. This was denied to them by the coal operators. What could they do but strike to obtain their just demand?

The steel workers, through the Steel Workers Organizing Committee, recently asked for a wage increase of only ten cents per hour. A conspiracy then existed among the major industries of the nation that a wage increase of only two cents per hour could be given. The steel workers obtained their wage increase, thereby smashing the conspiracy; but only the threat on the part of the Steel Workers Organizing Committee that their members would have to strike and the fact that, as free men, they could strike, compelled the steel companies to grant this wage increase.

The same situation prevailed in the case of the recent dispute between the United Automobile Workers and the General Motors Corporation. In spite of the profits being enjoyed by this corporation, it refused to concede a reasonable wage increase to its workers. After months of haggling and negotiations, the threatened exercise by its employees of their constitutional and God-given right to jointly lay down their tools and not work, led to the company conceding the request of the union and its members. Take away this right to strike, and the company could have continued saying, "No! No! No!" until the union had been successfully driven out of existence and the workers compelled to work under such conditions as the company desired to impose.

It is easy to condemn and to villify labor because some action which it has taken has stopped production; but to fail to investigate with an open and fair mind what are the causes which led the workers to take this action in spite of all the hardships that are involved for labor during a strike, leads to an exceedingly dangerous situation. It is the workers who must do the sweating and the toiling in producing the goods which this country needs for its defense and survival. To villify these people without justification, to condemn with ease, merely leads to a destruction of the morale of the common people and the imposition of economic slavery.

Compulsory mediation is not the answer to the problem of labor relations. The answer lies in maintaining and enforcing labor's full rights, including the right to organize, to bargain collectively, and to strike. Compulsory mediation, as Phillip Murray pointed out, is the negation of this.

It lies also in enforcement and strengthening of laws requiring employers to bargain and negotiate in good faith. The greatest step made to date in this direction was the passage of the Wagner Act. The people of the United States are in agreement with the policy laid down by this Act. Enforcement of this Act, by denying contracts to violators, by interpreting it as it was meant to be interpreted, would do more to prevent strikes and to settle them when they do occur than all the talk in Congress and in the employers' press about compulsory mediation or arbitration or cooling-off.

These proposals represent the main fronts of the attack on labor now being pressed in Congress and in the press. They are the current climax of a long range plan to achieve three main reactionary ends:

1. Destruction of the workers' rights to organize, bargain collectively and strike, and the imposition of forced labor.

2. Destruction of labor organizations as the barrier to unchecked monopoly profit.

3. Complete control of the national economy and the government by big business, not only for the period of the present "emergency" but for all time.

The prospect is not a pleasant one. If carried through, it will mean a big business dictatorship over this country, comparable to the fascist controls imposed on the people of warring Europe.

Labor is not taking the prospect lying down. The C.I.O. is putting its resources behind the fight against the Vinson and Ball bills. It is doing this in two ways; by fighting in Congress, and even more important, by fighting in the shop and on the picket line. The C.I.O. is carrying this fight successfully on many fronts—recent victories in steel, Ford, in coal mining, in the electrical and radio industry, in a score of industries where the C.I.O. has won contracts and wage raises. It is fighting also for the rights of all workers and common people—for the rights of Negroes, for the rights of aliens, for the rights of minority groups now under particularly vicious attack.

The basic problem in considering any legislation affecting labor relations should be whether it is conducive or detrimental to the defense of the nation. All reasonable arguments and facts would seem to point to the conclusion that the proposed legislation which I have discussed are menaces to the defense of the American people.

Labor peace, and the resultant steady flow of production, can best be achieved through fair dealing—not repressive legislation. Legislation proffered in good faith but capable of perversion is at least as dangerous as laws avowedly aimed at curtailing labor's freedom. Our experience during the First World War with attempts to prevent labor from striking indicates that such attempts tend only to bring on strikes. It should be clear to any patriot that the defense potential of our people is not raised by the reduction of their living standards (through confiscation of their bargaining weapons and the stealing of their basic liberties). Defense demands diametrically opposite policies and programs.

What then should be embraced in a program of defense legislation? The C.I.O. supports fully a proper defense program. We are also in favor of legislation which will effectively carry out such a program. We agree with the proponents of the legislation criticized by us that the continuance of production is essential to defense. Our effort, however, is to discover the basic causes for interruptions in production, with a view to eradicating them.

Impartial investigation over many years has indicated that the refusal of industry to permit labor to organize into unions of its own choosing and to bargain collectively has been the most frequent cause of strikes; this truth is embodied in the declaration of policy in the N.L.R.A. There can be no doubt that violations of this right as well as of others guaranteed by that act, are being committed daily and by leading figures in defense industries. This is the first and most important form of sabotage of national defense which must be disposed of. And what would be more effective and more in the interests of national defense than the enactment of legislation, adding criminal penalties for violations of the N.L.R.A. With one stroke we should thereby have created the legal machinery whereby we might really put a stop to the sabotage of defense on a colossal scale. This done, we could add a further ounce of prevention through the presidential issuance of an executive order denying government and defense contracts to such violators.

Other changes to further the defense of the nation might include vigorous enforcement of anti-trust laws to keep prices down; extension of the application of the Wage-Hour Law and the Walsh-Healey Act; furtherance of work relief and youth training; extension of social security and public housing; passage of the Coffee National Guard Bill prohibiting use of the National Guard for strike breaking purposes; and revival of the quiescent Civil Liberties Unit of the Department of Justice. And with the enactment of the La Follette Oppressive Labor Practices Bill outlawing the use of industrial spies, guns and munitions by employers against their employees, we should be so far on the road to industrial peace as to have a practical assurance of uninterrupted defense production.

This is the way the C.I.O. answers the conspiracy against labor and against the welfare of our country. It is the duty of progressives everywhere to support this fight—whether they are part of the labor movement or outside its ranks. It is their duty to oppose restrictions on the right to strike, to oppose attacks on labor and on minority groups, to give labor all the help they can. Labor will not be defeated if this help is not given, but labor's struggle will be advanced if it is given.

And liberals and progressives will justify their existence. I know of no other way for them to do so.

COMPULSORY ARBITRATION OF LABOR DISPUTES? [5]

I was born in the labor movement and joined a union before I was old enough to vote. Nevertheless, I would have a very poor opinion of myself if I approached a subject of such vital concern to my country solely from the point of view of the trade-union movement.

Americans should not countenance compulsory arbitration of industrial disputes or approve the proposal to limit, or perhaps entirely nullify, labor's right to strike, because both are thoroughly anti-democratic and, therefore, un-American.

At this moment the American people are as united in support of the institutions which have made their country glorious as they have ever been in their entire history. They are all concentrating on the supreme task of national defense. There are sharp differences of opinion concerning details, but there is gratifying agreement on the main objective—*the preservation of the precious heritage handed down to them by the Fathers of the Republic.*

No class is displaying a deeper devotion, or a more enlightened understanding of the exigencies of the situation, than the more than eight million members of the American labor movement.

Within the last month the metal trades and the building trades, powerful organizations which have been militantly defending what they conceive to be their rights, have voluntarily

[5] By Edward Keating. Editor-manager since 1919 of *Labor*, official weekly newspaper owned by 15 railroad labor organizations; former United States Congressman. *Rotarian.* 58:15, 56-8. March 1941.

submitted proposals which, for all practical purposes, will make strikes impossible during the period of the emergency. All they ask is that their employers meet them half way and in the same spirit of willingness to sacrifice for the common cause.

In the immense transportation industry, the carriers and the twenty-one standard railroad labor organizations have learned how to settle their differences at the conference table. The machinery provided for the adjustment of disputes by the amended Railway Labor Act of 1933 has worked so smoothly that during 1940, according to the latest report of the United States Mediation Board, there was only one insignificant "walkout." It affected a switching corporation owned by a steel company, and was disposed of in a week.

It should be emphasized that this beneficent legislation was drafted by the unions, and was passed by Congress, despite the opposition of a powerful lobby representing the carriers. Today it is universally hailed as a "model law"—a monument to the vision and statesmanship of free workers.

In other industries there is nothing to justify serious apprehension.

Of course, there are the exceptions which prove the rule, but, by and large, instead of seriously discussing a proposal which would literally dynamite industrial relations at a time when peace is absolutely vital, Americans should be on their knees thanking God that American workers, despite the almost unbelievable sufferings they have endured during the most appalling of depressions, have refused to be swept off their feet by the "isms" which threaten the very foundations of Christian civilization in a large part of the world.

Americans should remember, too, that there is nothing new about these proposals to "outlaw strikes." Almost all countries, and three or four of the states of the United States, have experimented along that line, and a candid examination of the record will demonstrate that in every instance a departure from the processes of democracy has provoked bitter class feeling, *but has utterly failed to end strikes.*

Proponents of anti-strike legislation fail to understand that it is one thing to outlaw strikes and quite another to compel freemen to labor under conditions which they regard as grossly unfair.

Our friend Governor Henry J. Allen twenty years ago set up an Industrial Court in my native State of Kansas. The Court adjusted a few minor strikes—the kind which could have been disposed of easily by any competent labor mediator—but when it undertook to enforce its mandate in major controversies, it simply didn't get anywhere.

I recall that on one occasion the Court atempted to restore peace in the Kansas coal fields. Some of the leaders of the strikers were sent to jail. Their followers refused to work until they were released. Even after the Miners' Union had declared the strike was unauthorized, only about half the men resumed the important business of digging coal. The others stubbornly held their ground. Of course, the Governor might have filled the jails with these men, but he was wise enough not to attempt it.

When the Court endeavored to compel an employer to accept what was an extremely conservative wage scale, he appealed to the courts. The United States Supreme Court, in a decision written by Justice Van Devanter, a most conservative gentleman, clipped the wings of the Industrial Court and it gradually faded out of the picture.

It might be well if businessmen and others who are disposed to look with favor on anti-strike legislation were to ponder the following paragraphs from Justice Van Devanter's opinion:

> The system of compulsory arbitration which the Act establishes is intended to compel, and if sustained will compel, *the owner, and employees* to continue the business on terms which are not of their making.
> It will constrain them not merely to respect the terms, if they continue the business, *but will constrain them to continue the business on those terms.*
> True, the terms have some qualifications, but as shown in the prior decision the qualifications are rather illusory and do not subtract much from the duty imposed.
> Such a system infringes the liberty of contract and rights of property guaranteed by the due process of law clause of the Fourteenth Amendment.

The learned Justice saw quite clearly that compulsory arbitration is a two-edged sword. *If the law can compel a worker to return to his job, although the conditions are unsatisfactory, it must be able to compel an employer to continue to operate, even if that means bankruptcy.* It is not a pleasant prospect for either workers or businessmen.

If we are to abandon the conference table, discard mediation, and rely on force to achieve industrial tranquillity, we must, of course, set up some tribunal or individual clothed with the necessary authority. That court or individual will be picked by the government in power and, unless we are willing to go a step further and deprive large groups of citizens of the right to vote, the make-up of the government will be determined at the ballot box.

It is not necessary to suggest that, in that event, employers and employees might be divided into hostile camps, each seeking to control the government in order that it might select a "czar" who would fix wages and working conditions satisfactory to a particular group.

The employers might have the "czar" today, but the workers, possessing a vast majority of the votes, might have him tomorrow. Even if we were to deprive voters of the ballot, and use sufficient force to drive them back to their jobs, we would still find we had not achieved industrial peace.

I have before me a survey I had something to do with making which shows just what happened wherever an attempt was made to settle industrial disputes by force. It is a story of bitter contest—and invariable failure. Space limitations will permit only two or three examples.

In 1910 France faced a general strike of railroad employees. It ended in six days, because the government of Aristide Briand, who at that time described himself as a "philosophical anarchist," called the striking employees to the colors and placed them under military orders. A ukase was then issued requiring the men to operate and maintain the railways. However, they never joined the Army, because they went back to work before the order became effective.

That sounds like a great victory for compulsion. But let's see what really happened.

The employees resorted to sabotage. No shipper was sure his freight would arrive at its destination on time. A shipment originating in Lyons and billed to Paris would disappear for weeks. Eventually it might turn up in the yards at Toulon or some other place.

When asked to explain, the workers pointed out that when they returned to work, 3,000 of their comrades had been refused reinstatement. These men, they asserted, were unusually competent, while their substitutes were very incompetent. That was not a convincing alibi, perhaps, but what could the officials do?

Curiously enough, the freight shipments which got into the most trouble were those billed to rich manufacturers and merchants.

Premier Briand did his best to save his face, but before six months had passed every demand made by the workers when they first threw down their tools was granted, and the 3,000 men who had been "blacklisted" were restored to their jobs.

Most of us have read a little English history, and, therefore, we know something about how workers were treated in England during various periods. At one time workers who dared talk about unions and higher wages were thrown into jail or exiled. Some suffered even more serious punishment. Eventually the rulers of Britain cast compulsion aside, not because they had suddenly become altruists, but because they had discovered that the system wouldn't produce results. Strikes came and went without regard to law, injunctions, or oppressive court decisions.

Always these disturbances affected more and more workers and increased the number of working days lost, both in general and in specific industries. In some instances these strikes took on the aspects of rebellion against the existing order of things.

So, in 1906, the Trades Dispute Act was passed and unions have flourished like a green bay tree ever since. British employers take unionization as a matter of course, and no one interferes with a strike unless it can be shown that it is directed against the Government.

This policy is paying rich dividends at this moment when Britain, with her back to the wall, needs the loyal support of every citizen. The workers have responded so loyally that Premier Churchill, an extreme conservative and regarded at one time as the archenemy of the unions, has placed Ernest Bevin in control of everything that has to do with labor, and Bevin is the chief of the Transport Workers' Federation, one of the most militant organizations in the country. Every trade-union leader is cooperating with Bevin. They will "deliver the goods," but they will deliver them as freemen, not as slaves.

Australia and New Zealand are often cited as countries where compulsory arbitration has been a success. As a matter of fact, after the setting up of compulsory tribunals, strikes increased, and soon industrial courts, even if they continued to function, were as valueless as Governor Allen's Court in Kansas. Occasionally they would settle a controversy, but, in the main, unions called strikes when they saw fit, and then proceeded to reach an agreement with their employers through the usual channels of negotiation.

As I said at the beginning, the situation as of today is in no sense alarming. Americans need not worry about the future if they will only keep in mind a few simple principles.

They must remember they are dealing with men who have read the Declaration of Independence and the Constitution and are proud of the fact that they are freemen.

Unionization should be encouraged, not discouraged; and labor should always retain the right to strike, but should use it only when other and better methods have failed.

Government can help by strengthening the mediation services in state and nation. Those services have done a marvellous job during the last quarter of a century and are constantly becoming more efficient, largely because they command the confidence of the employers as well as the employees.

Of course, there will be occasional flare-ups and, unfortunately, the newspapers will exaggerate their importance, placing scare headlines over stories which relate that 200 or 300 men are "out" and that the union is making "shocking demands"— like a minimum wage of 50c cents an hour.

Sensible people will not be disturbed by such developments. Such strikes will not endanger the republic or slow up national defense, and the contractor who is not willing to pay a minimum of 50 cents an hour is "chiselling" on his government as well as on his employees.

Let's keep our heads, develop our sense of fair play, and all will be well.

ECONOMIC ENQUIRIES AS A BASIS FOR
DEMOCRATIC ADJUSTMENT OF
LABOUR DISPUTES [6]

The object of this article is to show what can be done to insure that labor law will continue to develop along lines which will preserve independent workers' and employers' organizations on a democratic basis, by finding other methods of settling labor disputes than compulsory arbitration. The question of economic inquiries as a basis for the adjustment of labor disputes is discussed here with this end in view. In other words, the problem is not merely that of proving that economic inquiries are of value in any kind of determination of labor conditions, whether compulsory or voluntary, but that of showing how economic inquiries, combined with other action, can prevent the development of compulsory arbitration. This calls for a few introductory remarks to explain why compulsory arbitration should be avoided.

The essence of democracy lies in the right of the people to combine for the defense of economic and other interests, and in the possibility for conflicting interests to be adjusted by discussion and action within the limits of the law. Conceived in this light, the democratic culture of a nation finds expression in the economic sphere not only in self-governing unemployment and sickness funds, and the like, but also in independent trade unions and employers' associations. The freedom of action of these organizations is one of the advantages of democracy, and interference with it is an interference with the democratic rights of the people. This does not mean, of course, that such interference may not be necessary in particular circumstances; but it does mean that interference for the regulation and settlement of disputes may not go beyond what is necessary in the interests of the community as a whole, and should, so far as possible, take the form, not of direct prohibitions of particular acts, but of a policy and a machinery which avert acts injurious to the community as a whole. Correct balancing of respect for the freedom of action of the organizations against

[6] By Jørgen S. Dich, Economic Adviser to the Ministry of Social Affairs, Denmark. *International Labour Review*. 38:575-90. November 1938.

respect for the interests of the community as a whole, combined with an economic and labor policy in these matters that is both far-sighted and preventive, is in fact a necessary condition for the preservation of true democracy. It is dangerous from the democratic standpoint if the idea spreads that strikes and lock-outs are an anomaly in a well-ordered community, for this approximates to a conception of society based on the principle of dictatorship. From the democratic standpoint, strikes must be regarded as a justifiable exercise of the rights of organization that exist under the present forms of society.

A strike is important not merely as a means of achieving material improvements for the workers, but also psychologically as a demonstration of power, which compensates for the inferiority that the individual worker must feel in the modern community, especially in relation to the managements of big undertakings. By the activities of the organizations, that sense of equality which is the basis and object of all democracy is created in the economic sphere. The display of power helps to give the worker a feeling of security, in that he realizes that he himself has a share in deciding his economic status, and that he is not merely a defenseless victim of economic and political forces. To this extent a collective demonstration of power through organizations and strikes is important irrespective of the conflict of interests between workers and employers, but its importance is enhanced by that conflict. The conflict springs from objective conditions, and is not a mere illusion. And, since class feeling has an objective basis, it is incompatible with the idea of democracy to suppress this feeling among the workers and replace it by an ideology of economic harmony derived from other sections of society. The mental attitude of conflict, which in fact exists and which, being based on actual conditions, cannot be removed within the framework of any democracy, must therefore be taken into account as an important element in the real situation when judging the value of different methods of settling disputes.

These views imply no apology for class feeling nor do they imply its preservation. On the contrary, the experience of the Northern European countries has shown that it is precisely the activities of the trade unions arising out of this class feeling—including strikes—which help to bring about such improvements in the workers' conditions of life that class feeling is reduced. It may consequently be expected that trade union activity combined with government measures will ultimately remove the conditions on which the opposition is based, and will thus lead to the disappearance of class feeling. If such a development is to be promoted by means of the feeling of conflict, it must be the task of democracy not to suppress but to guide the activities that have their origin in this class mentality.

The principle to be applied is the same as that underlying all democratic statemanship: to strengthen those forces in the community which grow out of democratic culture and which act in the desired direction. The adoption of this principle in the field of labor law means that the powers within trade union democracy that work for peace are given an opportunity to make themselves felt. Any strike prohibitions to be issued must be issued by a moderate majority within the unions, after discussion between the moderate and militant elements. Such a prohibition is respected by all on account of its democratic origin. A minority does not usually strike on its own account; the energy and activity of the minority find a natural outlet in the effort to arrive at the desired majority. The potential energy of the organism accumulated by its more combative elements is consumed in speeches and applause at general meetings. There is no need for illegal associations formed to intensify the feeling of conflict still further, and to relieve the increased tension by fighting with the police and the authorities. If the trade unions are deprived of the right to strike, their activities may take such forms. That the minorities will break away is also a possibility that must be faced. The energy that hitherto found a natural outlet in democratic ways—in trying to win over the majority—within the trade union movement making for moderation are thereby set aside; an ally in the effort to avoid strikes is dismissed; instead of the democratic strike prohibitions which in numerous cases these moderate majorities have issued and for which they have gained voluntary respect, there is a prohibition issued by the government, whose only means of enforcing it lies in threats of punishment and fines. The ballot paper is replaced by penal law, democratic methods by dictatorial. Compulsory arbitration is thus an asset to those sections of the working class whose policy is to obtain advantages (or power) by direct action against the authorities, while it weakens the democratic and peacefully inclined sections of the working class in their endeavor to show that the workers can gain advantages by purely economic means in society as at present constituted. The splitting of the working class that follows from this can hardly be politically desirable, especially when it is borne in mind that the consolidation of extreme elements among the workers will provoke a corresponding consolidation of extreme elements on the other side, and will thus lead to a development which will endanger the continued existence of democracy.

It must also be remembered that the condemnation of strikes as illegal will create among the middle classes, on whom the words "legal" and "illegal" make a strong impression, a feeling of keen animosity towards any workers who infringe the prohibition. This animosity will probably tend to be directed against the working class in general, especially if the authorities are forced to take drastic action against trade unions on strike. The ground will thus be prepared for an attack on trade unions as such.

The forces which have led to temporary or permanent provision for compulsory arbitration in various countries have arisen from widespread or prolonged disputes.

General disputes which extend to a large number of trades and industries, owing to the inconveniences which they entail for the public, will in most countries cause the government to interfere and take steps involving a direct prohibition of the dispute. In Denmark this feeling against general disputes has in several cases led to the adoption of special legislation terminating individual disputes in a manner approximating very closely to compulsory arbitration.

If this is to be avoided, an attempt must be made to influence the causes leading to general disputes. There are two factors in particular that call for attention in this respect. The first is a matter of organization; the other is the extent of divergence between the workers' claims and the employers' counterclaims.

If the form of organization on the employers' and workers' sides is such that the power to decide on a strike or lockout in several or in all trades is intrusted to one and the same authority, there will be a constant latent threat that minor disputes will grow into general disputes. The efforts made to centralize this power are due to the employers' general desire to extend the area of disputes. The principal motive of employers for extending the area of a dispute, in countries like Denmark, arises from the form of organization chosen by the workers. Where the workers are organized in trade unions, the employers' position in an industry comprising several trades will be very weak if a dispute breaks out in only one of the trades, since the result will in most cases be to hold up production in the entire industry. A strike among painters, for example, may hold up building, and a strike among boiler and machine tenders may hold up nearly the whole of industry. The employers are thus led to adopt the policy of spreading the dispute as far as possible to all trades in the industry at once. Their reply to a strike in one of the trades is a lockout for all the trades, and this extends the stoppage of work to new industrial fields. The result is an approach to a general dispute, involving a number of trades and a number of industries.

As a remedy, it will be necessary to find measures which will render an extension of the area of a dispute less advantageous and more difficult for the employers. Two things are needed: an effort to bring workers' and employers' organizations and agreements into conformity with the natural grouping that arises from the development of modern industry; and a limitation of the employers' right to concentrate decisions for all trades in a single organization.

The first step in a policy of prevention must therefore be to promote reorganization of the workers' unions on an industrial basis. In countries such as Denmark, where the majority of the workers are traditionally organized by trades, it would hardly be possible to undertake a complete reorganization on an industrial basis, because of the opposition which would be encountered in the existing organizations. In these countries the problem will be that of trying to find a system combining the existing trade unions with a form of organization based on industries in such a way that separate agreements can be concluded, and separate labor disputes conducted, on behalf of the workers engaged in a particular industry. It is conceivable that, side by side with the trade unions, industrial unions or councils might be formed to represent the various trades in each industry. Ideas of this kind have lately been very much to the fore in the Danish union movement.

Apart from the need for restricting the scope of disputes, there are other arguments in favor of a system combining industrial and trade unions which are of importance in connection with the policy here proposed. As suggested below, a change should be made in the system of conciliation, to enable the conciliation institution to base its proposals on economic considerations. For example, it should be possible to ascertain by an inquiry whether wages can be paid at a particular rate. If an inquiry of this kind is to cover a whole trade, spread over industries with very different earning capacity, it will naturally be of little value. It is hardly possible to determine whether a particular wage rate can be paid to painters in general; but it is possible to inquire whether a particular industry is in a position to pay its workers, including painters, a higher wage. The conciliation institution will therefore be able to find an economic basis for its proposals much more readily when a dispute affects an industrial union than when it affects a trade union.

In addition to this, the possibilities of improving wages that are dependent on differences in the economic position of the various industries cannot be exploited without organization on some other basis than the trade. The idea that different wages can be paid to the workers in the same trade according to the industry in which they are employed cannot gain ground until the principle of industrial unionism has been adopted.

The change in the basis of labor organization suggested above is one of the two measures needed to prevent a development leading towards compulsory arbitration. The other consists in doing away with that concentration of authority to decide on disputes which employers have effected in Denmark and in some other countries. The decision to engage in open dispute here rests with a single body. Even though the conciliation institution puts forward a proposal which both the workers' and the employers' organizations in a particular trade or a particular industry would have accepted had it been submitted to a ballot of their members, these trades may have to continue the dispute because the authority to decide lies with the central organization.

In order to alter this state of affairs the conciliation institution must be given power to decide that the proposals it puts forward in the event of a threatened general dispute (and perhaps also in other cases) shall be made the subject of a separate vote for the field covered by each industrial union or trade union, in such a way as to prevent the employers affected from transferring their decision to a higher organization, and that the vote taken in each case, irrespective of the results of the voting in other trades, shall be decisive for the trade or industry concerned. In order to insure a completely democratic decision, based on the individual employer's judgment of the situation, the conciliation institution must be able to decide that the proposal shall be submitted to a general ballot (and it must of course have similar authority with regard to the workers). The vote in the various trades or industries must be binding, so that if the proposed agreement is accepted there can be no question of starting a new dispute and thereby leading to further ballots, until the agreement is due to expire. Under this system, in the industries or trades in which both employers and workers accept the conciliation proposals, the dispute is thereby terminated and work must be resumed, so that the dispute continues only in those industries or trades in which either or both of the parties have rejected the proposal. A point for discussion is whether these rules should be supplemented by a provision that the parties which accept the proposal, and which must resume work, may not contribute towards the support of those which continue the dispute.

There can hardly be any doubt that such rules would do much to reduce the scope of most of the general disputes that threaten to occur in the future. The proposal is in reality one for the decentralization of disputes, and its adoption would therefore naturally lead to a decline in the number and extent of general disputes, which to a very great extent depend on the centralization of power. The only restrictions on the right to declare sympathetic strikes and lockouts resulting from these rules are those which follow from the fact that in the event of a threatened general dispute this right cannot be transferred to any higher authority, and that the decision concerning sympathetic action must be taken by the local organization, before the result of the voting in the trade or industry directly concerned is known.

The policy suggested here disregards the argument that the workers' organizations should centralize authority as the employers have done. This argument is based on acceptance of the centralization of power effected by the employer. If a country follows this path, on which Denmark entered by adopting the Conciliation Act of January 18, 1934 (Section 8, subsection 2), which promotes the development of a bilateral centralization of power, a stimulus is given to a process which logically leads to compulsory arbitration. It must be realized that any policy which aims at avoiding compulsory arbitration must oppose the centralization of power in the employers' organization and thereby do away with the need for similar centralization on the part of the trade unions. But any such interference with the employers' right to centralize depends on the organization of the workers on an industrial basis, as proposed earlier in this article. The two parts of the policy cannot be separated. Simultaneous application of both measures is a necessary condition for obtaining satisfactory results.

The duration of a dispute depends partly on the economic resources at the parties' disposal and partly on the extent of their differences. In order to prevent disputes which last so long that government interference becomes necessary, measures must be devised that can influence these two factors. The growth of organization has meant that the workers in many countries, including the Northern European countries, have fairly large strike funds; and it will hardly be possible or justifiable to take any action that will limit the workers' right to accumulate these funds. Economic endurance in a dispute depends, however, partly on the assistance obtained from trades that are not involved in the dispute. From the standpoint put forward here it is therefore necessary to consider whether this form of assistance should not be restricted as regards both workers and employers. A general prohibition of the giving of economic assistance to persons engaged in a dispute would hardly be feasible, but the government conciliation institution might conceivably be given power in certain cases to decide, when putting forward its proposals, that economic assistance must not be received if the dispute is continued. An injunction might also be issued against giving assistance to a party rejecting the proposal. Provisions of this kind must be supplemented by others forbidding the taking of collections without approval by a higher authority, such as the Ministry of Justice. An Act to this effect was passed in Denmark on May 16, 1934.

The factor which has the strongest influence on the duration and intensity of disputes, however, is the degree of difference between workers and employers. In the clash of claim and counterclaim, conditions are created setting such violent passions in motion that only a prolonged dispute, entailing the exhaustion of one of the parties, can lead to practical results. The divergencies between the parties may be mainly political or emotional in character, or mainly economic. The possibility of avoiding the prolonged and bitter disputes that spring from emotional factors often depends on whether the sense of economic realities has spread among the workers to such an extent that the employers' fear of the unions is unfounded and the workers use their power in a reasonable manner. The spreading of this sense of reality necessarily takes some time, so that in countries which are suddenly faced with a strong development of the trade union movement there are bound to be disputes in which emotional factors exert such an influence that compulsory arbitration or other forms of government intervention may become necessary.

These observations bring the question of an economic basis for conciliation between the parties into the foreground among the measures intended to prevent disputes. Conciliation on the lines to be described below can also be justified, however, by various other considerations.

It is important for the workers to have their claims examined by a body on which they themselves are represented by experts, in order that the more far-reaching effects of their wishes or demands may be brought out and may play a part in the discussion of the question whether or not they shall insist on their claims. This does not necessarily mean surrender of the claims; it may lead to a demand for supplementary policies calculated to avoid the undesirable effects of the claims. In this way trade union policy is made to enter new and more constructive fields. It will become clear to the workers that an economic era has opened in which direct wage increases are no longer the only or the most effective means of improving their conditions of life, and that a lasting rise in the standard of living calls for the bringing of influence to bear on the general economic policy of the country in such a way that the necessary conditions for the raising of wages or the shortening of hours can be created without injury to the workers or to those classes of society who are in a similar position to that of the workers, or to economic development in general. The more theoretical side of this subject, which has largely been confined to the utopian plane, out of touch with the practical work of the trade unions, will thus be brought to bear directly on their day-to-day work and will enrich it with new ideas, while at the same time those ideas will become adjusted to the demands of the situation. In the more advanced democratic countries the trade union movement has now reached that stage in its development when this transition from direct to indirect and constructive methods is about to take place, and it therefore becomes necessary to create the machinery through which the process can be effected.

This problem of supplementing traditional trade union policy by more far-reaching plans raises the question of the relation between the economic policy of the government and that of the trade unions. Many of the supplementary measures which are to bring about the necessary conditions for better wages or increased employment can only be the result of political action. On the other hand, governments are now forced to regulate adjustment to the changes in economic conditions brought about by dynamic evolution, and this adjustment must in many ways take into account, or be directly affected by, the agreements on wages and hours concluded between employers and workers. A rational economic policy must therefore include some machinery for coordinating the various economic aims as far as possible. By means of this machinery, the objects pursued by the management of the Central Bank could also be treated as one of the economic factors that the parties have to take into account, or that they try to influence through their representatives in the government, in the management of the bank, or in some other responsible quarter. If the interests of the organizations are recognized from the democratic standpoint as deciding factors side by side with those of the state, and machinery is set up through which the mutual adjustment of interests can take place, and if steps are taken to insure that this adjustment in fact enters into the consideration given by the individual trade union members to their economic policy, then it will be seen that not only can the trade unions be fitted into a state-regulated system of economic adjustment but without them there can be no such system on a democratic basis, depending ultimately on understanding and recognition by the masses of the government's policy and its relation to the policy of the trade unions.

The work of a coordinating and advisory body of the type suggested may also lead to coordination of the workers' economic interests and the interests of those groups of society which are not organized. A trade union policy that is detrimental to smallholders, for instance, or to persons belonging to the commercial and clerical classes, who may be worse off economically than the workers, is unsatisfactory and creates conflicts which in the long run will be injurious to the workers themselves. If these facts are made clear by proper economic guidance, the existing sense of solidarity with the poorer classes of society may exert an influence on practical wage policy. In this way, by the action of the trade unions themselves, the public will in many cases be protected against the lack of consideration which is often put forward as a reason for intervention in the form of compulsory arbitration.

The logical outcome of all this is to set up a conciliation institution which in its work can and must take into account economic conditions, and which is given power to demand the necessary information for this purpose and to organize its own economic inquiries; further, it should be given the right to justify its conciliation proposals to the parties and the public on economic and other grounds. The position in most countries has hitherto been that the conciliation institution has allowed its proposals to depend solely on an estimate of the attitude of the conflicting parties and their relative strength, and not on an economic estimate of the effect of a particular wage change on prices, sales, and employment. Nor has the conciliation institution, at least in Denmark, tried to influence public opinion. When there is danger of a general dispute, it is particularly necessary that the institution should explain its action to the public by economic arguments which the parties are forced to take into consideration. In such cases the effect of a conciliation proposal depends in no small measure on how it is received by the public, and it is therefore only rational that the conciliation institution should be able, by giving the economic justification for its proposals, to influence public opinion and thereby also the parties.

This need for giving conciliation proceedings an economic basis becomes particularly pressing in cases where the parties expect that in the last resort the government will not allow an open dispute to break out but will intervene by enforcing compulsory arbitration. In such a case the parties will be governed in their negotiations solely by the desire to give the conciliation institution the impression that its proposal is received with decided antipathy. The attitude they adopt will be as stiff as possible, and as there is no risk involved the result will be that both parties unanimously reject the proposal. This means that the actual basis for settlement by conciliation in its present form disappears, since the procedure is founded on an estimate of each party's inclination or disinclination for direct action, and it must be assumed that the threat of such action is real. Therefore, if it is desired that the conciliation institution, and, should occasion arise, the arbitration authority to which the dispute is subsequently referred, should not have to reach a settlement without any basis at all, it becomes necessary to give the institution the means of making independent enquiries in order to obtain a firm foundation for its proposals.

Economic conciliation should be intrusted to a special body, an economic conciliation council, which should act before a possible dispute breaks out. The most natural course would no doubt be for the conciliation council to follow the negotiations which take place between the parties before any dispute. In Denmark collective agreements provide that negotiations must be opened half a year before the agreement expires, and a stipulation of this kind is highly desirable in order to insure that there shall be sufficient time for the necessary inquiries. When a representative of the conciliation council is present at the negotiations, the discussion will inevitably be raised to such a level of economic intelligence that the parties will be bound to take into account a number of economic facts. The conciliation council should also be given the right to make, at a specified date before notice of a strike or lockout is given, and in such form as it considers most suitable, a statement on the issues between the parties. And perhaps it should also be able to require the parties, through their bulletins or in some other way, to bring this statement to the knowledge of their members; but the parties must always have the right to add their own comments on any such statement.

The rationalizing, coordinating and educational activities in which such a council can engage will promote peace. In order to insure that this does not lead to neglect of any of the interests involved, it should be the duty of the council to enquire into and report on any methods other than those that may have been rejected which can lead to the desired results. Thus, if the council is opposed to a particular reduction of hours or increase of wages, it is not enough to give economic arguments for its view, showing, for instance, that such a claim is incompatible with a policy pursued by the government and otherwise approved by the parties, or that a proposed measure, such as a general rise in wages, is not likely to lead directly to the desired result—say a rise in the standard of living—to the extent anticipated. The council must also ascertain in what particular fields and under what particular conditions the claims put forward could conceivably be realized, and explain to the parties by what general economic policy on the part of the government and the Central Bank it would be possible to satisfy these claims on a broader basis. If the council is opposed to a claim for a reduction of wages in periods of depression, it must explain its view to employers by reference to the stabilizing influence of a steady wage rate on the economic situation, and in general try to show by what other measures it would be possible to give employers the economic facilities which are to them the necessary condition for the maintenance of production in the circumstances. A claim for wage reductions can thus be turned into one for foreign exchange measures, changes in banking policy, state regulation of production, or similar action, just as a claim for wage increases can in certain cases be turned into one for increased capital accumulation, or for state regulation and an amended foreign exchange and banking policy. In this way the council becomes an institution both for conciliation and for consultation.

It is obvious that this preliminary work in the field of consultation and conciliation cannot altogether prevent the outbreak of disputes. When that happens the same conciliation authority obviously must not come forward again, after the dispute has lasted for some time, and make further conciliation proposals. When an open dispute breaks out, it means that the relative strength of the parties in the particular situation must determine the settlement of the concrete issue. The conciliation procedure that has to take place later must therefore be able to depart from that which was based on economic grounds and was the work of the economic conciliation council, and must take into account the tactical strength of the parties or their psychological powers of resistance. A conciliation proposal of this kind must be put forward by another institution, since one and the same body cannot, without weakening its authority, lay before the parties at one date a proposal based on economic reasons and at a later date a proposal deviating from the first and influenced by tactical considerations. In particular cases, however, it is quite probable that the institution to which the dispute is referred will tend to keep fairly close to the conciliation proposal put forward by the council. This means that there will be very little to be gained from an open dispute, which of course is a factor making strongly for peace.

In order that the advisory economic conciliation council may be able to work in accordance with the ideas suggested above, it is essential that it should have power to collect all the information it needs for a complete judgment of the claims put forward. The council must therefore have authority to organize, if need be, special economic or statistical inquiries. At the same time, it will have to be given the right to demand information from employers as to the profits of their undertakings, prices, etc., since these matters may be of importance for judging the point at issue. The obligation for employers to give information is in fact a very important prerequisite for the work of the conciliation council. It will therefore be incompatible with the policy outlined above if that resistance to the giving of information on the economic situation of undertakings which is so general in business is maintained. The earnings of an undertaking cannot be regarded as a private matter when knowledge of them can help to create a state of industrial peace in which the whole community is interested. The need for making it compulsory to give information is seen to be still greater when it is remembered that secrecy increases the workers' suspicions with regard to the undertaking's earnings, and therefore tends to produce disputes.

A policy which aims at maintaining the influence of organizations in a democratic community, thereby leaving the way open to disputes, must include preventive measures to insure that the number, extent, and duration, of these disputes is limited to such a degree that provisions for direct prohibition and compulsory arbitration do not become necessary for social or political reasons. This means that the workers' organizations must on the whole be built up on the basis of industrial unionism, so that the tendency of organization on a trade basis to extend disputes from one industrial group to another may disappear. The employers' possibilities of concentrating the right to decide on disputes in a single authority should be limited and replaced by a more decentralized system. The right to take sympathetic action must in certain cases be restricted, and the same may apply to some extent to the right of outside organizations to give economic assistance to the parties to a dispute. A system of preliminary conciliation based on economic grounds must be organized for the purpose of making an objective economic inquiry into the issues, guiding the parties with regard to the possibilities of realizing their claims, coordinating the economic aims of the organizations with the economic policy of the government, and helping to make it possible for the organizations to take into consideration those sections of the population which are not organized. It must be made compulsory for employers to give information, so that the conciliation institution can collect the data that it needs for the settlement of disputes. These various measures do not mean that compulsory arbitration or similar compulsory action may not be necessary in certain cases—for example, in disputes in industries of great importance for production as a whole—but they help to limit the cases in which open disputes break out or in which they break out in such circumstances that direct intervention becomes necessary.

It will be seen that the four or five closely connected measures which have been proposed for preserving democracy in industrial relations consist as a whole in the establishment of conditions for a consistent application of democratic organization to certain aspects of social life. It is deviations from democratic principles and unsound psychological assumptions that produce conditions in which compulsory arbitration and other similar undemocratic methods have to be used for the settlement of disputes. In countries where culture is at so high a level and the appropriate structure of organizations so well developed that the special intellectual weapons which are characteristic of democracy can be used in industrial disputes, the necessary conditions are fulfilled for the protection of free trade unions and employers' associations, and of all the values connected with them.

SHALL STRIKES BE OUTLAWED? [7]

Those who advocate compulsory arbitration sometimes talk as though workers have in them some perverse streak which

[7] From pamphlet by Joel Seidman, Labor Economist; John Dewey Research Fellow for 1940. p. 4-8, 29. League for Industrial Democracy. New York. January 1938.

makes them want to strike. They have no understanding of the low wages, the long hours, the speed-up, the discrimination, and the petty tyrannies that drive workers to desperation. Nor do they understand that workers usually strike only as a last resort, for they work in order to obtain an income, and that income is interrupted by a strike. To a youth, tired of drab factory life, a strike may indeed bring a touch of adventure and excitement, but a worker with family responsibilities is sobered by the thought of mounting debts. It is no fun to pound the pavements for hours in a picket line, in rain or snow, summer heat or winter cold. It is not pleasant to be charged by mounted police, to be slugged by hired hoodlums, or to be the target for tear gas bombs. Workers strike because they have grievances beside which these terrors are as nothing, and because they have learned by long experience that only a militant union, able and willing to strike when that becomes necessary, can wrest concessions from powerful employers.

But why not arbitrate, and save the suffering of the strikers, the losses to the employer, and the inconvenience to everyone else? When unions are powerful and well established, and genuinely fair arbitrators can be found, arbitration may indeed prove satisfactory. In certain American industries, including coal mining and men's clothing, voluntary arbitration has been successfully employed over a period of many years. Needless to say, the crucial issue is who the arbitrators shall be, and what their social viewpoint. Often enough have supposedly impartial arbitrators revealed themselves as men with the employer's point of view to make workers somewhat suspicious, even of voluntary arbitration. And yet workers, both in the United States and in Great Britain, have called for voluntary arbitration many more times than have employers; for workers have usually been in the weaker position, and it is the weak who are most eager for arbitration. For arbitration usually insures some sort of compromise, whereas in battle the weaker party may expect complete defeat.

As for compulsory arbitration, that would place power in the hands of governmental appointees, who would doubtless reflect the attitude of the prevailing political party. Since American labor has been woefully weak on the political front, it is not surprising that it has consistently and vigorously opposed compulsory arbitration. That government whose police club strikers, whose judges issue injunctions against them, and whose troops smash picket lines should not feign surprise if its arbitrators are looked upon with suspicion. Indeed, it would be surprising if the awards of arbitrators, as of other government officials, did not express the social philosophy of the group in control of the government.

In many discussions of strikes and compulsory arbitration the losses due to strikes have been exaggerated, as the problems involved in compulsory arbitration have been minimized. In an economic system with busy and dull seasons, frequent lay-offs, competition, and limited purchasing power, it is possible that a strike may not involve any loss to the community. Its effect may be merely to transfer work from one employer to another, and from one group of workers to another. Time lost at the beginning of a season may be added on at the end, or may be made up by overtime. If the strike is won, the loss in income to the strikers may speedily be made up by higher rates of pay, and the greater purchasing power thereafter may prove of permanent value to the entire community. This does not deny that strikes are usually costly to the workers, the employers, and the community; it merely asserts that the conventional method of assessing the cost involves a very great exaggeration.

Should compulsory arbitration be adopted, however, will strikes be ended and their losses avoided? The history of compulsory arbitration everywhere suggests the contrary. Australia, New Zealand, Norway, and Kansas have all witnessed many illegal strikes under compulsory arbitration; and Canada and Colorado, under their systems of compulsory investigation, have had similar experiences. In all of these cases, moreover, the authorities have proved reluctant to invoke the penalties provided by the law for violations. For jail sentences do not mine coal, as the state of Kansas discovered, and thousands of strikers can scarcely be imprisoned. The authorities in many countries have learned that it is the course of wisdom not to threaten workers, but to seek to remove their grievances. A strike settled by compulsion, they have learned to their sorrow, is soon again unsettled. If the parties can voluntarily reach a mutually satisfactory agreement, however, the way to a lasting peace has been prepared. Thus the compulsory arbitration courts come more and more to function, for the most part, like mediators.

The task of any arbitrator is not an easy one. He may perform a useful service in remedying inequalities in pay between workers of the same skill, or between workers in different industries. He may avoid quarrels over movements in prices by adjusting wages to the cost of living. But how high should wages be? In forty years of effort arbitrators have been unable to develop a satisfactory formula, and indeed there can be none that will satisfy all parties. Labor properly demands an increasingly high standard of living; but how reconcile this with profits, productivity, and the demands of stock and bond owners?

And so the arbitrators have usually altered the distribution of income within the working class rather than between the working class and the employing class. The lowest wages have been raised, the sweated trades improved, and the unskilled laborer benefited. But the skilled workers in the better paying industries have seldom been helped. If countries with compulsory arbitration are compared to those without it, most authorities claim, the spread between the wages of skilled and unskilled is found to be much narrower. The unskilled and those in sweated trades, those who can form weak unions or none at all, those whose bargaining power is limited—these workers have usually been benefited by compulsory arbitration. But the skilled workers, who can form strong unions, win strikes, and bargain effectively, have usually gotten less than would have been theirs had free collective bargaining been allowed.

Still another result of compulsory arbitration is that wages remain relatively more stable than elsewhere, rising more slowly in periods of prosperity, and falling more slowly in times of depression.

Sometimes the industrial arbitration courts have functioned in practice more like minimum wage boards, with the additional function of mediation in other disputes. This has been true, for example, in the case of the Australian federal labor court, with power over disputes extending beyond a single state. Unions with fighting power have disregarded the court whenever they chose, and have reached their own agreements with employers. Their strikes were illegal, to be sure, but under the law there could be no prosecution without the court's consent. The court has thought it wisest to withhold such consent, to gain labor's good will. Those workers who have little fighting power and whose wages are at or near the minimum tend to accept the decisions, since their strikes would likely prove to be failures. Employers usually accept minimum wage boards because competition based on substandard wages is thereby eliminated. Unions are usually satisfied if they possess the right to establish wages above the minimum through collective bargaining.

This review of efforts to maintain industrial peace demonstrates that compulsory arbitration is not a promising device to employ. The inevitable bias of the arbitrators, and the absence of standards for those who seek to be fair, inevitably cause a lack of confidence in decisions, and periodic refusals to abide by them. Under modern capitalist economy, labor feels that its right to strike is its surest guarantee of fair treatment. Only when labor has great influence in the government can the determination of wages and hours be entrusted to governmental appointees. Agencies established to enforce compulsory arbitration again and again find themselves acting primarily as mediators, and refusing to punish participants in illegal strikes in order not to sacrifice good will. It is possible, of course, to enforce penalties against strikes rigidly, as it is possible to outlaw trade unions. Such actions may indeed enforce industrial peace, but at the expense of social justice.

The part of wisdom is to attempt, not to outlaw strikes, but instead to remove the just grievances of workers. If that is done, if employers are forced to bargain collectively, to establish proper working conditions, and pay adequate wages, relatively few strikes will be declared. The longest and most severe strikes have occurred, not where labor was powerfully organized and management willing to deal with it, but where the right to organize was not granted, and genuine collective bargaining denied. In the United States some industries, such as stove molding, have a history of many years of satisfactory collective bargaining without a strike. It is where unions are weak, not where they are strong, that strikes are to be most expected. No responsible and experienced labor leader will sanction a strike if continued negotiations offer promise of a satisfactory agreement. Most agreements, moreover, provide that there shall be no strikes until the expiration date has been reached. Where outlaw strikes occur, it is usually due to a combination of unfair practices on the part of the employer and inexperience on the part of the workers. Governments, both state and federal, will be wise to devote their attention to safeguarding the right to organize, and to promoting real collective bargaining.

COUNT TEN FIRST [8]

We in Minnesota feel that in order to realize the full value and advantage of mediation, it is necessary that machinery be set up so that the mediation and conciliation should take place before the strike or lockout occurs. In this way production continues and the workers continue to receive their pay checks. Furthermore, it usually is much easier to mediate a settlement before a strike occurs than it is afterward. A strike causes tempers to flare and sometimes violence breaks out, and the whole atmosphere makes it more difficult to have the two parties reach an agreement.

Two years ago Minnesota adopted the Minnesota Labor Peace Law based on these principles. We require that if management and labor cannot reach an agreement in a dispute, they shall notify the state labor conciliator. Then they must wait ten days, or, as we frequently refer to it, they must "count ten" and take one day for each count.

During these ten days the state labor conciliator calls the two sides into conferences and endeavors to have them reach a voluntary settlement of the dispute before production stops. Workers continue to work and the management likewise must maintain the status quo. The conciliator cannot force either side to agree

[8] By Harold E. Stassen, Governor of Minnesota. Part of five-way symposium on "How to Insure Industrial Peace." *Rotarian*. 58:29. June 1941.

to any points of settlement.   Public opinion is the only force behind the law.

The soundness of the principles has been demonstrated by the remarkable success of its operation.   In 1937 and 1938, 33,382 workers in Minnesota were involved in strikes; in 1939 and 1940, under the new law, this was cut to 5,859, although at the same time the national loss through strikes was increasing.

Even in these recent months of critical national-defense production, while many difficult disputes have arisen, there has not been a single important stoppage of work in Minnesota.   In fact, in the last five months, while over 200 disputes have reached the conciliator, only a few minor ones involving altogether 150 workers ever reached the point of strike or lockout.

Perhaps the outstanding example was the dispute at the Minneapolis-Moline Power Implement Company which arose at about the same time as the Allis-Chalmers dispute.   The company is engaged in the same industry and the union was the same union as in the Allis-Chalmers situation.   But while the Allis-Chalmers dispute was battled out on the picket lines, with many long weeks of stoppage of defense production and great loss to the workers in wages, the Minneapolis-Moline dispute was settled around the conference table.   In fact, when all preliminary conferences failed, we were able to have the National Defense Mediation Board, of which Clarence A. Dykstra is Chairman and Mr. Davis is Vice Chairman, take jurisdiction before the work stopped. They summoned both sides to Washington, and the employer and employee representatives continued conferring on the train on the way to Washington and reached a settlement there before they met with the National Defense Mediation Board.   The settlement was based upon the recommendations of the Minnesota Mediation Commission.

I believe this has been the first and only national-defense dispute that reached the National Defense Mediation Board before production stopped rather than after work stopped.   This example reemphasizes the basic soundness of the principles that have been demonstrated over and over again the last two years in Minnesota.

If the sound principles of mediation of Mr. Davis's decision are to have opportunity to work to their fullest, a notice to the government before a strike or lockout and a brief waiting period, or cooling-off period, or mediation period, while production continues and conditions remain the same, are essential steps. They represent practical mechanics for the functioning of democracy with public opinion as the force that brings results.

THE POLICY OF THE AMERICAN ARBITRATION ASSOCIATION ON COMPULSORY ARBITRATION [9]

This [American Arbitration] Association has been asked to state its policy with respect to compulsory arbitration. It does so with pleasure.

The Association was founded in 1926 to advance the knowledge and practice of arbitration. From the beginning, it adopted the centuries-old concept that arbitration is the *voluntary* act of the parties as to their agreement to arbitration, as to their choice of arbitrator and as to the kind of proceeding they would like to have. Arbitration is the very antithesis of force. If its voluntary character is removed and compulsion substituted, it is not arbitration—no matter what label is appended.

Said the *Compleat Arbitrator*, the English classic in 1731:

Arbitrament is the determination of two or more persons, at the request of two parties at least who are at variance, for ending the controversy without publick authority.

Said Blackstone's *Commentaries*:

Arbitration is where the parties injuring and injured submit all matters in dispute, concerning any personal chattels or personal wrong, to the judgment of two or more *arbitrators,* who are to decide the controversy; and if they do not agree, it is usual to add, that another person be called in as *umpire* (*imperator* or *impar*), to whose sole judgment it is then referred: or frequently there is only one arbitrator originally appointed. This decision, in any of these cases, is called an *award*. And thereby the question is as fully determined, and the right transferred or settled, as it could have been by the agreement of the parties or the judgment of a court of justice.

[9] American Arbitration Association. New York. 3p. mim. December 4, 1944.

Said Judge Thacher in *United States* v. *Paramount-Famous Lasky Corporation, et al*, 34 F. (2d) 984 (1929):

> By agreement of these distributors, exhibitors who were not represented in the adoption of the uniform contracts have been constrained to accept their terms regardless of their wishes, and by the compulsory system of arbitration, sanctioned and enforced by the collective action of the distributors, have been constrained to perform the contractual obligations thus assumed. In fairness it cannot be said that the restraint imposed upon these exhibitors is voluntary because they accept and agree to be bound by the contracts. They can have none other, because the defendants have agreed that they shall not; and, unless something more than the mere acceptance of all they can get is shown, they must be said to have acted under an involuntary restraint, imposed and continued by the defendants to the end that the contracts shall be signed and their terms obeyed. . . .
>
> Upon settlement of the decree the parties may suggest provisions, if such be feasible, under which uniform contracts containing arbitration clauses may be voluntarily adopted by the members of this industry without coercion or other unlawful restraint.

Conflicting as the laws often are, inconsistent as judges sometimes are, united opinion has prevailed as to the voluntary nature of arbitration and the safeguarding of this right.

The so-called pacific processes of settling controversy have since their origin thousands of years ago been voluntary. No outside person could force his way into a dispute as a conciliator, mediator or arbitrator. Consent was deemed necessary even among the nomads who often ceased fighting only long enough to select an arbitrator by agreement and mutual selection. It is of the very essence of arbitration that this primary principle be maintained lest arbitration perish and the force of arms or of law again prevail.

These are the principles to the preservation of which the American Arbitration Association was dedicated in 1926. These are the principles about which all of its procedure and administration are built. These are the principles the Association has carried throughout its war service. These are the principles it proposes to carry into the post-war period in all of the reconstruction problems that lie ahead.

Believing that this is the only kind of arbitration that can survive as an instrument of equality and justice, this Association will not undertake to act under any compulsory form of arbitration; it will not ask members of its panels to serve in any compulsory process; it will not lend its aid to the negotiation of any arbitration agreement, not voluntarily sought by the parties; it will neither create nor administer any rules which create any form of duress by which the rights of any party to a fair and just determination of his dispute will be prejudiced.

The Association administers for the parties the following types of tribunals: commercial, labor, accident claims. These tribunals are competent to decide local, national or international controversies.

They all operate under rules that grant the parties full voluntary rights. At no step in the proceeding is a party forced to do anything beyond what he has voluntarily agreed to do in his arbitration agreement or by stipulation thereafter.

The Association believes now as it always has that arbitration, being a persuasive process and opposed to all forms of force, is *arbitration* only to the degree to which it remains voluntary. When the will of one party is imposed upon another it ceases to be arbitration. When the will of an arbitrator or outside intervener is imposed upon another, it ceases to be arbitration. When a person not agreed to by the parties is named arbitrator that person is not a person chosen by the parties, as the tradition and law of arbitration decree. Whenever arbitration is ordered by directive or duress in any form, at that instant it ceases to be arbitration as men understand it, believe in it and trust it as an act of their own free will.

Any form of administration, not openly and voluntarily arrived at by the parties this Association is not willing to arbitrate.

COMPULSORY ARBITRATION [10]

The National Association of Manufacturers has, under normal conditions, been unalterably opposed to compulsory arbitration as an infringement upon the rights of workers and management

[10] From article "Labor Arbitration in Wartime," by William P. Witherow, past President, National Association of Manufacturers. *Arbitration Journal.* 6: 16-18. Winter 1942.

alike. In wartime there is no reason to change that long-term conviction, even though it may, in effect, have to be waived for the duration of the war, depending upon how the [National War Labor] Board interprets the President's Executive Order.

Today—threatened as we are from all sides and from the air by totalitarianism—the right and the privilege of settling our own affairs becomes more precious than ever. True, the burden of responsibility upon the disputing parties to arrive voluntarily at an early agreement is heavier. But citizens of the great democracies are fast coming to a greater understanding of the fact that with every privilege and right goes a responsibility and a duty. And this is well.

Let it be hoped that arbitration, if arbitration it is to be, may be *voluntary*.

Compulsory arbitration by law establishes government control over collective agreements regulating wages, hours and working conditions. Settlements which are the result of such outside coercion and compulsion neither solve the points at conflict nor reconcile existing misunderstandings.

John L. Lewis referred to compulsory arbitration as "involuntary servitude" and a "death stroke at national unity." The late Samuel Gompers wrote that "the only real effect (of compulsory arbitration laws) is to . . . . make wage-earners dependent upon a political agency to carry industrial problems into politics." Thus has labor expressed itself.

Wherever compulsion enters, freedom leaves. Where freedom leaves, democracy as we know it ceases to exist.

Voluntary arbitration, on the other hand, is one of the highest expressions of civilization. With it is preserved man's sacred right of choice of action. Unless we prove we are unworthy of it, let us keep it at all cost.

One factor contributing to the growing use of voluntary arbitration has been the ability of labor and management to agree on issues they were willing to arbitrate. Some issues have been withheld from arbitration because they involve questions of principle which neither side would be willing to leave to an arbitrator, either because of conviction that the issue cannot be compromised or because it is of such grave public importance that private citizens, acting as arbitrators, should not undertake to resolve it.

One such question is labor's participation in functions for which management has full legal and moral responsibility. Another is the controversial closed-shop question, namely, whether management should join hands with labor unions and make union membership compulsory. So far, government has insisted that employees be given absolute freedom to join or not join any labor union, and the law forbids interference by the employer with the exercise of that freedom. If the government compels an employer to sign a closed-shop agreement, or any modification of it, the government destroys the right of free choice.

Even more important, in a period when maximum production means national safety, is the conviction of management that it must have the right to hire and retain men who are competent and efficient—whether or not they are union members.

So fundamental is it to the preservation of the very principles for which we are fighting that no compromise [should] be made with *principle* in arbitration in wartime. . . .

This is no time for the introduction of new questions of policy, no time for a new industrial revolution. This is the time for the mutual acceptance, by industry and by labor alike, of the *status quo* existing before Pearl Harbor and Manila on such fundamental questions as who shall "manage" and who shall "work" and who shall determine which workers shall work.

This is no time to put up for discussion or make arbitrable such vital and emotional questions as the closed shop. Rather is this the time to get to work, using the rules of the game as they applied toward the end of 1941.

The closed shop conflicts with two fundamental liberties: (1) the right of the worker to work as he wills, and (2) the right of the employer to employ men or not to employ them with a view toward operating efficiency, regardless of their race, religion or political views. It is a question of the greatest importance and must not be treated either lightly or in haste.

With the country involved in a struggle for its very existence, neither employer nor employee should use the emergency to effect changes in the bargaining relationship.

EXCERPTS

A study of compulsory arbitration in all its aspects, reveals three new concepts for determining collective labor conditions that are significant in their potential importance.

1. Government compulsion on the part of both employer and employees to submit their disputes to an outside agency, would withdraw the controversy from the jurisdiction of the two parties concerned and place it, instead, in the hands of an external agency less familiar with the problems at issue, and in consequence, less apt to resolve the points of difference to the satisfaction and acceptance of both employer and employees.

The award (the terms and conditions decided upon by the arbitration agency in the settlement of the dispute) would then constitute the regulation of working conditions either by government direct or through the authority vested in its agent, rather than the voluntary and optional determining of these working conditions by employer and employees.

In the final analysis, this method would tend to establish, in practice, the regulation of working conditions by government authority.

2. With working conditions thus regulated by government authority, political influence and power become increasingly important as a weapon for both employers and workers.

It may be seen that such compulsory arbitration by government might tend to introduce a long, bitter battle for political strength in order to influence labor politics and legislation.

In his book *An Introduction to the Study of Labor Problems*, Gordon S. Watkins says: "It is commonly believed that compulsory arbitration functions in the interest of those who constitute the economic and political power."

3. Compulsory arbitration tends to move away from the principle of self-government in industry. In its consistent operation, it would necessarily substitute arbitrary, legislative labor standards or standards established by government arbitrators, or both, for the practical terms and conditions jointly determined by the parties involved.

The logical application of compulsory arbitration would quickly tend to place increasing emphasis on government regulation of economic freedom for both industry and labor.—*"Compulsory Arbitration of Labor Disputes." National Association of Manufacturers. New York. n.d. mim. p. 12-14.*

American labor is not prepared to accept compulsion. If people cannot agree, there is no alternative. Compulsory waiting periods or cooling-off periods for which proposals have been advanced are founded on the idea that American workers should be forced to work against their will.

This assumption is false and shortsighted. The record proves that no compulsory cooling-off periods have even accomplished their intended purpose. In Canada the Industrial Disputes Inventigation Act, providing for a compulsory waiting period, has served to demonstrate this. While 90 per cent of 536 disputes were settled under the act in the first 20 years of its operation, there were 425 *illegal* strikes which were of greater consequence to the country than the ones adjusted.

Compulsory waiting periods, like all unreasonable restraints, only serve to breed lawlessness and unrest. Certainly the record of operation of such state laws in Michigan and Minnesota demonstrates that they are ineffective as a means of insuring industrial peace.

The American Federation of Labor is unqualifiedly opposed to the enactment of any legislation providing for the settlement of disputes through waiting periods or other forms of compulsion not only because such laws are restrictive and repugnant to democracy, but also because labor knows that they will not work. Labor believes that the best protection against industrial strife is an honest attempt to seek to avert threatened disputes by timely recognition and elimination of their causes.

We in America must show to the world that as a free people, through the contribution of free and unrestricted labor we can far exceed the accomplishment of workers subjected to regimented compulsion or of labor herded into concentration camps.

The only cause I plead in urging the policy of voluntary cooperation is the cause of free democracy. I hope with all labor that this plea will gain inalterable acceptance. Its rejection can only mean the admission of failure of the whole democratic process. Such failure the American people are not ready to admit.—*William Green, President, American Federation of Labor. In "We Work for the Future."* '41. *p.* 21-2.

In just such historic periods as these we are now passing through, there is grave danger that hysteria will be substituted for clear-thinking, and feeling for sound judgment. This dangerous, psychological condition is now being shown by some Members of Congress, editors of newspapers, and others who influence public opinion.

Some of those referred to advocate the enactment of repressive, anti-labor, and anti-strike legislation. They think in terms of compulsion, when our national needs call for the highest type of voluntary service. They would, if they had their way, make rebels out of working men and women who are enthusiastically and willingly giving all they have and all they can to the government and to society. They totally disregard the sacred prohibition against compulsory labor, which is included in the 13th amendment to the Constitution of the United States, reading as follows:

Neither slavery nor involuntary servitude, except as a punishment for crime whereof the party shall have been duly convicted, shall exist within the United States, or any place subject to their jurisdiction.

Forced labor, the concentration camp, and compulsory service may be imposed upon Labor in totalitarian countries, but never in a democracy where the guarantees of freedom, liberty and justice are written into the organic law.

We can reduce strikes to a minimum; we can develop efficiency and the highest degree of cooperation between management and labor, by applying the principles of mediation, conciliation and voluntary arbitration in the settlement of industrial disputes.

Legislation providing for compulsory service; compulsory arbitration—compulsion of any kind—will provoke strikes, social unrest, and destroy efficiency.

The right to strike is fundamental. The workers must always be accorded the right to give or withhold service. However, the recognition of the right to strike does not mean that strikes should take place during periods of national emergency. This is particularly true during these days when the government is engaged in the execution of a far-reaching defense policy. Workers must exercise self-discipline, must work and serve in the interest of national defense, and must make such sacrifices as the exigencies of the situation demand. All working men and women who fully appreciate the value of freedom, liberty and democracy, will do so.—*William Green, President, American Federation of Labor. "Labor and National Defense." Rotary Club of Pennsylvania. Ap. 2, '41. p. 11-12.*

There is general agreement that one provision of the new legislation should be the enforcement of a "reasonable" waiting period in advance of strikes, during which the processes of collective bargaining, mediation, fact-finding or voluntary arbitration may have a peaceful opportunity to go forward. . . .

But some Administration leaders and others in Congress talk easily of going on from there to give the President power to order compulsory arbitration if at the end of the waiting period he thought such action desirable. If Congress is to pass such legislation, let it at least do so with its eyes fully open to the implications of such legislation and what is most likely to happen under it. Those who favor such legislation evidently imagine that these compulsory arbitration powers would be used only in a few rare instances. What they overlook is that they would affect nearly every labor dispute that arose, because the disputants would be aware from the beginning of the existence of this Presidential power and would bear it in mind in whatever moves they made.

Just as union leaders today do not accept a wage increase from an employer through collective bargaining if they think they can get a bigger increase from the Mediation Board, so union leaders would not accept a recommendation of the Mediation Board if they thought they could get a better one out of a special board of arbitration. John L. Lewis has already given an illustration of this process. Employers, on the other hand, disappointed by a Mediation Board decision, might see hope in an appeal to a compulsory arbitration board.

In one way or another, in short, once compulsory arbitration is admitted as a final resort, the percentage of disputes going to it would probably be very high. Boards of arbitration could not adopt the chaotic policy up to now of the Mediation Board, of "deciding each case on its own merits." Soon or late they would have to make their awards in accordance with a plainly understood set of standards regarding the closed and open shop, wage increase policy, and so on. But this would mean that the government and not the unions and employers was fixing wages and working conditions. What this would ultimately do to an independent labor movement or to the private enterprise system it is too early to foresee.

On the other hand, it should be quite clear that the mere proposal for an obligatory "cooling off" period would not be in itself sufficient to deal with the present labor problem. We cannot ignore our legislative sins of omission or commission that have done so much to provoke and intensify disputes while proposing a remedy that treats the final symptoms of the strike evil and leaves the causes untouched.—*Editorial. New York Times.* N. 26, '41. p. 22.

Due to the fact that different psychological, geographical, and economic factors influence each country differently, it is difficult to make generalizations as to the most successful method for industrial peace. However, from the experience of the above mentioned countries [Great Britain, Australasia and Canada] certain factors common to all instances of governmental intervention are discernible.

First, it is obvious that laws, regardless of the nature, cannot effectuate a state of industrial peace in industries which are striken with some fundamental economic defect. The coal mining industry, for example, has been overdeveloped in practically every industrial country and at present the supply of miners greatly exceeds the demand. Consequently in England, Australasia and Canada methods for industrial peace which are effective in other industries have been unable to relieve the strife in the coal fields. Hence it is not to be expected that the mere passage of mediation, conciliation, or arbitration laws will remove industrial unrest. Laws can be enacted and boards can hand down awards, but if the defect is inherent in the industry itself flagrant violations will inevitably occur.

Secondly, the experience of the foreign countries studied has proved that the present trend is toward greater and greater use of non-coercive methods for industrial peace. England's only attempt at compulsion failed even during the war, a time when patriotism was urging employers and employees toward greater cooperation. At other times the British voluntary agencies have made as good a record in settling and preventing disputes as has any country which has utilized coercive methods. The best records of compulsion are found in New Zealand and Australia where labor is highly organized, and, for the most part, controls the dominant political parties. However, in New Zealand compulsory arbitration was unable to stand in the face of the pressure of recent economic depression. In Australia the coercive features have remained intact, but there is a trend for both the Commonwealth and the state governments to resort primarily to conferences and mediation rather than to arbitration. Although the Canadian Disputes Act has compulsory provisions they are rarely used because the major portion of the disputes are settled by conciliation.

In the third place, much of the success or failure of any system for industrial peace depends on the type of men who constitute the personnel of the administrative unit. The New Zealand system fell in 1932 largely because the court of arbitration had fixed wages so high that the refusal to cut them made the economic position of the employers intolerable. In our own country Title 3 of the Transportation Act became a source of industrial strife instead of peace primarily because the act's administrators were openly anti-union in their actions. On the other hand the Canadian Disputes Act has been highly successful due to the open-minded attitude of the Minister of Labour and his appointees, and their consistent refusal to invoke the compulsory features of the act. They have used the compulsory features only as a mild threat to open the way for conciliation. Industrial peace agencies cannot function unless the attitude and activities of the administrators are so impartial that the confidence of the disputants and the public is always retained.

Today in the United States the question of industrial relationships is delicate and fluid, and until the issue of unionism is definitely settled any program for governmental intervention will meet with opposition from those whose views do not coincide with the objects of the program. Nevertheless, the interests of the industrial community as a whole demand that employers and employees accept the responsibility of keeping industry going, and when they refuse to accept this responsibility the government is justified in stepping in. The end of governmental intervention should be voluntary and amicable collective dealing between labor and capital, and this can be achieved only when both sides are free to develop as equals.—*George T. Starnes, Associate Professor of Labor Economics, University of Virginia; and John R. McCutcheon and James M. Stepp, Graduate Students in Economics, University of Virginia. "A Survey of the Methods for the Promotion of Industrial Peace." Bureau of Public Administration. University of Virginia. Charlottesville. '39. mim. p. 76-7.*

It is much too simple to dismiss the Connally-Smith War Labor Disputes Act as a badly drafted law and let it go at that. Testimony that there is something wrong with it can now be offered by more than 200 employers on the basis of direct experience. In a little over two months of the law's operation, unions have used it 214 times to put pressure on an employer, or through him on the government, for some concession that was being refused. And the use of the law by organized labor for this purpose is increasing at an accelerating rate.

The lineup on the bill when it was before Congress led industry to believe that it had a vital and positive interest in the measure's passage. With a remarkable unanimity, organized business and its allies in the House and Senate fought hard and long for its enactment. The unions and their cabal in government opposed it to the limit of their strength and the end of their stratagems.

Conceived as an instrument that would divest organized labor of some of its power as a pressure group and eliminate some of the frictions in employee relations, the law has had a directly opposite effect. It serves a purpose completely alien to that which was intended by its sponsors. Instead of curbing labor's bargaining strength, the section of the act that provides for plant seizures in the event of labor trouble or the threat of labor trouble has armed the unions with a new weapon.

Instead of neutralizing labor's political influence through its inclusion of a ban on direct political contributions by the unions, the act has been responsible for a resurgence of political activity in the A.F.L. and C.I.O. which promises to make itself felt distinctly in 1944.

Instead of discouraging wildcat stoppages by its provision of penalties for strikers and leaders, flash strikes and quickies have increased since June. . . .

Most important of all, the famous 30-day cooling-off period which must now elapse between announcement of intent to strike and the taking of a strike vote has become in practice a heating-up period during which campaigning and agitation have precipitated the employee relations of more than one important war plant into chaotic disorder.

It is popular to say now that this inversion of the law's purpose came about because, while the idea behind the measure had been long considered and discussed, the bill itself was hastily written to take advantage of the favorable legislative opportunity for its enactment that was presented by John L. Lewis' feud with the government. This explanation is dangerously simple. It assumes that a different drafting into law of the Connally-Smith intent would assure the attainment of the desired end. This might be true, but it is by no means certain. It is dangerous doctrine because it focuses on the mere language of the law that attention which business should be giving to the theory behind it.

The fundamental question is how much can be done by legislation to influence a social dynamic like labor relations. We have, by judicious lawmaking, regulated strong-running currents.

The Sherman Act and the law creating the Securities & Exchange Commission are examples of such regulation. But when we legislate in the hope of reversing a trend and in so doing make a too radical attack on established patterns, we risk intensifying the very hazards we seek to escape.

In the intensely practical, but delicately balanced competition of labor relations, the concepts of politicians written into law may have unpredictable and intolerable consequences. The interests of business will best be served by leaving the details of collective bargaining and personnel policy to its industrial relations experts. Better than anyone else, they know what hazards inhere in further government intervention of any sort.—*Editorial. Business Week.* S. 11, '43. *p.* 108.

CASE FOR COMPULSORY ARBITRATION

SHOULD COMPULSORY ARBITRATION OF LABOR DISPUTES BE INSTITUTED IN THE DEFENSE INDUSTRIES? [1]

Never before in the history of the Republic has labor been accorded such favorable legislative recognition as has characterized the past seven years.

Labor has been granted the opportunity for collective bargaining and collective agreement under the sanction of law.

The employment conditions of an increasing number of workers have been improved by the Walsh-Healey Act (1938), under which employees engaged on any government contract that exceeds more than $10,000 in value are assured of basic hours of not more than eight per day and 40 per week, and pay at a rate not less than the prevailing minimum wage of the industry and locality as determined by the Secretary of Labor. Under this act all government contractors are required to guarantee that their employees will work under safe and healthful conditions. Under it employees in 31 industries have benefitted.

In addition, labor is protected under the Fair Labor Standards Act, the National Mediation Board, the National Labor Relations Act (regarded by labor itself as the Magna Charta of labor), and the Social Security Act. Certainly, government has dealt generously in the protection of labor.

In addition to these and other measures enacted in behalf of labor, the United States Conciliation Service, the oldest federal agency dealing with employer-employee relations in the United States, long has placed its services at the disposal of labor in

[1] By Edward Eugene Cox, Democratic Representative from Georgia since 1925; Member, House Committee on Rules. *Modern Industry.* 1:57-61. February 15, 1941.

the interest of industrial peace and the reduction of idle days due to threatened, impending, or existing strikes.

Within but a few days of the creation of the Advisory Council on National Defense, the United States Conciliation Service was designated as the federal agency to deal with labor disputes; and the Secretary of Labor selected a group of the most experienced commissioners of conciliation to work with such industries as oil, aviation, manufacturing, machine tools, rubber and chemicals, building construction, ship-building, and steel—all vital to the nation's existence not only in times of threatened insecurity but even in times of peace as well.

But despite all the efforts of Congress and the general public interest in the welfare of labor during recent years, labor has exhibited but little inclination either to promote peace within its own ranks or to aid in the promotion of industrial peace generally. Since 1937 labor has been engaged in an unprecedented number of strikes of serious concern to the nation. Within recent months it has not hesitated to strike in defense industries.

Strikes are of serious concern not only to labor. They also affect the entire nation. They are of concern to every individual in the nation. In times such as these they tend to affect the very existence of the nation.

Today, America is engaged upon the greatest peacetime program of defense in the history of the Republic. Our future depends upon the effective production of men and machines. America now calls upon all its resources—human as well as material—in order to prepare against an ever-increasing and ever-impending threat to its national safety and security.

By the Act of September 1940, the "Selective Service and Training Act," America seeks to provide for its defense by increasing its armed forces and by training those forces for effective and efficient service in the event of invasion from abroad. In pursuance of that Act, 16 million young men between the ages of 21 and 36 registered on October 16.

But industry, too, is conscripted under the terms of the Selective Service Act, which confers upon the President the power to require manufacturers to accept and to execute orders for defense materials or, in the event of non-compliance, to take immediate possession of any plant whose owner refuses, and to manufacture therein any product or material that may be required for defense purposes, with the further power of imposing a penalty of imprisonment for three years and a fine of not more than $50,000.

In announcing its policies, the Advisory Commission of the Council of National Defense declared among other things that the primary objectives are the production of materials required by our armed forces and the assurance of an adequate future supply of such materials with the least possible disturbance to the production of supplies for the civilian population. The Commission holds that the scope of our present program entails bringing into production many of our unused resources of agriculture, manufacturing, and manpower.

The Commission also reaffirmed the principles enunciated by the Chief of Ordnance of the United States Army during the World War in his order of November 1917, concerning the relation of labor standards to efficient production.

We are embarking upon a program of vital importance to the national security and safety. The months ahead will demand an attitude of cooperative enterprise among all groups in the nation. We have conscripted the manpower of the nation, we have authorized the conscription of industry when the President deems such conscription essential. The selective service forces of the nation must serve; industry must cooperate; only labor is free to strike, to stop the wheels of industry, to retard the national progress, to threaten the national security, and to endanger the national welfare. Labor, indeed, has been granted a preferred status.

Labor is not required to conciliate. Neither the Secretary of Labor nor the Director of the Conciliation Service nor the Commissioners of Conciliation possess any power to compel labor to agree to conciliation. The officers of the United States Conciliation Service have no mandatory power. Both labor and industry may reject their tender of service.

True, there has been some growth in arbitration. But such arbitration as prevails today is purely voluntary; and it has been resorted to largely merely for the purpose of settling disputes that arise over agreement interpretations. It never has been resorted to even voluntarily for the settlement of disputes over fundamental issues. In short, while men may be drafted to serve in the armed forces of the nation, and while industry may be compelled to produce, there is no power over labor, not even the power of compulsory conciliation or arbitration—of determining a controversy and imposing a settlement.

Surely such a status is not conducive to the efficient performance of the program which the people of America have been compelled to assume for their national safety and security. If the nation is to produce effectively there must be no obstacle in its path. Not even labor can be permitted to jeopardize the national welfare. Labor must adopt the spirit of cooperation for national security. It must adopt the same spirit of sacrifice demanded of all the rest of the nation. Both labor and industry must accept a system of compulsory arbitration at least for the duration of the existing emergency. And Congress should enact a measure of compulsory arbitration into law.

At the end of January, 1940, there were 92 strikes in progress in American industries. Those strikes involved more than 39,000 workers and were the cause of more than 239,000 idle man-days in that month. At the end of February 1940, 111 strikes were in progress, involving almost 37,000 workers and causing almost 285,000 idle man-days during that month. In March of that year, 98 strikes were in progress, involving more than 42,000 workers and causing almost 381,000 idle man-days during that month. In April 1940, 113 strikes were in progress; they involved more than 51,000 workers and caused more than 442,000 idle man-days. In May of that year, 99 strikes were in progress. They involved more than 75,000 workers and caused the loss of more than 664,000 man-days. In June 1940, 108 strikes were in progress at the end of the month; 52,000 workers were affected, and almost 466,000 man-days were lost.

The second half of the year was the same. In July, 108 strikes were in progress at the end of the month; almost 76,000 workers were involved, and 552,000 idle man-days were the result. In August 130 strikes were in progress at the end of the month, affecting 73,000 workers and causing 615,000 idle man-days. In September 1940, the last month for which statistics are available at this writing, 140 strikes were in progress at the end of the month, involving 95,000 workers and causing 725,000 idle man-days.

During 1933, almost 1,700 strikes were in progress, causing almost 17 million idle man-days during that year. During 1934, more than 1,800 strikes were in progress, causing more than 19 million idle man-days. In 1935 more than 2,000 strikers were in progress, causing more than 15 million idle man-days. In 1936 more than 2,000 strikes were in progress, causing almost 14 million idle man-days. In 1937, 4,740 strikes were in progress, causing more than 28 million idle man-days. In 1983, 2,772 strikes were in progress, causing more than nine million idle man-days. And in 1939, 2,613 strikes were in progress, causing more than 17 million idle man-days.

On the average, well over a million workers were affected each year during that seven-year period in which the nation was recovering from a serious depression characterized by extensive unemployment and when it might have been reasonable to assume that labor, returning to work, would have indicated a desire to remain at work.

But labor, apparently, was reflecting the spirit of its own factional discontent during those years as it still continues to do. For despite all the efforts of its best friends, including the President, labor still refuses to resolve its internal strife and embark upon a course of peace. And even as labor is unwilling to suppress the discontent within its own ranks, it is unwilling to modify its discontent with management and enter voluntarily upon a general program of cooperation or conciliation.

COMPULSORY ARBITRATION OF
LABOR DISPUTES? [2]

The United States is filled with the clamor of industrial disputes which make for confusion and dislocation. In every dis-

[2] By Henry J. Allen, Governor of Kansas, 1919-1923; since 1935 Editor of the Topeka *State Journal. Rotarian.* 58:13-15. March 1941.

cussion as to why the actual work upon the defense program does not go forward faster, labor is mentioned as either the first or the second cause of the delay.

William S. Knudsen, director of defense production management, recently took the public into his confidence in a most poignant discussion, declaring that there was a lag of 30 per cent in aircraft output alone. He emphasized that the labor difficulty constituted the first barrier to needed progress. He mentioned specifically the need of correcting the schedule of labor hours which now blacks out the industry from Friday night until Monday morning.

An exactly similar thing happened in France, where the left-wing labor racketeers, establishing a government within the government, controlled the energies of labor. France pays today in tragic despair for the ruin of a brave land which tried to save itself on a 37-hour-week labor program interrupted continuously by sitdown strikes, apathy, and other disorders. While France, crippled by this situation, produced less than 35 airplanes a month and allowed labor to live in semi-idleness, Germany worked furiously producing 1,500 planes a month.

In America the reaction of public opinion on the subject of national security is significant. A poll recently taken by Dr. George Gallup reveals that over 70 per cent of the people of the United States blame labor for the retardation of the defense program. It would not be just, of course, to blame labor individually, or as a mass: the system responds to the labor leaders; they must face the rising tide of public censure.

The labor situation is even more difficult than it was during World War I. Even then it was bad enough. It may be recalled that between April 8, 1917, and November 15, 1918, there were 6,000 strikes in industries which were producing the sinews of war in the United States. Some were strikes on New York docks, which retarded the loading of ships taking supplies to the men in the battle lines. Most of the old faults are reappearing with added emphasis.

Last week I visited with an industrial leader who is building an oil refinery in southern Illinois. The company had fixed six months as the normal time for construction, but the job has been running nine months now and has at least three months to go. The cost has almost doubled the original estimate.

The day I was there a shortage of pipe fitters had brought an emergency. Over 70 pipe fitters from the union in Chicago had been sent to the job. Irrespective of their qualifications, the contractor had to pay a $1-a-day fee for each man to the union officials. It costs $300 to join that union, and the apprentice supply thus had been restricted. Of the 70 men, the youngest was 62 years of age.

Common labor on this job is getting $1 an hour; skilled labor getting from $1.50 to $1.70. The contractor must negotiate constantly with the business agents of 12 separate unions. An expensive lot of time has been wasted by jurisdictional quarrels.

At Fort Riley the government is now building 700 houses for troops. More than 9,000 so-called workers have already been mobilized. The situation presents a confused scene, vividly reminiscent of the spectacle I saw there 24 years ago. Now, as then, the buildings are being constructed on the cost-plus (pluck) basis. Common labor is getting top prices for short hours. The process through which any man may get a job is somewhat as follows:

He must first have a clearance from the unemployed rolls, then he applies at Ogden, a village near Fort Riley, to a labor leader who charges him $40 for a union card. He is then at liberty to enter into a conspiracy with the contractor to add his name to the lengthening payroll and thus effect the cost of the job upward to the mutual profit of them both. Sometimes he misses a job with the contractor, but he doesn't get back the $40.

The shocking story thus begins with union labor's collection of approximately $360,000 for union fees on a simple Army job at an interior point. The reckless pressure of haste and numbers will complete the simple, temporary buildings, but at a cost altogether out of proportion to the needs, even of this grim hour.

When you contemplate the confusion encountered everywhere through the lack of coördinated program, it may seem absurd to debate leisurely the constructive proposals of a remedy that has been receiving some attention for over two generations. It would seem to demand of the government a firm hand.

The National Labor Relations Board (N.L.R.B.), brought into existence by the Wagner Act, was created as an instrument of labor's resistance to employing capital. It should have been entitled "An Act for the Regulation of Capital by Labor."

Probably capital, in the dark ages of its early days, never figured out a program which obtained so watertight a grip upon labor as that which labor has now established for its control of employer relations. The severity of this modern-day labor control is not justified by the ruthless, early-day control by capital.

The National Labor Relations Board is a semijudicial body whose judges are also the prosecutors, and at times the detectives and witnesses who gather evidence on the cases in which they pass final judgment. Those who read the reports of the recent Congressional investigation of the N.L.R.B. must realize how utterly unimportant and without dependent value this expensive arm of the service has been from the beginning. It represents labor statesmanship at its very worst.

There have been honest efforts to create workable, compulsory programs for the solution of labor controversies. Something over a quarter century ago, the industrial tribunals of New Zealand and Australia gave us some hope. They were organized originally with the thought that collective bargaining might be given an even, balanced justice by court procedure and discipline. Space is not sufficient to discuss the acts' many sensible provisions.

In the United States, probably the most important effort in this direction was the Kansas Court of Industrial Relations. It was not an act for compulsory arbitration, but rather for compulsory adjudication. The theory was that the controversies between capital and labor in essential industries could be solved by impartial adjudication, that the trial of the causes could be surrounded by every solemnity that surrounds other court procedure, and that it would be safe to set up the broad principle that courts of justice which find equitable solution for every other relationship in life, can find it for labor.

Elaborate provisions for research, for hearing, and finally for appeal to the higher courts were provided. Collective bargaining was recognized. Its rights were standardized and protected.

The justification for the law was in the thought of the authors that a strike in an essential industry, such as food, clothing, transportation, was a conspiracy against the general public, which had a right to protection against this attack upon its safety.

The law was exceedingly popular. Other states and nations studied it. In Kansas it wrote a new chapter in the possibilities of just adjudication of labor disputes. Mussolini fashioned his "Syndicalist Labor Act" after the argument of the Kansas Industrial Court. He took its provision against strikes in essential industries and its accepted arguments. In fact, he took the north half of the law, leaving out the court. He himself became the court, thus distorting it from a thing of impartial justice to an instrument of tyranny. Other dictators borrowed it from Mussolini.

Thus, the Kansas Court had gained wide recognition before the Supreme Court of the United States crippled the act by reversal on what appeared to be a minor point, but which in reality provided a major consideration.

The Kansas Industrial Court Act provided that during the consideration of a controversy over wages between workmen and employers, a minimum wage might be established by the Court which would prevail during the hearing. The Supreme Court of the United States held that the state should not have the power to establish a minimum wage under any circumstances, since such latitude would give the state power to interfere with contractual relations between labor and capital.

This position of the Supreme Court has since been deeply affected, if not indeed completely repealed, by subsequent opinions upon the same question, but at the moment it deprived the Kansas law of its balance of justice.

The Industrial Court had functioned for several years with satisfactory results. Its acts had received approval of the State Supreme Court. However, after the Supreme Court of the United States had limited the powers of the state body, it lost its usefulness, since, obviously, it would be unfair to forbid strikes without allowing labor, in a court of justice, the fullest latitude for protection and relief.

In writing its Industrial Court Act in 1927, England was conscious of what the Kansas Industrial Court was trying to do. In its forms the doctrines and philosophies of the Kansas Industrial Court Act are suggested.

The British Industrial Court system probably is the most effective effort mankind has seen to solve the labor problem. In 1938 President Roosevelt appointed a commission to visit England and give him a report upon the effectiveness of the English experience. The report reveals that an honest effort on the part of the government, the public, and labor leadership is producing a system which is solving the problems. There is no more racketeering by greedy and self-conscious leaders. The labor unions have become possessed of legal status and are responsible for their conduct. Strikes and lockouts had disappeared long before the present grip of war placed all capital and all labor under the grim control of an endangered government.

The first consideration, when contemplating America's labor problem, has to do with its emergent character. Defense orders have been given the right of way in the order of need. The term "bottleneck" has appeared with a new meaning—to describe the labor delinquency more frequently than in connection with any other blockade.

When the war is over, Americans will face the colossal task of reconstruction, which will test their resourcefulness no less than does national defense. It would be wise, of course, to prepare for the emergency of this kind which awaits the hour of peace, as well as for the emergency the nation now encounters.

Already states are stirred by industrial problems. A national organization is advising united action on the part of state legislatures to create industrial tribunals. It would seem to me that the simplest, most practical, and most enduring relief points to the remedy which Great Britain found in her Industrial Courts and the machinery established under the carefully thought-out statutory law. There is a clear pathway of accomplishments providing for America the definite wisdom of experience. The British Industrial Court Act, with its attendant legislation, has received the approval of the President's Commission on Industrial Relations in Great Britain. These enactments would give valuable machinery for immediate progress away from the present confusion and waste.

STRIKES IN A DEMOCRACY [3]

Strikes and lockouts in any industry which are causing widespread and serious hardship or suffering among the public might reasonably be subject to compulsory arbitration. It should be noted that this proposal is not designed to prevent the occurrence of disputes that are likely to result in hardship or suffering. It is not intended that there should be a "waiting period" before the strike begins or any cessation of hostilities while an investigation is being made. But when suffering actually becomes sufficiently acute to constitute a genuine emergency, then government should intervene. Some responsible government agency should be empowered to determine when a state of emergency exists. An investigation should therupon be undertaken, with a view to developing findings and recommendations that might serve as a basis for the settlement of the dispute. The recommendations should be those thought most likely to be acceptable to the disputants, and considerations of justice to any of the parties concerned, including the public, should be purely and distinctly incidental, if indeed they should be entertained at all. Findings and recommendations should be submitted to the disputants. Should the disputants fail to reach an agreement on the basis of the recommendations, they should then be given the option of establishing their own arbitral agency to settle the dispute or of submitting it to an agency established or designated by the government, preferably to one especially established for that particular dispute. Acceptance of the award for a reasonable length of time should be made compulsory. This procedure would constitute real interference with the right to struggle for status, but it is an interference that can be justified on the ground of public welfare, and if not too much abused will not seriously violate any tenet of democracy.

[3] From article by Domenico Gagliardo, University of Kansas. *American Economic Review.* 31:53-5. March 1941.

It would be within the bounds of democratic procedure to prescribe another restriction. Limited production of commodities and services might reasonably be required during strikes in some industries and occupations. . . .

Refusal by unions or employers to follow the procedures here suggested—compulsory adjudication of disputes involving rights arising out of law or custom or involving interpretation or application or collective agreements, the arbitration of all industrial disputes in public utilities, the arbitration of disputes resulting in genuine and serious public emergencies, and limited production in some instances—should be declared to constitute unfair labor practices, for both unions and employers. Approximate penalties for those guilty of such unfair labor practices should be provided, and suitable legal procedure for their trial developed. But in the final analysis this means that the orders of the state, whether involving the interpretation of a collective agreement or the arbitration of disputes over new terms, if not voluntarily obeyed would be put into effect by force. Only in the most extreme circumstances would it be necessary or desirable for the state to operate an industry, but that should be undertaken if necessary.

The suggested restrictions on the actions of organized labor and capital are not really severe, they would arise out of and be based upon the machinery and processes of widespread collective bargaining, most of which is voluntary, and they would be applicable for the most part only after organized workers and employers failed to agree upon settlement. Many disputes involving interpretations of agreements and some involving new terms are now voluntarily and successfully adjudicated and arbitrated. The suggested alternative of allowing the disputants to establish their own machinery will drastically limit the need for state action, and constitutes a satisfactory answer to the charge that arbitrators rarely have adequate knowledge of individual technique. It is at present not uncommon for unions to permit limited production of vitally essential commodities and services during strikes. And when the public is seriously threatened, all parties to the dispute expect the state to intervene, forcibly if necessary, and workers and employers are resigned to that intervention, although they are sometimes vociferous in their denunciations. Legal enactment would thus merely crystallize, institutionalize, and extend somewhat practices that are now already fairly widely accepted and followed, and by bringing into relief the elements of a beneficial policy would stimulate further refinements of that policy. The right of a group to struggle for status, which is quite properly considered fundamental in a democracy, would continue to exist largely unimpaired, but the struggle would be carried out on a higher plane, on a plane in which the public interest, which is also fundamental in a democracy, would receive due consideration.

A NATIONAL PUBLIC LABOR RELATIONS POLICY FOR TOMORROW [4]

We have as a people certain elementary conceptions of personal right and social relationship inherent in the nature of our institutions, the traditions and ideals of our people which are peculiarly pertinent to our topic. Let us note at the threshold of discussion, that, whether we be employers or employees, corporations or labor organizations, we cannot assert "rights" without recognizing that whether we speak of individual or collective action, we find corresponding "duties" whether we look into the field of morals or law. My right to life carries with it the duty to risk it if necessary in the defense of the nation. My right of liberty is limited by the duty to recognize the equal and reciprocal rights of others by which we preserve freedom for all. My right of property is accompanied by the duty not to use it to the injury of others. Finally all rights in society are necessarily limited by the superior, indeed paramount considerations of public interest. This does not lessen the value or minimize the importance of the individual person or his rights. For American restrictions and limitations are self-imposed. We live by liberty under law. We are not the less a free people because we live

[4] By James A. Emery, Lawyer, Washington, D.C. Address before the National Founders Association, New York, November 17, 1943. 13p. National Founders Association, Chicago.

under self-imposed restraint. Indeed, the difference between those who enjoy constitutional liberty and those who do not, is that the former place limitations upon their own conduct, while the latter live under restrictions imposed without their consent.

One of the great natural rights is that of association. Man is a gregarious animal. He seeks the company of others for protection, assistance and fraternity. He promotes and defends his own interests through the aid and cooperation of others. The result of this characteristic of man is the rights of organization and combination. When men subordinate themselves through association for the achievement of some common purpose by common methods, they become not a mere aggregate of individuals but a new moral personality, the power and influence of which will grow in accordance with its success in subordinating the will and judgment of each participant to the purpose and methods accepted.

Within our nation thousands of our people associate for worship, fraternity, the investment of their savings and the protection of their interests as farmers, workers or managers. Because of their numbers and their general objectives, we properly treat with special liberality the organization of the workers, to advance and protect their hours, wages and working conditions. On the other hand, the laws of the state and the nation represent multiplying controls and regulations to establish responsibility and liability, especially among business groups for every form of combination which they may assume.

The natural right of association is limited by corresponding duties, not only in the interest of their members but of all with whom they have relations. For as combination gives power it becomes obviously more necessary to recognize a paramount public interest in the methods by which that power is applied and made effective. For experience has taught us that all combinations of men have possibility for evil as well as good. Like individuals the morality or legality of combined effort is measured by its purpose and the means of accomplishment.

Thus in labor disputes of peace time the public comes to have a vital interest in the methods and objectives of the disputants quite different from that of the adversaries. This springs from the complex and interdependent nature of our industrial society. With the growth of populous cities, personal dependence on distant production, the extensive and inter-related system of distribution, transportation and communication, there rises a supreme social interest in a serious interruption of our economic process which may become as threatening to the maintenance of our individual and community life as attack or siege by a public enemy. We may endure a local strike or lockout causing inconvenience, indeed, hardship. We may accommodate ourselves to a temporary and partial interruption of communication or transportation, but we cannot endure for long on any great scale paralysis of the public services or grave interruption of the production and distribution of the necessities of life.

"There are some things," said President Wilson, commenting on a threatened railroad strike, "in which society is so profoundly interested that its interests take precedence of the interests of any group of men whatever."

Any combination to deprive the United States of fuel, transportation or communication, as a means of enforcing its demands, plainly ought to be unlawful in peace as well as war. Confronting just such an attempt twice during his administration, President Wilson stated the fundamental issue in unforgettable terms:

> The difficulty about all situations like that which we have passed through is this—that the main partner is left out of the reckoning. These men were dealing with one another as if the only thing to settle was between themselves, whereas, the real thing to settle was what rights had the 100 million people of the United States. The business of government is to see that no other organization is as strong as itself; to see that no body or group of men, no matter what their private interest is, may come into competition with the authority of society.

Until there arose a vested political interest in the non-enforcement of such principles, there was no doubt of their necessity or the public interest in their enforcement.

Let us recall that history. In 1896 Grover Cleveland was confronted with a breakdown of transportation by rail. Not because of any dispute between railroad managers and their men; but in a sympathetic endeavor of the American Railroad Union to compel the Pullman Company to accept demands made upon it. To accomplish this purpose the movement of even mail trains with pullman cars was to be stopped until demands were granted. The President undertook to remove the obstructing combination from the rails. He had the power to do it by force. He undertook to do it by reason. He offered the persuasive order of a court rather than the bayonet of a soldier. The Supreme Court held, in the proceeding that followed, that this Government, by the very terms of its being, with powers and duties to be discharged for the supreme welfare, had the right to apply to its own courts: "For any proper assistance in the exercise of the one and the discharge of the other."

Again, in 1916, the Railroad Brotherhoods sought an eight-hour day and the determination of a standard unit of train service without decrease in compensation. Presidential mediation failed, arbitration was refused, a strike vote was taken. In that crisis President Wilson recommended a legislative answer. Congress wrote a contract between the parties by the passage of the Adamson Act. Upon attack in the Supreme Court it was held, in a famous opinion (*Wilson* vs. *New,* 243 U. S.), that when a dispute of the character presented threatened a national catastrophe through the general interruption of railroad service, the Congress, as a regulation of commerce, could write a contract between the disputants which they were bound to observe in order to prevent a paralysis of transportation, and that contract was effective until the parties substituted for the compulsion of legislation, a voluntary agreement of their own.

Again, in October 1919 the United Mine Workers demanded a 30-hour week and a 50 per cent wage increase. There was in existence an agreement between the miners and the operators for "the duration of the war." While the Armistice had taken effect in November 1918, we had not yet concluded a treaty of peace and a million American soldiers were in service abroad. Fuel was essential to supplies and the moving of them. All our domestic utilities, production and the flow of all forms of traffic were dependent to a greater extent than now on coal. Conciliation and mediation failed. In the face of a Presidential appeal Mr. Lewis announced that he would call a general strike. In a public statement describing the situation confronting the country, the President declared: "A strike under these circumstances is not only unjustified, it is plainly illegal."

Congress by joint resolution supported the President. On November 8th the President instructed the Attorney General to enjoin the calling of the strike and it was done.

Three years later, confronted by a police strike, the then Governor of Massachusetts declared a principle never before questioned in private as well as public service: "There is no right to strike against the public safety by anybody, anywhere, any time."

In recent years public authority has forgotten those great principles. Special legislation and judicial interpretation have taken preventive remedies from private persons, and judicial construction has made it lawful and right for one group to do that which remains unlawful and wrong when done by others in like circumstances. Even in the midst of war the voice of Government addressed to the deliberate interruption of essential production has been that of persuasion, not command. Its remedy for the desertion of war production has been to punish the willing by seizing their property that the unwilling may return to service. As a remedy it is a distortion of law as appropriate as beating the wife of a deserter to punish his abandonment of the service he owes. As a policy it excites increasing demands for the seizure of plants on the slightest pretext.

The American public is plainly dissatisfied with the surrender of the Executive to threats at home while resisting coercion from abroad with national force. The effect of weakness, hesitation and favoritism in the assertion of public authority has deluded thousands of otherwise loyal citizens into believing they may desert war work and thus serve the public enemy without realizing the nature of their conduct.

Nothing I have said is to be construed as lessening the public obligation to fully recognize and protect the right of workers to freely choose their own form of organization and representation without coercion from any source, and to effectively assert and enforce legitimate demands by every legitimate means. It is the abuse, not the use of the power of organization by corporation or union to which this country objects.

The principles I have asserted in no way deny or restrict the appropriate place of the labor organization in our American life. The issue is not whether we shall have labor unions or corporations, but what kind of labor organizations and corporations we shall have. If that is a reactionary assertion let me recall a notable statement of Mr. Justice Holmes among his Harvard papers and which he regretted he did not publish:

I have no doubt that when the power of either capital or labor is asserted in such a way as to attack the life of the community, those who seek their private interest at such cost are public enemies and should be dealt with as such.

"Power," said Pericles, "measures the man." He might have added, responsibility sobers him.

I suggest from the facts submitted and the principles asserted, certain fundamental conclusions follow:

1. Power without corresponding responsibility is today a characteristic of the American labor combination. It is not in the interest of the American worker that such a condition should continue. It will inevitably lead to a reaction that will dangerously threaten the workers' legitimate rights of association. Surely upon reflection, the worker must give equal recognition to the principle which he properly insists must apply to every form of associated effort save his own: that there is no place in a complex, interdependent, industrial civilization for the development and use of organized power without corresponding responsibility for its use.

2. As a public necessity there should be clearly restored to the national government and exercised by it as occasion arises, the authority to enter its own courts on any appropriate occasion for the control or dissolution of any, not merely some combinations which may threaten the public order, the public safety or the public supply of the necessities of life as a means of enforcing its demands.

In the field of medicine, engineering, sanitation, preventive remedies represent the advance of civilization. Why should they not be restored in the field of law for the use of government, representing the social self-defense of the people?

3. Our political and economic structure rest upon the rights of the individual separated from the mass. Morally it recognizes the nobility, dignity and worth of the human individual as the handiwork of God; economically it preserves his opportunity and security in the fruit of his effort, because he is the dynamo of social progress. The individual has no greater right than that of selecting and pursuing any lawful calling without interference or coercion from any source. Every voluntary organization may invite whom it pleases into its ranks, but it may not undertake to control and prevent those who do not join its ranks from enjoying the personal liberty which is their right. For that principle our soldiers die on alien soil.

"No man," said Lincoln, "is good enough to govern another man without that other's consent."

4. An elementary part of the voluntary right of association is the right not to associate. We exercise the right by negative not less than affirmative action. In business or social intercourse, in worship or fraternity, we not only join others, we refrain from doing so. We extend credit or refuse it. We worship with some, not with others. In marriage there is rejection as well as acceptance. Compulsion is not the basis of association.

5. If there are to be statutory tribunals to offer mediation, conciliation and arbitration in order to anticipate the threat that private labor disputes may become public dangers, let their terms apply equally to the parties involved. Let any privileges they confer depend for their continued enjoyment upon good conduct. But finally, let them operate with equality or they will not be practically effective, for no public remedy will work well which operates in an atmosphere of continuing injustice.

If these seem hard principles, I suggest the test is whether or not they be true principles. In that connection let us recall that in the hour when the fate of the Constitution hung in the balance, when compromises which threatened the very foundation of the undertaking was pressed upon the Constitutional Convention, Washington spoke for the first and last time.

It is true probably, [he said] that no plan we propose will be adopted. Perhaps another dreadful conflict is to be sustained. If to please the people we offer what we ourselves disprove, how can we afterwards defend our work? Let us raise a standard to which the wise and the just may repair. The event is in the hands of God.

The assertion of the supremacy of government over all private forms of association, great or small, corporations or labor unions, is vital to the integrity of our political system. Experience demonstrates that under popular institutions elections may become auctions if privilege can be purchased by political contributions. Moreover, if any private group, whether in the field of business or of labor, becomes so powerful as to successfully challenge government itself, the people no longer rule. They do not govern, they are governed by that which dominates their life.

I am sure the more we reflect upon these principles the more we must perceive that they are indispensable to the restoration of the authority of government, the preservation of order, and the restoration of equality among our citizens. They rest upon the due recognition of all the great rights of association, of freedom to organize and to promote individual and collective interests for every legitimate purpose. But they check combination at the deadline of public interest. Beyond that it has no claim to proceed. Nor can any group make secure their own rights unless they accept the responsibility that goes with growing power, for they themselves may otherwise become the victims of the precedent they create.

THE ADJUSTMENT OF LABOR DISPUTES IN WARTIME [5]

The existence of war or other great national emergency alters the setting within which the adjustment of labor disputes is attempted. Strikes may normally be expected to decrease in these circumstances, since there is apt to be and is now, a wave of public indignation over those strikes which do occur. In this war, the major unions have given no-strike pledges, and . . . these pledges have been observed fairly well. The labor, employer, and public members of the National War Labor Board have unanimously resolved that "no grievance, however great, justifies an interruption of war production. Under these circumstances, a decrease in the number of strikes is the natural thing.

[5] Howard S. Kaltenborn, University of Nebraska; Chief Wage Analyst, Regional War Labor Board, Detroit, Michigan. In his *Governmental Adjustment of Labor Disputes.* p. 221-4. Foundation Press, Inc. Chicago. 1943.

Although strikes decrease, there is no reason to assume that labor disputes will normally diminish. There is nothing inherent in a state of war to reduce employee grievances, and in fact war may carry with it forces operating to increase employee grievances. In the present war, the number of strikes has decreased materially, but the number of labor disputes of the non-strike variety has certainly not diminished and appears to have substantially increased. The number of cases coming before the United States Conciliation Service has materially increased since the declaration of war, and there has been a very definite upsurge in recent months in the number of dispute cases coming before the War Labor Board.

Labor relations students generally agree that it is easier to adjust a labor dispute before a strike has occurred rather than afterward. Thus, the coming of war tends in this one respect to increase the effectiveness of governmental agencies in adjusting labor disputes, since the great bulk of the cases will be non-strike cases.

In wartime, as well as in time of peace, mediation should remain the basic governmental method of intervention. To provide otherwise would mean refusal to use the most effective single adjustment process available. However, it is very important to realize that mediation is not of itself sufficient during time of war. There are always sure to be labor disputes which defy successful mediation. In time of peace, such disputes are apt to eventuate into strikes and this may be tolerated since the public interest is less evident than during time of war. It is, however, necessary in a period of war to supplement mediation by other adjustment processes so as to minimize the possibility of strikes.

Under normal conditions, the governmental adjustment process usually ceases if mediation fails and arbitration is refused. In a subsequent portion of this manuscript, it is recommended that ad hoc emergency boards be appointed to make a public report on such disputes where the public interest may be affected substantially and adversely. Of course, the scope of the public interest is broadened tremendously by the existence of a great national emergency. Disputes which normally would have little importance become fraught with great public significance in the emergency period. The former National Defense Mediation

Board was in effect a mediation board and a standing emergency board combined. Where its mediation efforts were unsuccessful, it issued public recommendations which were not legally binding on the parties. The National Defense Mediation Board was replaced in January 1942 by the National War Labor Board. Until January 1943, the latter board was in effect a mediation agency and a compulsory arbitration board combined. At that time the Board . . . announced its abandonment of mediation, but the Board still has the authority to "finally determine" disputes.

The past experiences with compulsory arbitration, and even with the somewhat milder compulsory investigation, have not been too favorable. The use of compulsory arbitration at the present time is, however, justified for several reasons. First, mediation is retained as the basic process, and this is supplemented by voluntary arbitration. The Conciliation Service attempts mediation and, where mediation fails, urges arbitration. Thus, the voluntary adjustment processes are used first, and only where these do not suffice to settle the dispute is there resort to more coercive measures. Second, if all strikes are to be prevented during wartime, some arrangement must be made to insure final settlement of labor disputes by means other than stoppages of work. Public recommendations by either standing or ad hoc emergency boards will operate in time of war to prevent strikes in most cases where mediation has failed and arbitration has been refused, but strikes will still occur in some instances. Several examples of this in the present war have been cited in previous chapters, the leading illustration being the Captive Coal Mines strikes. If all strikes are to be prevented, arrangements must be made for final decisions in cases defying mediation and voluntary arbitration, and these final decisions must be enforced by the government. This is compulsory arbitration. At the present time, the War Labor Board is given authority to "finally determine" issues coming before it, and the President has always been willing to enforce the Board's awards by commandeering company plants if necessary. It appears probable that such an arrangement would not work at all successfully in this country in time of peace, but it is working successfully now and public opinion supports the arrangement. Third, the War Labor Board has tripartite representation, and consequently both employers and labor have a part in any decisions that are made by the Board. Compulsory arbitration in this country is generally detested by both employers and unions, but where it seems necessary they will accept it more readily if they have a share in the administration of the plan.

The present arrangements for adjusting labor disputes are by no means perfect, though the general outlines are sound. Thus, although mediation is retained as the basic process, the Federal Government's mediation activities could be considerably strengthened. . . .

The present arrangements include mediation, voluntary arbitration, and compulsory arbitration. With the coming of peace, compulsory arbitration should be abandoned. Until that time, however, compulsory arbitration will probably continue to perform a necessary role.

MICHIGAN MEDIATION [6]

When in Michigan the legislature enacted a law which became effective on the 1st of July, 1939, called the Labor Mediation Act, the Governor asked me to organize that work and become a member of the Michigan Labor Mediation Board.

We had very little precedent—in fact, practically none—in Michigan. There are very few states in the Union that had had any experience with such a law. We found, though, that the experience in mediation and arbitration work generally could be applied to this work of this board, and I was glad to be of assistance.

We then proceeded and organized the board and its work, adopted rules as found necessary, and went to work.

[6] By A. C. Lappin, former member, Michigan Mediation Committee. Statement before House Committee on the Judiciary, February 18, 1941. United States. House of Representatives. Committee on the Judiciary. Delays in National Defense Preparations; Hearings, February 17-March 24, 1941. p. 29-36. 77th Congress, 1st session. 1941.

In the first year of our experience we were served with 666 notices of impending strikes. The law provides there a so-called cool-off period of five days in ordinary cases, or thirty days where a public utility or a hospital is involved, or, in the language of the act, any other industry which is affected with a public interest.

I happened to be the only attorney on that board, and the informal opinions or interpretations were first expressed by me. We had no guide, no precedent, no Supreme Court decisions of the state.

Quite recently, in order to be of greater service in connection with the defense program, in which Michigan is playing a very important part, especially Detroit, I expressed the opinion that any industry wholly or largely engaged in connection with the defense program is an industry affected with a public interest. The Attorney General, at the request of our board, officially confirmed that informal opinion. The result has been that during the last sixty days or thereabouts the board has ruled that such an industry, being affected with a public interest, and involved in connection with an impending strike, must have thirty days' notice served instead of five days' notice before a strike actually takes place.

There was considerable objection on the part of two or three of the unions, who felt that the board was writing something into the act. Personally we did not think—I am sure I am quoting the other members of the board accurately—that we were changing the law in any particular. We were simply exercising our best judgment in the interpretation of the law.

On the whole the unions have cooperated almost 100 per cent. There has been an exception here and there.

In the very beginning, in the very inception of the law, you might say, I am sorry to say that one of the principal labor leaders in Michigan made a public statement condemning the law, condemning the board, and advising union presidents and business agents and representatives of one kind or another to ignore the law. Strikes were issued. He was so emphatic in his statement, and I believe that I am quoting him correctly when I say that he said, "There are not enough jails in Michigan to hold all the violators of the law." I am happy to say, however, in that connection that the unions did not heed the statement of this leader.

After two or three months had elapsed, we gained the confidence of practically all the union leaders, all the representatives and spokesmen and attorneys for industry; so much so that on numerous occasions they confided in us privately, told us what they would be willing to do, what would be their minimums and maximums, what compromises they would make, so that we would to that extent be assisted in our negotiations.

I said . . . that we had 666 notices during the first twelve months of the existence of that board. Less than 10 per cent of them resulted in strikes, and, as nearly as I can remember, less than a dozen involved any substantial number of employees.

The record for the first six months of the year 1940-41, which would be from the 1st of July, 1940, to the end of December, corresponds with the first year so far as numbers are concerned. That is, we received about two and a half to three notices per day. But the number of strikes has been materially reduced. In charge of the Detroit office I had about 300 notices during those three months. Less than a dozen resulted in strikes.

You will probably be interested in knowing that the board as a whole and I personally give the unions and the employers and their representatives and attorneys credit for this commendable situation. . . .

Some of the unions have complained about the cool-off period. The objection has been technical and otherwise.

I honestly do not think that there is any justification on the part of any intelligent, honest man objecting to that so-called cool-off period. The fact of the matter is that the unions generally have anticipated this cool-off period, and very frequently forwarded these notices to the board so that the time would begin to run while negotiations were still pending.

So that I doubt if there is one case in a dozen, or one case in a great many more, at which notice was served, where the union could be guilty of honestly complaining about the effect of the so-called cool-off period.

Of course, the objection is that it prevents them from striking; that this is a free country, and so forth. But it does not do anything of the sort. They still have their right to strike after the cool-off period has elapsed, and they sometimes do strike after that period has passed.

We encounter quite a number of difficulties, of course. I think the principal difficulty that we now have to contend with in Michigan is the question of jurisdiction.

Until three or four months ago this involved only the question of determining between the C.I.O. and A.F. of L. Now, during recent months we have run into this anomalous situation: Within the A.F. of L. ranks—I don't believe that we have had a single case of it in the C.I.O. ranks—but in the A.F. of L. ranks we have had questions of jurisdiction. A.F. of L. unions have for the first time, at least for the first time in my knowledge, been willing to walk through A.F. of L. picket lines.

A notable instance is one in which we recently were obliged to call upon William Green and ask that some committee or some individual be assigned to handle this question of jurisdiction; and he denied any authority. We called upon the international president of the two unions, and he denied authority. The unions appealed to the mayor and the Governor, but in vain.

There was a question of jurisdiction between, to use an example, the Teamsters and Drivers' Union and the Brewery Workers' Union, which still remains unsettled. This question of jurisdiction does give us, and perhaps gives other communities, plenty of headaches.

Recently we have run into this situation on several occasions: A contract was signed with one union, and then the other union claims a majority and threatens a strike. Our hands are tied. We are absolutely helpless. There is nothing that we can do.

Both the Supreme Court and the National Labor Relations Board ruled recently that they will not go behind a contract, that they will assume that the existing contract is valid, and will not aid the other union in attempting to force a second contract.

We have recently had tied up in Detroit an industry of considerable magnitude, not involving the defense program, but nevertheless employing several hundred people, in which one union had claimed a majority of nearly 90 per cent and the other union likewise claimed a majority; and picket lines followed despite the existence of a valid contract with the first union.

There has been quite a stream of transients flowing into Detroit during the last few months. One of the newspapers estimated them at 100,000.

We are receiving a lot of inquiries and complaints at the offices about racketeering in one form or another. That reached the stage at one time where we privately consulted the F.B.I. man in Detroit. There were complaints about fees being charged by unions. There were complaints about percentages of salaries that must be deducted in order to be permitted to work. One man told me within the last four days that he was obliged to pay $2 per day in order to pursue his trade as a roofer.

I think, from the experience that we have had there, we must adopt nationally, at least during this period of the defense program, some plan that corresponds with the Railroad Mediation Act, and possibly goes a step further. I think in this period that that is absolutely essential.

That should be followed by the second step, namely, mediation; and that, if necessary, at least in connection with the defense program, should be followed by compulsory arbitration as a last step.

Unions have as a whole objected to compulsory arbitration. We thought that industry did too. But within recent weeks I had occasion to discuss that with the attorney for the Manufacturing Association in Michigan, and he agreed with me that under existing conditions compulsory arbitration may be desirable in certain instances. . . .

Now, I think I understand the unions' chief objection to any kind of arbitration. And, mind you, they asked for arbitration in numerous instances in these lesser cases. In fact, during the last six months it was my privilege to sit as arbitrator at least two dozen times where the question that delayed the settlement was whether one or more men were discharged for cause or discharged for union activity.

I don't believe that that justifies the continuance of a strike. I think the objection on the part of the unions—and I am a so-called union man and claim to be friendly to the unions—is that they feel that the type of man appointed as arbitrator may be unfriendly to labor, may not be liberally minded.

I think that that objection may be easily overcome by not resorting to that method of permitting each side to appoint an arbitrator, who naturally becomes a pleader for his respective appointer, the one to whom he is responsible for his appointment. . . .

I think [compulsory arbitration would bring about a complete understanding or composition of the differences between the two sides] if the arbitrators are agreed upon by both sides, not each appoint an equal number and that equal number appoint a so-called umpire. . . .

It is well to remember that the Conciliation Service of the Labor Department [sends] arbitrators around the country who do nothing but arbitrate. They are designated as arbitrators. They are immediately acceptable to both sides. In fact, they ask for such an arbitrator in advance if they know of the existence of that service. . . .

I want to make this perfectly clear: I am advocating compulsory arbitration only as a last resort, because, if it is properly applied, it really is not compulsory as long as they have confidence in the system. . . .

Having a very weak law, we have read into the law certain implied powers, for instance, the power to arbitrate as a last resort, or the power to appoint an independent auditor to check the company's records, or the power to continue our supervision over the election. Those three implied powers have been of very great assistance in avoiding or settling a goodly number of strikes. . . .

[The workers generally would rather arbitrate their differences than strike.] I don't think there is any question about that. They would rather arbitrate or mediate or negotiate.

Very often, when we sit around the table, the issues will seem to be very important, and they make mountains out of them. Then, after they empty their chests, so to speak, and we let them do so for half an hour, they reduce themselves to their lowest common denominator; and before we know it we are making headway.

As a rule, you will find that there is one primary issue involved. They may raise half a dozen questions; but when that primary issue is settled in some fashion, the rest of the issues almost fell in line of themselves."

EXCERPTS

On the question of compulsory arbitration, I should say that it would have to be hedged about with considerable safeguards. Under the present situation, where labor has great political power, the machinery of arbitration could be stacked in its favor. You would then have not compulsory arbitration but predetermined decisions granting labor whatever it decided it could take without arousing too great opposition in the rest of the community. I am in favor of compulsory arbitration, but the technical administrative safeguards would mean the difference between success and failure.—*Elisha M. Friedman, Consulting Economist, New York. Quoted from a letter of December* 20, 1944.

The remarkable feature of the whole [industrial arbitration and conciliation] system [in Massachusetts] is that it really is compulsory, yet always self-imposed. Efforts at conciliation are mandatory, so it is compulsory at least to try to agree. In the next place, many employers and employees have made standing agreements to submit disputes to arbitration. In increasing numbers those agreements contain a provision that *all* questions which may arise in the future be submitted to the board for final adjustment. There, certainly, the arbitration is compulsory. But the parties themselves have made it so. Finally, it is compulsory for the board to investigate and report blame when all else fails, yet the report has no legal effect. Then comes the compulsion of public opinion, which is probably the strongest compulsion of all.

In these days we need a strong, united nation. In this country, at least, the way to achieve unity is not through the relationship of mastery and submission. It is by the art of getting along well together. That is what Massachusetts is trying to accomplish through conciliation and arbitration in its labor relations—*Leverett Saltonstall, Governor, Commonwealth of Massachusetts. State Government. S. '40. p. 168.*

Supporters of state intervention in the regulation of labor conditions reply that state conciliation and arbitration is, on the whole, to be regarded and organized, not as a judicial but, from the nature of the subject, as an administrative function, which cannot be performed without exposure to political influence; that the state naturally acts on political grounds in other spheres of administration—industry, tariffs, public services (railways, gas, water, electricity), taxation and, in particular, social policy; and that to have a wages policy is therefore at least not illogical. The supporters of compulsion may deprecate abuses in "political wage-fixing," but hold the view that to distinguish between admissible and inadmissible influence in individual cases is very difficult, and that "hard cases make bad law." In their opinion really important labor disputes in the modern state have become political matters and can be decided only in accordance with the general policy of the government, which must be consistent if it is to be successful; and they will perhaps finally declare that in countries whose conciliation legislation does not recognize authoritative intervention by the state, the pressure of public opinion—educated politically far more than economically—is quite or nearly equivalent to compulsion by the state.—*International Labour Office. Geneva. Studies and Reports. Series A, no. 34. '33 p. 133-4.*

There have been significant changes over the last eight years in the attitudes of sections of the Australian community toward the arbitration system. Before the depression, employers, and the well-to-do classes generally, regarded it with hostility. It unwarrantably interferred with a man's right to run his business as he liked. By bringing employers and employed into the realm of litigation it prevented cooperation, and created or intensified bitterness between them. It forced up wages unnaturally, and caused a vicious spiral of rising costs and rising prices. It introduced red-tape and a mass of harassing restrictions into the conduct of industry, making economy and efficiency impossible. It did not promote industrial peace, for everyone knew that Australia was the most strike-ridden country in the world. And when the depression came, "the slump psychology that in all countries sought a scapegoat," in Australia as in New Zealand, "found one in the arbitration court."

Since 1931, these views have been profoundly modified. It is now fairly generally accepted that the days when a man could run his business as he liked have gone, and that the abolition of the arbitration system cannot bring them back. In every civilized country where the economy is an individualist and capitalist one, an increasing consciousness amongst the workers of their rights and their power when organized has made it inevitable that their voice should be heard in determining the conditions of labor, and that "union rules" should have to be taken into account to a growing extent in the management of industry. It is dimly realized that "the abuses of inelasticity, departmentalism, detailed regulations and restrictions, are the result of any attempt in the modern industrial system to place industrial relations on an organized basis; and that the legalism and technicalities of compulsory arbitration have merely intensified conditions which would exist without it. It is also coming to be understood that much of the former opposition to the arbitration court was really opposition to collective bargaining; that with labor conscious and organized collective bargaining cannot be avoided; and that collective bargaining can be carried on with less strife and loss through the machinery of the court.—*Norman Cowper, Sydney, Australia. Economic Record (Melbourne). Je. '38. p. 16-17.*

In spite of the fact that it has never for a moment hesitated to use coercion against employers, when it thought them even partly responsible for holding up war production, the administration has argued that to use coercion against workers to prevent strikes is "an infringement on liberty." Yet even this one-sided excuse is lacking at Akron. We read of pickets forming a shoulder-to-shoulder barricade at the gates of the rubber plants and turning back men who came to work. This means that even in wartime, while the right to strike is protected, though it plays directly into the enemy's hands, the right to work, the right to supply our fighting men with the tools they must have, is not being protected.

So far from taking any extra steps in wartime to prevent strikes, the supposed law-enforcement authorities of the country are not even taking the most elementary steps that ought to be taken in peacetime. The administration has step-by-step been wiping out even the natural penalties against striking. Under the Wagner Act of 1935, for example, it has deprived the employer of his former right to discharge a striker and permanently hire some one to take his place. Now, in the most costly and momentous war in history, our government authorities timidly tolerate violence and coercion on the part of strikers. The Federal Government will no doubt blame this on local authorities, though it is clearly one-sided Federal intervention that has brought about so many of the situations with which the local authorities are asked to deal. Yet however Federal and local officials may seek to shift the blame to each other, the picket lines at Akron are a humiliating confession of governmental weakness. They mean a breakdown in governmental authority.— Editorial. *New York Times.* My. 26, '43. *p.* 22.

It is a waste of time to talk about whether or not the employer may be to blame. The employers of America are crushed. However blind, or stupid, or greedy they may have been, or whatever small percentage of them may have been blind, stupid, or greedy, they have paid and paid dearly for it. Labor is having its own way with industry and business and government. Investors practically no longer have any certain assured rights. They do not have the right of free speech. They cannot even threaten to shut down their business, not even though continued operation means bankruptcy.

The contention of labor leaders that they are striving to better the condition of the worker is true only in part. Their main purpose is to gain for themselves more and more economic and political power. The politician quails before them and does their bidding. The officeholder becomes their pliant tool and conspires to turn the government over to them.

Labor insists that compulsory arbitration involves the application of governmental coercion and force. How empty this contention becomes when we remember that coercion and force runs through all labor laws and was put there because of the insistence of labor leaders. How hollow it appears in the light of the fact that it is coercion and force that constitute the principal weapons used by labor.

It is un-American and dangerous to our liberties for labor to refuse to mediate or arbitrate its disputes and to continue to insist on stopping work on defense projects. It is just as reasonable to assume that because an army does not like the way some of its officers act, or the rules laid down for its government, that it would refuse to go out and meet the enemy.—*E. E. Cox, United States Representative from Georgia. Congressional Record. F. 17, '41. (current) p. A738.*

The nation today awaits with feverish anxiety the outcome of a strike of a half million men which may determine the destiny of millions of men under arms. In advocating the passage of the bill under consideration, we cast no reflections on honest labor or the rights of men to organize in their trades or vocations, but we do insist that the power which one individual is exerting at this time is more power than a good man would want and a lot more power than a bad man should be privileged to exercise. Under the leadership of one . . . [who has a] selfish desire for power and wanton lack of consideration for the success of our arms, the war effort is being retarded.

We, as a nation, are demanding of the Axis powers an unconditional surrender. Are we, then, to cringe on our knees in cowardly fashion before an unscrupulous dictator in this country and beg for a negotiated peace? Every day, every hour these mines remain closed means the lack of support those men on the battle fronts have a right to expect from us. Are we to permit the souls of those men in the uniform of the American soldier to be bartered for the selfish advancement of an unscrupulous, selfish leadership in our own country? Let us rededicate ourselves to a program of conduct under a government by law. Let us assert in our own country the ideals we are fighting for in other continents.

There is but one answer to the question that is in the minds of many people today as to whether or not any individual is bigger than the United States—that question must not go unanswered—and the answer to that question is to be made by the Seventy-eighth Congress. Let us measure up to the standards of patriotic Representatives of a people who look to us for an order of leadership that will bring a peace in all disturbed relations of the world.—*Jim McCord, United States Representative from Tennessee. Congressional Record. Je. 3, '43. (current) p. 5418.*

When labor squabbling becomes unbearable to the public, the traditional remedy in a democracy is legislation imposing some form of compulsory arbitration, under which a disinterested agency is empowered to dictate a settlement to the disputants. This form of governmental control over employer-employee relations is exercised widely in Australia and New Zealand, though it has made slight headway in Britain and America.

A decade of strikes, sit-downs, and lockouts, however, may have changed America's reluctance to adopt compulsion in such matters, officials of Labor Peace for California, Inc., believe. For that reason, the organization—backed by professional and small-business interests—last week prepared to submit to the voters as a state constitutional amendment the first measure of its type to reach the promotional stage in recent years.

The California proposal would create a state mediation board of five members to be appointed by the A.F.L., the C.I.O., the California Chamber of Commerce, the California Farm Bureau Federation, and the Governnor respectively. This board would seek to mediate all labor disputes and, where such efforts failed, would have the power to prescribe settlements. Its orders would be enforced by the courts.

In addition to creation of the board, which would function only in labor disputes, the California group seeks to tighten the state's labor law by providing a list of unfair labor practices, such as discrimination against union men, engaging in sit-downs, and illegal picketing, which, unlike the curbs applied by the Wagner Act, would bear as heavily upon unions as upon employers.

The compulsory-arbitration movement in California is indicative of the bitterness of some sections of the public—notably professional men, small businessmen, and small farmers—who have been constantly pushed around by strikes on the water front, the farms, and on the roads. By going directly to the public, backers of the movement will sound out current sentiment on this type of arbitration which has been dormant in America since the Supreme Court of the United States knocked out the Kansas industrial court law in 1923—to the rejoicing of the public as well as labor and employers.—*Newsweek, F. 19, '40. p.50, 53.*

Political compulsion in labor disputes is usually adopted either because of a rapid multiplication of the number and severity of strikes or because of the existence of a particular extreme emergency. The latter cause is important in perhaps nine out of ten instances.

The moving force behind the adoption of this compulsion is sometimes the general public inconvenience resulting from industrial disputes and sometimes the political pressure of the group (always economically the weaker) that expects to gain most by submission to neutral authority. An example of the latter is the support of compulsory arbitration by the weaker unions of New Zealand in 1892-1894, while the stronger unions opposed it. As all the unions there became stronger they favored the use of conciliation procedures but, when they were weakened again by the depression of the 1930's they again supported compulsion and caused its readoption in 1936.

Compulsory conciliation and/or arbitration have been adopted in modern times by the following states and countries (excepting emergency war decrees during the Great War): New Zealand,

1894 and 1936; New South Wales and West Australia, 1902; Australian Commonwealth, 1904; South Australia and Queensland, 1912; Norway, 1916; Kansas, 1920; Mexico, 1925; Italy, 1926; Germany, 1934 (quasi-compulsory arbitration had been in effect since 1923); United States of America, 1935 (compulsory conciliation only); France and Denmark, 1936.

In some countries such as Australia, most or all industries are affected by compulsion. In others, only public utilities (variously defined) are so affected. Similarly, the degree of compulsion varies from an absolute ban on all strikes and associated activities, as in Germany, to the provision that if one side carries the dispute to court, the other must cease belligerent activities and come into court likewise, as in Norway and New Zealand. Ordinarily, there is provision for conciliation and mediation as preliminary steps, but occasional disputes may go direct to arbitration, as in New Zealand between 1901 and 1908.

In general, the trend has been away from compulsory measures to voluntary and predominantly conciliatory techniques, for very rarely have compulsory measures given continually satisfactory results. All types of compulsory machinery have had their greatest periods of success at the beginning, usually under extremely able administration and before opposition has had a chance to crystallize around the fundamental defects of such systems.—*Samuel P. Hayes Jr. "Psychology of Conciliation and Arbitration Procedures." In "Industrial Conflict; a Psychological Interpretation." p.399-400. Cordon Co. Pubs. New York. 1939.*

The National War Labor Board has informed me that on February 27 the National War Labor Board notified you of its decision that you should arbitrate under the auspices of the National Mediation Board the pending dispute on the Toledo, Peoria & Western Railroad, of which railroad you are president.

The history and significance of this case is recited in the final appeal of the National War Labor Board sent you on March 13, 1942, as follows:

The defiance of the Government of the United States by the Toledo, Peoria & Western Railroad Company has raised issues far beyond the dispute between the company and the railroad brotherhoods. This government of the people in time of war cannot afford to permit the special or private interest of any labor union or corporation to break down the national agreement between management and labor, that labor disputes shall be settled for the duration of the war by peaceful means.

A private quarrel between a company and a union cannot be allowed to continue in the midst of a total war.

The Government of the United States, which through four successive public agencies, proposed patiently but unsuccessfully a peaceful settlement of this dispute, cannot be flouted by private interests.

Before Pearl Harbor, both sides refused arbitration proposed by the National Railway Mediation Board. Since Pearl Harbor, a number of Federal agencies have attempted to settle this dispute by peaceful means.

First, the National Railway Mediation Board proposed arbitration. The unions accepted but the company rejected.

Second, the director of the Office of Defense Transportation proposed arbitration. The unions accepted but the company rejected.

Third, a three-member panel of the United States Conciliation Service proposed arbitration. The unions accepted but the company rejected.

Fourth, the National War Labor Board unanimously directed arbitration under Section 8 of the Railway Labor Act and under the auspices of the National Railway Mediation Board, set up by Congress for that purpose. The unions accepted but the company rejected.

Fifth, the National Railway Mediation Board sent its mediator to Peoria to carry out the directive order of the War Labor Board for arbitration. The unions again agreed to cooperate and the company refused.

This rejection of established peaceful and lawful procedures for settlement of this labor dispute tends to breed violence and a disrespect of lawful processes.

We denounce any violence, any disregard of law and any defiance of peaceful procedures. The national crisis demands the use of the peaceful means of settlement established by the government.

The government has been patient, but there is a point beyond which patience becomes an act of disloyalty to a people who have seen stronghold after stronghold of freedom go down because men and materials to save them arrived too late. The people of the United States have a right to demand that their government prevent a private quarrel from checking the national will.

In this time of dire necessity for the quick maximum transportation of all materials as part of total war, any refusal to settle a railroad labor dispute involving a small but vital link in overland transportation between the oceans is intolerable to the American people in their struggle to remain free.

The National War Labor Board, in the name of the Government of the United States, again unanimously, and for the last time, calls upon the management of the Toledo, Peoria & Western Railroad Company to accept arbitration of this dispute in accordance with the decision of the board.

In these times of war, I must insist that the national agreement that there shall be no strikes or lockouts for the duration of the war and that the procedures for the peaceful settlement of labor disputes as set forth in the Executive Order creating the National War Labor Board must be complied with by all American employers and labor groups.

As President of the United States and Commander in Chief of the armed forces, I hereby request you to comply with the order of the National War Labor Board immediately.—*Letter by President Franklin D. Roosevelt to George P. McNear, Jr., President of the Toledo, Peoria & Western Railroad Company, March 14, 1942. New York Times. p. 16. March 17, 1942.*

This administration, that labor is daring and defying at every opportunity, passed the National Labor Relations Act and the Fair Labor Standards Act, in which every privilege and right was bestowed upon labor and protected. Frankly, it is my opinion that is was never intended that man, individually or collectively, should enjoy a privilege without discharging a corresponding duty. However, these acts confer every privilege on labor without imposing the first duty. Further, for the protection of labor, the War Labor Board has been set up, to which, under the law, it is provided that any grievance should be referred for adjudication and adjustment. No fair-minded person can ever contend that this Board has not gone out of its way to lean in favor of the requests of labor. In fact, it has very nearly surrendered to labor and made itself subordinate to its dictates.

Let us see where the rights of the taxpayer come in on this question. I have made an investigation and have learned that the pay roll of the National Labor Relations Board for the month of April 1943 was $227,380; that the pay roll of the Wage and Hour Division of the Department of Labor was $753,-563.72; and the War Labor Board estimated as an approximately

correct figure its pay roll for the month of April 1943 as $350,-
000; all of which aggregate $1,330,943.72 the taxpayers of the
United States of America expended in the single month of
April 1943 to provide a legal means by which any grievance,
either real or imaginary, that labor may have could be adjusted.
Yet in the face of this, these gangsters rise up as monsters and
defy the very law that the sons of the taxpayers of this nation
are fighting to defend. April was not a month of exception
by any degree, and by the application of a little mathematics, it
can be seen that the taxpayers of America spend in these three
divisions in one year $15,971,324.64 that there may be no neces-
sity for strikes in America, this huge sum in the face of millions
spent to operate the Labor Department.

When you taxpayers of this nation go to pay your taxes I
want you to bear these figures in mind and further remember
that these same enemies of democracy following defense industries like vultures, assessed the American workman from $50
to $250 each for the right to make weapons for your boys to
defend the shores of this nation; these sums being collected by
the agents of this invisible empire who account to no one. It
is impossible to estimate the aggregate so collected, but I say to
you that it has run into the billions of dollars, which sums come
again directly from the pockets of the taxpayers of this nation.
Yet, in the face of these outrages practiced upon the people,
they have the audacity to tell you and me they will defeat us if
we do not yield to their demands. Before I would sell my
people short and be a traitor to the causes of American liberty,
I would gladly surrender my right to ever hold another public
office.—*John S. Gibson, United States Representative from
Georgia. Congressional Record. Je. 2, '43. (current) p. 5395-6.*

So far as the voluntary idea is concerned, so long as all of
the workers of the United States voluntarily submitted perhaps
that was enough. But we now have a case of the representatives
of labor in one of the largest industries, who have said that they
are no longer bound to submit, that conditions have changed
since the agreement was made, that it no longer binds them, and
they refuse to submit to it. That is the issue today. On Sunday

night last, the President of the United States made an appeal to the miners to submit their case to the National War Labor Board. They had refused to do so. That is the issue today before the United States. It seems to me that on that issue the Senate should say that if they are not voluntarily willing to submit their case to the National War Labor Board they should be compelled to do so. . . .

I have not provided a criminal penalty for not finally complying with the order of the War Labor Board because it seems to me that it is doubtful whether we ought to go that far and because it is doubtful how effective it would be. Instead I have provided an injunction, that is, a formal hearing before the Circuit Court of Appeals, before three judges of outstanding character, in every circuit, who shall determine whether the hearing was fair and properly conducted and whether the government—not an individual, but whether the government—is entitled to have the order enforced by injunction. Once the order is issued, the President can take steps to carry it out through the court and the steps are clearly defined with the general agreement on the part of everyone and knowledge that the case has been thoroughly tried and everyone has been heard and the court has in definite terms said what should be done and what should not be done. . . .

MR. TYDINGS. As I understand the Senator's proposal, the net effect of it in disputes similar to the mine dispute would be to make arbitration compulsory?

MR. TAFT. That is correct.

MR. TYDINGS. As I understand, even though, after all the hearings, a final decision was handed down, it would not bind anybody to accept it, and a man could refuse to work.

MR. TAFT. It is declared to be binding but the only penalty provided is that the government may go into the circuit court of appeals to enforce the order by injunction.

MR. TYDINGS. I do not think I made myself clear. There is nothing in the bill that would compel a man to work.

MR TAFT. No; but, when it comes to the injunction, and I have read that provision several times—it is only against the leaders, only against instigation to strike, only against using union funds to support a strike and such other action to promote or further a strike as may be taken.

MR. TYDINGS. So, the net effect is that, instead of having a matter undecided, the Senator's proposal is to have compulsory arbitration, and, once the arbitration is had, if the individual does not commit any overt act against the government, he does not have to work unless he wants to do so. There is no compulsion to work.

MR. TAFT. There is one final step we could take if this procedure does not work. Rather than impose criminal penalties against individuals for not working, I would say the last step would be the drafting of the men into an American labor force and sending them into the mines. That is a step I am opposed to taking; I am opposed to the Austin-Wadsworth bill; I hope we never come to that; but, if we are not going to be forced to it, it seems to me we must take a reasonable step today, one that puts things on a legal basis, one that affords a procedure under the laws of justice laid down by Congress to prevent strikes against the war effort.—*Robert A. Taft, United States Senator from Ohio. Congressional Record. My. 5, '43. (current) p. 4031-2.*

I have no quarrel with organized labor. Quite to the contrary is my attitude. Collective bargaining is right, fair, and just. With labor I stand foursquare in all of its legitimate rights and fair undertakings. I concede to it the right to organize, the right to bargain collectively, the right to picket peacefully, the right to petition its government for redress, the right of peacetime strike. Yet I have no patience with the labor racketeer, nor the capitalistic racketeer and profiteer. Their unnecessary and unreasonable demands, forced walk-outs, shut-downs, and strikes are retarding our progress in this fight and simultaneously adding unreasonable risks to our fighting forces and the perpetuation of our Republic. Incidentally, I come from a labor town. Those people are my friends. I know and am happy to report to you that they are patriotic. So are the other men of labor in my district. They, I can assure you, are doing their utmost,

But they and hundreds of thousands of other patriotic labor affiliates, because of the unconscionable conduct of a few selfish, racketeering, sabotaging leaders, are being humiliated and embarrassed, and their brotherhoods and orders are nearing the chasms of disrepute. This legislation is as essential to vital war industry as Selective Service is to the armed forces. It does not deny to labor the right to strike. It continues for them that privilege under prescribed reasonable conditions even in government operated war industry.

Many arguments have been currently advanced in defense of John L. Lewis closing down hundreds of coal mines. None of them are reasonable; none are feasible; none will stand the test. They argue that labor is doing a good job. Yes, indeed, a commendable job, I agree. They also argue that because patriotic labor is being embarrassed with isolated strikes, we should not enact this legislation and thus further embarrass the patriotic laborer; that it would be a reflection upon him. Only those who violate the law are embarrassed thereby. No, no, my dear friends, this would not embarrass the patriotic war worker. On the contrary, he would most assuredly welcome it. Why? Simply because it would put his house in order and eliminate the scurrilous activities of the unpatriotic.

Others say that antistrike legislation would affect labor's morale. Well, goodness me, what about the morale of the people as a whole? What of the morale of the young man in uniform? Does not their morale merit your consideration? Every day they see these strikes headlined in the press. What a terrible tonic for them. It makes good reading for no one. It has positively brought the spirit of our people and fighting forces to the breaking point.

Frequently I receive letters from parents of servicemen, from the servicemen themselves, begging and pleading for legislation to put a stop to the unnecessary strikes in war industry. I know that you have received the same. Only a few days ago a young man from my district, a soldier of Uncle Sam, sat with me in my office and related in no uncertain terms the attitude of the American soldier on this question. He stated that the boys do not understand why it is that they, by a law of Congress, are drafted and forced to fight when at the same time the Congress neglects to enact legislation that would guarantee the utilization of a maximum of manpower in the production of war essentials. I agree with them. As long as blood flows in my veins, I shall stand by and cast my vote for them, the threats of John L. Lewis upon my political future notwithstanding. It is not fair for a man back home to go on strike in war industry when the soldier is looking to him for weapons to defend himself and this nation. —*Thomas G. Abernethy, United States Representative from Mississippi. Congressional Record. Je. 3, '43. p. 5402-3.*

There are some persons who claim that this legislation is not necessary for the reason that the spokesmen for labor have solemnly promised that there would be no strikes during the war. This in the face of the fact that the great coal strike is now on and 500,000 miners not on the job. What is the record of the War Labor Board in regard to strikes and labor disputes? Since it was created several months ago the W.L.B. has disposed of only 786 disputes, or an average of 50 cases per month. It now has pending before it some 2,000 unsettled cases, which, based on previous experience, will require 3½ years to settle. It is these disputes . . . from which strikes result. Furthermore, the records indicate that in 1942 there were a total of 2,968 strikes in this country, the greatest number for any year in our history, except in 1937 and 1941. During the month of April just past there were 395 strikes, establishing a record which, if maintained for a year, would total more strikes in one year than have occurred in all the combined years since the Department of Labor was created. Strikes are a serious and menacing problem and require the immediate attention of the Congress.

It has been asserted by those who are opposed to this bill that to enact it would be tantamount to an attack upon labor as a whole and charge them with unfaithfulness and disloyalty in time of war. What a silly and preposterous argument. Because laws are passed providing punishment for murder does not mean that all people are suspected of being guilty of murder. Because it is illegal to steal does not imply that everybody is a thief. Because a law is proposed to reduce strikes in the interest of the successful prosecution of the war does not mean that all workers are guilty of violation of the pledge of labor not to strike. No laws would be necessary if everyone were honest and fair and honorable. It is to punish the few and to suppress the temptation of some that laws are made. Honest labor has no reason for offense at this bill—it is only those whose conscience hurts who complain.

No one questions the loyalty and determination of the great majority of workers in this country. Their sons are in the field of battle and on the high seas the same as the boys of the employer and the office worker. They realize the grave danger in which our country rests; they know the importance to the success of our men at the battle fronts that there be no suspension of war production; they are willing to and have worked long and arduous hours; most of them have refused to strike even though they have felt themselves to be aggrieved. It is not those people whom this bill would affect; rather, it would curb the very, very small minority of laborers and labor leaders who persist in practices which are accepted in peacetimes but which have no place when their nation, their homes, their lives, and their jobs are in peril. Some of them have even gone so far as to defy the power and authority of the Chief Executive and the Commander in Chief. Those men who believe themselves above and beyond the power of government and who seek to make selfish gains for themselves during the exigencies of war, can and must be checked.

By what right, sir, can this government arbitrarily take a young man from his school, or his profession, or his business, and his home, compel him to give up substantial earnings, tear him away from his wife or mother or children, clothe him in the uniform of a soldier, put a pack on his back and a gun in his hand, command him to go forth to battle a common foe and expose himself to the shot and shell and hell of war and, at the same time, permit any person or group of persons, for personal and selfish reasons, to refuse to work and make the very things which that young man needs to protect himself from the enemy or to inflict harm to the enemy? By what right, I ask, can that same government confiscate the excessive earnings of a corporation, which have been occasioned by the war, or commandeer the plant, equipment, or property of any corporation or individual for the purpose of increasing war production and, at the same time, permit a worker or group of workers to stop production because they are dissatisfied with the wages they receive? There must be a uniformity and fairness of treatment for all the people, else the powers of government are misguided and abused.—*W. Sterling Cole, United States Representative from New York. Congressional Record.* Je. 3, '43. (*current*) p. 5386.

BIBLIOGRAPHY

An asterisk (*) preceding a reference indicates that the article or a part of it has been reprinted in this book.

BIBLIOGRAPHIES

Gagliardo, Domenico. Kansas Industrial Court. p. 255-9. University of Kansas. Lawrence. '41.

Garland, J. V. comp. Federal regulation of labor unions. (Reference Shelf. Vol. 15, no. 3) p. 269-86. H. W. Wilson Co. New York. D. '41.

Harris, Arthur. Government mediation and arbitration in industrial disputes. p. 25. mim. Bureau of Public Administration. University of California. Berkeley. Mr. 29, '39.

Kaltenborn, Howard S. Governmental adjustment of labor disputes. p. 304-10. Foundation Press. Chicago. '43.

Muller, Helen M. N.L.R.B. to enforce arbitration of labor disputes. *In* Phelps, Edith M. ed. University debaters' annual, 1937-1938. H. W. Wilson Co. New York. '38.

National Association of Manufacturers. Compulsory arbitration of labor disputes. p. 71-3. The Association. New York. '38.

Nichols, Egbert R. and Logan, J. W. comp. Arbitration and the National Labor Relations Board. (Reference Shelf. Vol. 11, no. 7) p. 41-76. H. W. Wilson Co. New York. D. '37.

Patterson, S. H. Social aspects of industry. p. 423-4. McGraw-Hill Book Co. New York. '43.

Phelps, Edith M. ed. Compulsory arbitration of labor disputes. *In her* University debaters' annual, 1919-1920. p. 244-6. H. W. Wilson Co. New York. '20. o.p.

Phelps, Edith M. ed. Compulsory arbitration of labor disputes in public utilities. *In her* University debaters' annual 1922-1923. p. 145-51. H. W. Wilson Co. New York. '23. o.p.

Phelps, Edith M. ed. Compulsory arbitration of railway labor disputes. *In her* University debaters' annual, 1919-1920. p. 188-91. H. W. Wilson Co. New York. '20. o.p.

Pierson, Frank C. Collective bargaining systems. p. 212-20. American Council on Public Affairs. Washington, D.C. '42.

Starnes, George T.; McCutcheon, J. R.; and Stepp, J. M. Survey of the methods for the promotion of industrial peace. p. 143-6. Division of Publications. Bureau of Administration. Charlottesville, Va. '39.

United States. Department of Labor. Library. Conciliation and arbitration in industrial disputes: a selected list of recent references. 15p. mim. Washington, D.C. O. 25, '37.

United States. Library of Congress. Legislative Reference Service. Labor in wartime (April 1941-March 1942) (Bibliographies of the world at war, no. 5) 92p. mim. Washington, D.C. '42.

Virginia. Labor Relations Commission. Report of Labor Relations Commission, submitted to the Governor and General Assembly of Virginia. (Senate document no. 3) p. 153-5. Division of Publications and Printing. Richmond. '40.

GENERAL REFERENCES
BOOKS, PAMPHLETS AND DOCUMENTS

Agar, Herbert. Labor relations are not a class problem. *In his* Time for greatness. p. 184-217. Little, Brown & Co. Boston. '42.

American Arbitration Association. Labor arbitration in wartime; report of the Industrial Arbitration Tribunal of the American Arbitration Association. 23p. The Association. 9 Rockefeller Plaza. New York. '42.

American Arbitration Association. Voluntary labor arbitration tribunals of the American Arbitration Association; rules of procedure and manual for their use in wartime. 30p. The Association. 9 Rockefeller Plaza. New York. '42.

*American Federation of Labor. Compulsory arbitration. 6p. mim. The Federation. n.d.

American Management Association. Management's stake in collective bargaining. (Personnel series no. 81) 51p. The Association. 330 W. 42d St. New York. '44.

Bing, Alexander. War-time strikes and their adjustment. 329p. E. P. Dutton & Co. New York. '21.

Bowers, John H. Kansas court of industrial relations. 133p. A. C. McClurg & Co. Chicago. '22.

Bowman, Dean O. Public control of labor relations; a study of the National Labor Relations Board. 504p. Macmillan Co. New York. '42.

Carpenter, Oliver C. Arbitration of labor disputes. *In his* Debate outlines on public questions. 7th rev. ed. p. 308-14. Minton, Balch & Co. New York. '32.
Includes references.

Chamber of Commerce of the State of New York. Further curbs on strikes during war times. 3p. The Chamber. 65 Liberty St. New York. F. 3, '44.

Chang, Ducksoo. British methods of industrial peace; a study of democracy in relation to labor disputes. (Columbia University Studies in History, Economics and Public Law, no. 425) 332p. Columbia University Press. New York. '36.

Council for Democracy. Public and strikes. (Democracy in action, no. 6) 38p. The Council. 285 Madison Ave. New York. '41.

Davis, Forrest. 300,000 guinea pigs. 31p. Toledo Associates. 240 Huron St. Toledo, O. '39.

Eliot, Thomas H.; Fraser, Cecil; and Saltonstall, Leverett. How can we prevent strikes from stalling defense. (New England Town Meeting on the Air. Vol. 1, no. 2) 32p. Bacon, Percy & Daggett. Northport, L.I., N.Y. Ap. 9, '41.

Feldman, Herman. Problems in labor relations; a case book presenting some major issues in the relations of labor, capital, and government. 353p. Macmillan Co. New York. '37.

Fisher, Thomas R. Industrial disputes and federal legislation. (Columbia University Studies in History, Economics and Public Law, no. 467) 370p. Columbia University Press. New York. '40.

Foenander, Orwell de R. Solving labour problems in Australia. 168p. Melbourne University Press in collaboration with Oxford University Press. Melbourne & London. '41.

Gagliardo, Domenico. Kansas Industrial Court; an experiment in compulsory arbitration. (Publications, Social science studies) 264p. University of Kansas. Lawrence. '41.

Gannett, Frank E. and Catherwood, B. F. eds. Industrial and labour relations in Great Britain; a symposium. 364p. The Authors. New York. '39.

Garland, J. V. comp. Federal regulation of labor unions. (Reference Shelf. Vol. 15, no. 3) 286p. H. W. Wilson Co. New York. D. '41.

Griffin, John I. Strikes, a study in quantitative economics. 319p. Columbia University Press. New York. '39.

Harris, Arthur. Government mediation and arbitration in industrial disputes. (1939 Legislative problems, no. 10) 25p. mim. Bureau of Public Administration. University of California. Berkeley. Mr. 29, '39.

Hayes, Samuel P. Jr. Psychology of conciliation and arbitration procedures. In Hartmann, George W. ed. Industrial conflict; a psychological interpretation. p. 368-438. Cordon Co. New York. '39.

International Labor Office. Labor courts; an international survey of judicial systems for the settlement of disputes. (Studies and reports. Series A, no. 40) 220p. The Office. 734 Jackson Pl. N.W. Washington, D.C. '38.

International Labour Office. Conciliation and arbitration in industrial disputes. (Studies and reports. Series A. no. 34) 696p. Geneva. '39.

Johnsen, Julia E. National labor relations act; should it be amended? (Reference Shelf. Vol. 13, no. 9) 416p. H. W. Wilson Co. New York. Ja. '40.

*Kaltenborn, Howard S. Governmental adjustment of labor disputes. 327p. Foundation press. Chicago. '43.
Review by W. R. Maclaurin. Mechanical Engineering. 65:812-13. N. '43.

Kellor, Frances. Arbitration in action; a code for civil, commercial and industrial arbitrations. 412p. Harper & Bros. New York. '41.

Labor organization and the question of strikes in the defense industries. (Public Affairs News Service Bulletin no. 6, series no. 5) 11p. mim. Womans Press. New York. My. 5, '41.

Labor's Non-Partisan League. Who causes strikes? 16p. The League. 1037-46 Earle Bldg. Washington, D.C. n.d.

Lewis, Elmer A. Compilation of laws relating to mediation, conciliation, and arbitration between employer and employees. 534p. Supt. of Docs. Washington, D.C. '43.

McCabe, David A. and Lester, Richard A. Labor and social organization. 374p. Little, Brown & Co. Boston. '38.

National Conference of Social Work. Proceedings. 1939:209-25. Factors in industrial peace: National Labor Relations Board. L. L. Jaffe; Conciliation and arbitration. A. P. Randolph.

Nichols, Egbert R. and Logan, James W. comp. Arbitration and the National Labor Relations Board. (Reference Shelf. Vol. 11, no. 7) 345p. H. W. Wilson Co. New York. D. '37.

Patterson, S. Howard. Industrial conciliation and arbitration. *In his* Social aspects of industry; a survey of labor problems. p. 402-24. McGraw-Hill Book Co. New York. '43.

Phelps, Edith M. ed. Compulsory arbitration of labor disputes. *In her* University debaters' annual, 1919-1920. p. 193-246. H. W. Wilson Co. New York. '20. o.p.

Phelps, Edith M. ed. Compulsory arbitration of labor disputes in public utilities. *In her* University debaters' annual, 1922-1923. p. 87-151. H. W. Wilson Co. New York. '23. o.p.

Phelps, Edith M. ed. Compulsory arbitration of railway labor disputes. *In her* University debaters' annual, 1919-1920. p. 155-91. H. W. Wison Co. New York. '20. o.p.

Phelps, Edith M. ed. N.L.R.B. to enforce arbitration of industrial disputes. *In her* University debaters' annual, 1937-1938. p. 243-89. H. W. Wilson Co. New York. '38.

Pierson, Frank C. Collective bargaining systems; a study of union-employer responsibilities and problems. 227p. American Council on Public Affairs. Washington, D.C. '42.
    Bibliography, p. 212-20.

Rich, Bennett M. Presidents and civil disorder. 235p. Brookings Institution. Washington, D.C. '41.

Robbins, James J. Government of labor relations in Sweden. 367p. American Scandinavian Foundation. New York; University of North Carolina Press. Chapel Hill. '42.

Roth, Almon E. and others. Toward a national labor policy. (Personnel series no. 72) 40p. American Management Association. 330 W. 42d St. New York. '43.

Senturia, Joseph J. Strikes. 2d ed. 58p. University of Chicago Press. Chicago. '40.

Smethurst, Raymond S. War Labor Disputes act. *In* Pitzele, M. S. and Smethurst, Raymond S. What to expect in labor legislation. (Personnel series no. 68) p. 15-24. American Management Association. 330 W. 42d St. New York. '43.

Smith, Everett R. What shall we do about it? 121p. Macfadden Publications. New York. '44.

Smith, Rembert G. Great need of this hour, the outlawing of strikes! 14p. The Author. Box 2123. Tulsa, Okla. '39.

Stark, Louis. National Labor Relations Board—why and how. (Social Action. Vol. 4, no. 9) 39p. Ag. 15, '38.

Starnes, George T.; McCutcheon, J. R.; and Stepp, J. M. Survey of the methods for the promotion of industrial peace. (Report. Series B, no. 4) 146p. mim. Division of Publications. Bureau of Public Administration. Charlottesville, Va. '39.

Twentieth Century Fund. How collective bargaining works; a survey in leading American industries. 986p. The Fund. 330 W. 42d St. New York. '42.

Twentieth Century Fund. Labor and the government; an investigation of the role of the government in labor relations. 413p. McGraw-Hill Book Co. New York. '35.

United States. Bureau of Labor Statistics. Arbitration provisions in union agreements. (Bulletin no. 780) 18p. Supt. of Docs. Washington, D.C. '44.

United States. Bureau of Labor Statistics. Report on the work of the National Defense Mediation Board, March 19, 1941-January 12, 1942. (Bulletin no. 714) 285p. Supt. of Docs. Washington, D.C. '42.

United States. Bureau of Labor Statistics. Strikes in the United States, 1880-1936. Florence Peterson. (Bulletin no. 651) 183p. Supt. of Docs. Washington, D.C. '38.

United States. Department of labor. Report of the Commission on Industrial Relations in Great Britain. 146p. Supt. of Docs. Washington, D.C. '38.

United States. House of Representatives. Committee on Military Affairs. Defense plant operations and labor relations; hearing, June 1-2, 1943, on S.796. 74p. 78th Congress, 1st session. Supt. of Docs. Washington, D.C. '43.

United States. House of Representatives. Committee on Naval Affairs. Conciliation and mediation of labor disputes affecting the national defense program; report to accompany H.R. 4139. H. Report no. 427. 3 parts. 77th Congress, 1st session. Supt. of Docs. Washington, D.C. Ap. '41.

United States. House of Representatives. Committee on the Judiciary. Delays in national defense preparations; hearings, February 17-March 24, 1941. (serial no. 3) 388p. 77th Congress 1st session. Supt. of Docs. Washington, D.C. '41.
  *A. C. Lappin. p. 29-36.

United States. Library of Congress. Compulsory settlement of labor disputes. (Legislative Reference Service. Bulletin no. 6). 28p. mim. Je. 6, '41.

United States. Library of Congress. Legislative Reference Division. Strikes in defense industries. (77th Congress, 1st session. Senate document no. 52) 141p. Supt. of Docs. Washington, D.C. '41.

United States. Maritime Labor Board. Report to the President and to the Congress, March 1, 1940. (76th Congress, 3d session. House document no. 646) 262p. Supt. of Docs. Washington, D.C. '40.
    Also: Supplemental report to the President and to the Congress, March 1, 1942. 20p. Supt. of Docs. '42.

United States. National Labor Relations Board. Division of Economic Research. Governmental protection of labor's right to organize. (Bulletin no. 1) 174p. Supt. of Docs. Washington, D.C. Ag. '36.

United States. National Mediation Board. Ninth annual report for the fiscal year ended June 30, 1943. 96p. Supt. of Docs. Washington, D.C. '44.

United States. Senate. Committee on Commerce and Committee on Education and Labor. Amending the Merchant Marine Act of 1936; hearings, December 8, 1937-March 24, 1938, on S. 3078. pts. 1-13. 1336p. 75th Congress, 2d-3d sessions. Supt. of Docs. Washington, D.C. '38.

United States. Senate. Committee on Education and Labor. National Labor Relations Act and proposed amendments; hearings, April 11, 1939-February 7, 1940, on S. 1000 [and others]. 24 parts in 4 vols. 76th Congress, 1st and 3d sessions. Supt. of Docs. Washington, D.C. '39-'40.

United States. Senate. Committee on Education and Labor. To amend the National Labor Relations Act; hearings, August 13-September 16, 1940, on H.R. 9195. 286p. 76th Congress, 3d session. Supt. of Docs. Washington, D.C. '40.

United States. Senate. Committee on Education and Labor. Violations of free speech and rights of labor; hearings, August 21, 1936-July 1, 1940, pursuant to S. res. 266. 75 parts. 74th Congress, 1st session to 76th Congress, 3d session. Supt. of Docs. Washington, D.C. '36-'41.
    See also reports of the Committee.

Virginia. Labor Relations Commission. Report of Labor Relations Commission, submitted to the Governor and General Assembly of Virginia; including A survey of the methods for the promotion of industrial peace, by G. T. Starnes; J. R. McCutcheon; and J. M. Stepp. (Senate document no. 3) 155p. Division of Publications and Printing. Richmond. '40.

Wunderlich, Frieda. Labor under German democracy; arbitration 1918-1933. 101p. Graduate Faculty of Political and Social Science. New School for Social Research. New York. '40.

Ziskind, David. One thousand strikes of government employees. 279p. Columbia University Press. New York. '40.

PERIODICALS

American Bar Association Journal. 28:4-7. Ja. '42. What laws should be passed to prevent strikes in defense industries. H. W. Smith.

American Bar Association Journal. 28:7-19. Ja. '42. Repressive labor legislation; an analysis of the Smith bill. Emil Schlesinger.

*American Bar Association Journal. 28:106-12. F. '42. Industrial law under the new constitutionalism. E. F. Albertsworth.

American Economic Review. 29:299-312. Je. '39. Labor disputes on rights and on interests. J. V. Spielmans.

American Economic Review. 33:1-20. Mr. '43. Collective bargaining and the common interest. E. G. Nourse.

American Economic Review. 33:247-63. Je. '43. Public regulation of labor relations, the Wisconsin experiment; National Labor Relations Act contrasted with Wisconsin Employment Peace Act. C. C. Killingsworth.

American Federationist. 45:258-63. Mr. '38. Collective bargaining in Great Britain. Dorothy Sells.

American Federationist. 45:1231-2. N. '38. Mediation in New York City. P. L. Robertson.

American Federationist. 48:14-15+. Ja. '41. Move away from legal bondage. J. A. Padway and B. A. Green.

American Federationist. 49:11. Mr. '42. Congress told of conspiracies by employers.

American Federationist. 50:12-13+. Ja. '43. Collective bargaining and the war. W. H. Davis.

American Federationist. 50:20-4. Ap. '43. Labor and the public. Julius Hochman.

American Federationist. 50:10-13. My. '43. Fascism comes to America; [anti-labor bills in the states.] J. A. Padway.

American Federationist. 50:3-5. Jl. '43. Involuntary servitude. J. A. Padway.

American Federationist. 51:21. Ja. '44. This is American labor's war—and we know it! William Green.

American Federationist. 51:13-14+. Ap. '44. Important decision; collective bargaining rights supersede individual contracts. J. A. Padway.

*American Federationist. 51:27-8. Ag. '44. Oppression of labor. R. M. La Follette.

American Magazine. 119:20-1+. Ja. '45. Labor faces a crisis; ed. by B. Smith. W. M. Leiserson.

American Mercury. 42:129-54. F. '38. Case against the labor board. H. L. Varney.

American Mercury. 58:667-74. Je. '44. Why unions must be regulated. O. G. Villard.
    Reply. S. E. Garner. American Mercury. 58:250-1. Ag. '44.

American Political Science Review. 31:1116-24. D. '37. Municipal government and labor disputes. William Anderson.

Annals of the American Academy. 224:1-195. N. '42. Labor relations and the war. Herman Feldman, ed.

Articles by various authors under the following headings: Recent developments in labor organization; Issues of wartime labor standards; Labor's cooperation in the national effort; Industrial peace and national labor policy; Planning against postwar tension; Bibliography.

Antioch Review. 2:76-89. Mr. '42. Labor relations and the war. W. M. Leiserson.

Antioch Review. 3:311-27. Fall '43. Labor in the war—and after. V. G. Reuther.

Antioch Review. 3:328-40. Fall '43. Antilabor front. V. H. Bernstein.

Antioch Review. 3:391-404. Fall '43. New patterns of democracy. C. S. Golden.

Antioch Review. 3:405-17. Fall '43. Bureaucracy and democracy in labor unions. Will Herberg.

Antioch Review. 4:315-17. Je. '44. Anti-labor offensive. L. Corey.

Arbitration in Action. 1:11. Ja. '43. What is arbitration?

Arbitration in Action. 1:6-7. S. '43. Difference between voluntary but enforceable arbitration, and compulsory arbitration.

Arbitration Journal. 2:29. Ja. '38. Compulsory industrial arbitration in the Philippines.

Arbitration Journal. 2:31-4. Ja. '38. Plan for adjusting labor disputes.

Arbitration Journal. 3:224-33. Jl. '39. How railroads keep the peace. R. M. Blagden.

Arbitration Journal. 4:85-90. Ap. '40. Arbitration supplants strikes in stopping textile stretchout. Solomon Barkin.

Arbitration Journal. 5:65-74. Ja. '41. Three years of arbitrating labor disputes; the American Arbitration Association.

*Arbitration Journal. 5:132-77. Ap. '41. Arbitration in national defense.

Titles: *Divide and conquer: the menace of disputes to national defense. Frances Kellor; Mobilization of voluntary arbitration resources. E. E. Young; Conciliation and national defense. J. R. Steelman; Arbitration and government contracts; Effect of the war on labor arbitration in Europe. I. Bessling.

Arbitration Journal. 5:239-44. Summer-Autumn '41. Coordinate mediation and arbitration in labor relations. Frances Kellor.

*Arbitration Journal. 6:11-20. Winter '42. Labor arbitration in wartime. W. P. Witherow.

Arbitration Journal. 6:24-33. Winter '42. War and industrial arbitration in Australia. P. A. Dodd.

Arbitration Journal. 6:102-7. Spring-Summer '42. Arbitration of job assignment disputes. Solomon Barkin.

Arbitration Journal. 6:122-9. Spring-Summer '42. Wartime report of the Industrial Arbitration Tribunal.

Arbitration Journal. 6:130-5. Spring-Summer '42. War Labor Board looms as a labor supreme court. Benjamin Werne.

Arbitration Journal. 6:235-46. Autumn '42. Decisions of the National War Labor Board; their effect on management and labor prior to October 3, 1942. Marion Dickerman.

*Arbitration Magazine. 2:7-8. Ja. '44. Compulsion, under the name of arbitration.

*Arbitration Magazine. 2:5-11. S. '44. How to select an arbitrator; blind man's buff—or an open-eyed choice? Paul Fitzpatrick.

Atlantic Monthly. 162:13-21. Jl. '38. How peace came to Toledo. E. F. Grady.

Atlantic Monthly. 165:81-8. Ja. '40. Wagner act: an evaluation. Robert Littler.

Atlantic Monthly. 165:758-65. Je. '40. Labor must decide. G. W. Alger.

Atlantic Monthly. 168:686-93. D. '41. Strikes, with a vengeance. S. B. Heath.

Atlantic Monthly. 171:74-82. Ja. '43. How much trade-unionism as usual? S. H. Slichter.

*Atlantic Monthly. 172:70-4. Ag. '43. Is nation-wide bargaining ahead? A. E. Roth.

Atlantic Monthly. 173:37-41. F. '44. Labor crisis. S. H. Slichter.

Business Week. p. 32-3. S. 3, '38. Norse-Swede labor system; there's compulsory conciliation but not compulsory arbitration in Sweden and Norway.

Business Week. p. 15-16. Mr. 1, '41. No walkout on labor policy; proposals to use compulsion in labor disputes seem unlikely to change law.

Business Week. p. 16. Mr. 1, '41. A B C of voluntary conciliation.

Business Week. p. 44+. Je. 28, '41. NDMB job: to keep talk going.

Business Week. p. 61+. Ja. 17, '42. NDMB into NWLB; Mediation Board becomes War Labor Board with only few changes.

Business Week. p. 58+. My. 23, '42. Steelman stymied; Montgomery Ward rebuff to Msgr. Haas.

Business Week. p. 74. Je. 5, '43. No bargaining by force in Canada.

Business Week. p. 100+. Mr. 25, '44. Bounds defined; National Labor Relations Board and National War Labor Board agree on distribution of powers.

Business Week. p. 112+. Ap. 22, '44. Up to Roosevelt; Ward strike forces showdown on NWLB authority.

Business Week. p. 104-5. Je. 3, '44. Arbitration boom.

Business Week. p. 95-6. Jl. 15, '44. Alabama reneges; conflict between state law and Regional War Labor Board's order involving maintenance-of-membership.

Business Week. p. 110+. O. 7, '44. Strikes rising.

Canadian Congress Journal. 20:21-3. D. '41. I.L.O. and war-time collaboration. J. A. D'Aoust.

Canadian Journal of Economics and Political Science. 9:331-47. Ag. '43. Trends in collective bargaining: a study in casual analysis. H. A. Logan.

Canadian Journal of Economics and Political Science. 9:348-56. Ag. '43. Problems of legislation relating to collective bargaining; with discussion. S. Midanik.

Canadian Journal of Economics and Political Science. 10:476-8. N. '44. State and collective bargaining. H. A. Logan.

Christian Science Monitor Weekly Magazine Section. p. 3+. My. 29; 14. D. 11, '43. Feather bedding on the railroads. G. P. McNear, Jr.

Christian Science Monitor Weekly Magazine Section. p. 2+. S. 4, '43. Featherbed rules; reply to G. P. McNear, Jr. D. B. Robertson.

Columbia Law Review. 33:1366-91. D. '33. Function of arbitration in the settlement of industrial disputes.

Commerce (Chicago) 39:16-18+. Je. '42. Arbitration speeds the war effort. D. F. Nicholson.

Commercial and Financial Chronicle. 158:25+. Jl. 1, '43. Congress overrides President's veto of anti-strike bill; with text of President's veto message.

Commonweal. 39:300-3. Ja. 7, '44. Labor on trial; A.C.L.U. study Democracy in trade unions. J. C. Cort.

Commonwealth Club of California. Transactions. 31 (Commonwealth. Vol. 12, no. 29, part 2):1-44. Jl. 21, '36. Compulsion in industrial relations.

Commonwealth Club of California. Transactions. 38 (Commonwealth. Vol. 20, no. 1, part 2):47-98. Ja. 3, '44. Labor relations in war and peace.

*Commonwealth Review. 23:1-19. Mr. '41. Scope of arbitration in labor disputes. W. L. Morse.
    Same. Labor Relations Reporter. 8:828-30. Ag. 11, '41. Same condensed. Management Review. 30:442-4. D. '41.

Conference Board Bulletin. 11:49-60. My. 4, '37. Government regulation of unions.

Conference Board Management Record. 3:53-7. My. '41. Management views the labor situation. H. F. Browne.

Conference Board Management Record. 3:81-5. Jl. '41. Labor policy in total defense. H. F. Browne.

Congressional Digest. 16:293-320. D. '37. Compulsory arbitration of labor disputes; with pro and con discussion.

Congressional Digest. 20:99-128. Ap. '41. Congress investigates defense labor problems; fact material and pro and con discussion.

Congressional Digest. 20:258-88. N. '41. Proposed federal regulation of American labor unions; fact material and pro and con discussion.

Congressional Digest. 22:163-92. Je. '43. Hobbs bill to outlaw labor racketeering; fact material and pro and con discussion.

Congressional Record. 88:(current file)A3036-8. Jl. 18, '42. Dictatorship in American music. Fred Bradley.

Congressional Record. 89:(current file)A2239-41. My. 3, '43. Legislative attempts to prevent strikes. Lindley Beckworth.

Congressional Record. 89:(current file)A2247-8. My. 3, '43. John L. Lewis and the coal strike. J. E. Rankin.

Congressional Record. 89:(current file)4030-54. My. 5, '43. Strikes in defense industries; Senate debate.

Congressional Record. 89:(current file)5304-30. Je. 2, '43. House debate on S.796.

Congressional Record. 89:(current file)5380-428. Je. 3, '43. House debate on S.796; Connally-Smith bill.

Controller. 11:9-15. Ja. '43. Labor disputes and the War Labor Board. G. K. Munson.

Current History. n.s. 1:434-40. Ja. '42. America faces the strike problem. R. V. Harlow.

Current History and Forum. 52:16-18. My. '41. Steelman and associates. Stanley High.

Debaters' Digest. 11:53-67. N. '37. Should the National Labor Relations Board be given the power to enforce compulsory arbitration? analysis, briefs and references.

Economic Record (Melbourne). 14:14-22. Je. '38. Towards industrial peace in Australia. Norman Cowper.

Economic Record (Melbourne). 17:45-56. Je. '41. Court of arbitration in New Zealand; the evolution of a legislature. W. R. Tuck.

Economist (London). 140:621-2. My. 10, '41. Arbitration in Australian labour disputes.

Editorial Research Reports. 1, no.6:99-116. F. 12, '41. Labor and the defense program. B. W. Patch.

Editorial Research Reports. 1, no.12:211-28. Mr. 29, '41. Labor as partner in production. Bryant Putney.

Editorial Research Reports. 2, no.19:343-59. N. 19, '41. Labor policies of the Roosevelt administration. C. E. Noyes.

Employers' Review (Sydney, Australia). 14:64-8. D. 31, '41. Commonwealth and state systems of industrial arbitration. R. Ashburner.

Far Eastern Survey. 10:164-5. Jl. 28, '41. Australia adapts industrial arbitration to wartime conditions. E. J. Riches.

Food for Thought (Toronto). 2:8-17. N. '41. Collective bargaining in Canada: in peace and war. Bora Laskin.

Fortune. 23:70-1+. Je. '41. Fortune survey: labor agrees with the public on banning defense strikes; the public agrees with labor on allowing others.

Fortune. 23:82-3+. Je. '41. Strike doctors.

Harper's Magazine. 180:625-34. My. '40. Violence and collective bargaining. M. J. Barloon.

Harper's Magazine. 182:598-637. My. '41. Labor mediators. Irwin Ross.

Harvard Business Review. 19:429-37. Summer '41. Labor peace in Pacific ports. Paul Eliel.

Harvard Business Review. 20:21-33. Autumn '41. Living with collective bargaining. B. M. Selekman.

Harvard Law Review. 38:753-92. Ap. '25. Constitutional limitations on compulsory industrial arbitration. S. P. Simpson.

Harvard Law Review. 50:1071-117. My. '37. Half century of legal influence upon the development of collective bargaining. Calvert Magruder.

Harvard Law Review. 53:754-91. Mr. '40. Mechanics of collective bargaining. Chester Ward.

Industrial Canada. 39:43-7+. S. '38. Mediation, conciliation and arbitration of labour disputes in Canada. G. V. V. Nichols.

Information Service (Department of Research and Education. Federal Council of the Churches of Christ in America). 20, no.28:1-4. S. 13, '41. Labor and the law.

International Labour Review. 37:463-72. Ap. '38. Labour courts. Henri Binet.

International Labour Review. 41:479-505. My. '40. Collective bargaining in the United States of America. Florence Peterson.

International Labour Review. 42:252-5. O. '40. Compulsory arbitration in Great Britain.

International Labour Review. 46:525-68. N. '42. Industrial relations and the determination of conditions of employment in wartime. I. Bessling.

International Labour Review. 47:367-9. Mr. '43. Government-employer-worker collaboration in Peru.

International Labour Review. 48:500-4. O. '43. Prevention of industrial disputes in the United States; the War Labor Disputes Act.

International Labour Review. 48:504-7. O. '43. Strikes in the United States in 1942.

Iowa Law Review. 27:232-49. Ja. '42. Highlights of our national labor policy. R. B. Watts.

Iowa Law Review. 29:145-348. Ja. '44. Symposium on labor law in wartime.

  See especially Arbitration and the War Labor Board. A. H. Frey. p. 202-20; Adjustment of labor disputes. H. S. Kaltenborn. p. 221-33; Post-war labor relations: the contributions of the War Labor Board. L. L. Jaffe. p. 276-96; Wartime arbitration of labor disputes. C. M. Updegraff. p. 328-48.

Journal of Business of the University of Chicago. 11, part 2:1-65. Ap. '38. National Railroad Adjustment Board. W. H. Spencer.

Journal of Political Economy. 35:657-83. O. '27. Eleven years of compulsory investigation of industrial disputes in Colorado. C. E. Warne and M. E. Gaddis.

Journal of Political Economy. 49:59-89. F. '41. Mediation, arbitration, and investigation of industrial disputes in New York State, 1937-40. W. P. Arenwald.

Journal of Political Economy. 49:722-31. O. '41. Strikes under the Wagner Act. J. V. Spielmans.

Journal of Political Economy. 50:750-60. O. '42. On strike analysis; plan for a new type of analysis. J. V. Spielmans.

Journal of Political Economy. 52:97-111. Je. '44. Organized business in America. Neil Chamberlain.

Journal of Retailing. 19:99-102. D. '43. Industrial peace for the retailer. S. R. Zack.

Labor Information Bulletin. 7:7. Jl. '40. Work of the Newark, N.J., Labor Relations Board. L. H. Garner.

Labor Relations Reporter. 8:31-2. Mr. 10, '41. CIO opposes new mediation body.

Labor Relations Reporter. 11:397-8. N. 30, '42. Final determination of disputes; address before American Arbitration Association, New York, November 23, 1942. W. H. Davis.

Labor Relations Reporter. 13:28-9. S. 13, '43. Arbitral review policy of WLB.

Labor Relations Reporter. 15:56-7. S. 18, '44. Peacetime War Labor Board. L. M. Gill.

Labour Gazette (Ottawa). 41:1272-6. O. '41. Organized labour and the defence of democracy. R. R. R. Brooks.

Ladies' Home Journal. 60:128-9+. O. '43. Is Pegler fair to labor? No. J. B. Carey; Yes. Westbrook Pegler.

Law Society Journal. 8:409-15. F. '39. Obligations of collective bargaining. R. M. Goldstein.

*Lawyers Guild Review. 1:40-5. Je. '41. Right to strike and compulsory arbitration. Lee Pressman.

Lawyers Guild Review. 2:1-7. Mr. '42. Collective bargaining in government enterprise. J. A. Padway.

Literary Digest. 124 (Digest. 1):17. Jl. 17, '37. Unfair to mediation boards!

Magazine of Wall Street. 69:180-2+. N. 29, '41. Labor: public issue no. 1; what should be done. H. F. Travis.

Michigan Law Review. 39:1065-108. My. '41. Evolution of the duty to bargain concept in American law. R. A. Smith.

Michigan Law Review. 43:329-82. O. '44. Authority of the National War Labor Board over labor disputes. L. B. Boudin.

Modern Industry. 2:22-4+. D. 15, '41. Labor's family feuds; jurisdictional strikes are all management's potential problem.

Monthly Labor Review. 45:269-77. S. '37. Industrial relations in Denmark. E. Gjessing.

Monthly Labor Review. 45:1411-13. D. '37. Tribunal for voluntary industrial arbitration.

Monthly Labor Review. 46:1047-67. My. '38. Review of strikes in the United States. Florence Peterson.

*Monthly Labor Review. 49:1023-44. N. '39. Adjustment of labor disputes. Florence Peterson.

Monthly Labor Review. 49:1045-9. N. '39. Municipal labor boards of Toledo and Newark. W. L. Nunn.

Monthly Labor Review. 49:1050-74. N. '39. Industrial-relations machinery in democratic foreign countries. M. H. Schoenfeld.

Monthly Labor Review. 54:1107-29. My. '42. Strikes in 1941. D. Q. Crowther.

Monthly Labor Review. 56:1170-4. Je. '43. National conciliation machinery for British coal-mining industry. E. M. Hodgkinson.

Monthly Labor Review. 57:46-57. Jl. '43. Recommendation of Emergency Board in dispute of railroad nonoperating employees.

Monthly Labor Review. 57:305-7. Ag. '43. War labor disputes act, or Smith-Connally act.

Monthly Labor Review. 57:935-6. N. '43. War Labor Board policy on review of arbitration awards.

Monthly Labor Review. 58:525-8. Mr. '44. Wartime regulation of industrial relations in Canada.

Monthly Labor Review. 58:927-47. My. '44. Strikes in 1943. D. Q. Crowther and R. S. Cole.

Monthly Labor Review. 58:1207-19. Je. '44. Effect of elimination of unfair labor practices on extent of collective bargaining. E. C. Brown.

Monthly Labor Review. 59:796. O. '44. Compulsory arbitration of labor disputes temporarily decreed in Colombia. W. E. Dunn.

Monthly Labor Review. 59:1001-13. N. '44. Arbitration provisions in union agreements. Abraham Weiss.

Nation. 157:124-6. Jl. 31, '43. How to choke unions; technique of the Christian American Association. Victor Riesel.

Nation. 158:68-71. Ja. 15, '44. Why war workers strike; case history of a shipyard wildcat. V. H. Johnson.

National Municipal Review. 29:174-7. Mr. '40. Communities settle their labor problems: Toledo Industrial Peace Board. W. L. Nunn.

National Municipal Review. 29:248-52. Ap. '40. Newark makes labor peace. W. L. Nunn.

National Municipal Review. 29:784-91. D. '40. Local progress in labor peace; many cities offer service for mediation. W. L. Nunn.

National Municipal Review. 33:195-7. Ap. '44. Controversies between cities, organized labor cause critical situations.

Nation's Business. 25:18-20+. O. '37. Specialized first aid in labor ills. J. R. Steelman.

Nation's Business. 28:30+. Ap. '40. Minnesota's year of labor peace. W. H. Kelty.

Nation's Business. 28:24+. Je. '40. First aid treatment for labor ills. Webb Waldron.

New Republic. 93:298-300. Ja. 19, '38. Attack on the NLRB. Leo Huberman.

New Republic. 103:825-6. D. 16, '40. Strikes in defense industries; how they can be avoided. W. H. Davis.

New Republic. 104:629-30. My. 5, '41. These workers don't strike; how Parafine Companies solved its labor-relations problem. A. Marsh.

New Republic. 108:790-2. Je. 14, '43. Union regulation by the states. L. B. Milner and P. Brissenden.

New Republic. 109:74-5. Jl. 19, '43. Trade unionist on F.D.R.; reaction to the Smith-Connally bill. V. H. Johnson.

New York Sun. Jl. 3, '43. How featherbed rules fare in courts. E. M. Friedman.

New York Times. p. 16. Mr. 17, '42. President urges T.P.W. to arbitrate.

*New York Times. p. 8E. F. 21, '43. Railroads viewed as factor in manpower problem. E. M. Friedman.
    Same. Congressional Record. 89:(current file)A750-2. F. 22, '43.

New York Times. p. 16. Je. 14, '43. Anti-strike bill.

New York Times. p. 3E. Je. 27, '43. Plan for compulsory arbitration is revived. Louis Stark.

New York Times. p. 12. Ja. 22, '44. Permitted violence.

New York Times Magazine. p. 11+. Mr. 30, '41. For peace in industry, a conciliator's creed. Cabell Phillips.

Newsweek. 22:64+. Jl. 5, '43. Angry Congress deals labor biggest setback in 10 years; reversal of Roosevelt veto on anti-strike bill.

Personnel. 17:177-84. F. '41. Arbitration of labor disputes. W. J. Graham.

Personnel Journal. 20:82-9. S. '41. Mediation and arbitration. Irwin Stalmaster.

Personnel Journal. 20:134-46. O. '41. Arbitration; getting a just award; an unfavorable award. C. S. Slocombe.

Personnel Journal. 21:151-6. O. '42. Negotiation and arbitration. C. S. Slocombe.

Personnel Journal. 21:258-64. Ja. '43. Wartime labor relations policy. Albert Earl.

Political Science Quarterly. 55:161-75. Je. '40. Turning point in American labor policy. Leo Wolman.

Political Science Quarterly. 59:264-74. Je. '44. Labor unions in peace and war. James Quarles.

*Propaganda Analysis. 4:1-14. Ap. 28, '41. Strikes, profits, and defense.

Public Affairs (Halifax). 7:136-40. Spring '44. Government adjustment of labor disputes in the United States. G. W. Taylor.

Public Opinion Quarterly. 5:17-37. Mr. '41. Citizen's committees: their role in industrial conflict. L. G. Silverberg.

Public Management. 19:99-103. Ap. '37. I went through a strike. Henry Traxler.

*Public Management. 19:103-7. Ap. '37. Maintaining industrial peace. L. S. Moore.

Public Management. 19:163-4. Je. '37. Plan for adjusting labor disputes. C. A. Prosser.

Public Opinion Quarterly. 8, no.3:376-90. Fall '44. Labor's role in the election. Joseph Rosenfarb.

*Public Opinion Quarterly. 8, no.3:407-15. Fall '44. Wanted: a national labor policy for industry and labor. S. H. Slichter.

Public Utilities Fortnightly. 28:795-805. D. 18, '41. We'll probably pass a law. Herbert Corey.

Public Utilities Fortnightly. 31:610-17. My. 13, '43. Gentle art of cooling off. Herbert Corey.

Quarterly Journal of Economics. 57:522-42. Ag. '43. Theory of union wage rigidity. J. Shister.

Quarterly Journal of Economics. 58:359-87. My. '44. Nature and scope of collective bargaining. Neil Chamberlain.

Quarterly Journal of Economics. 59:92-106. N. '44. Strikes and lockouts in Great Britain. E. L. Gomberg.

Reader's Digest. 44:37-40. Ja. '44. Labor against itself; measures to prevent the misuse of labor power. Thurman Arnold.

Reader's Digest. 45:56-9. N. '44. Labor reform by labor. W. W. Cenerazzo.

Rubber Age. 55:376-8. Jl. '44. Conciliation—and the rubber industry. J. R. Steelman.

Saturday Evening Post. 214:19+. Ap. 18, '42. Will labor lose the war? D. R. Richberg.

Scholastic. 38:9-10. Ap. 21, '41. Can mediation solve the defense tangle?

Scholastic. 43:5-6. S. 27, '43. Checkreins for labor; how War Labor Disputes act restricts strikes in war industry.

*Society for the Advancement of Management Journal. 4:45-8. Mr. '39. Arbitration—an analysis. W. E. Hotchkiss.

Sociology and Social Research. 29:96-104. N. '44. Labor under review, July, 1943-June, 1944. M. J. Vincent.

South Atlantic Quarterly. 40:146-53. Ap. '41. Future of the ordinary man. W. J. Matherly.

Southwestern Social Science Quarterly. 19:312-18. D. '38. Some aspects of the work of the National Labor Relations Board. E. A. Elliott.

Southwestern Social Science Quarterly. 20:292-9. D. '39. Relationship of the National Labor Relations Act to industrial and political democracy. E. A. Elliott.

State Government. 13:169-70+. S. '40. Getting results from arbitration; a case study of the organization and operation of industrial arbitration and conciliation in Massachusetts. Leverett Saltonstall.

Survey Graphic. 27:275-8+. My. '38. Promise of industrial arbitration. Webb Waldron.

Survey Graphic. 30:547-51. N. '41. Labor relations in the crisis. W. H. Davis.

Survey Graphic. 30:594-5+. N. '41. Management in evolution. W. R. Burrows.

Survey Graphic. 30:606-9. N. '41. Calling all employers! M. L. Cooke.

Survey Graphic. 30:611-14+. N. '41. Public and labor relations. W. M. Leiserson.

Survey Graphic. 32:277-81. Jl. '43. What's the matter with labor? Louis Stark.

Survey Graphic. 34:19-20. Ja. '45. Labor problem with a future; Western Union dispute over representation. Diana Lewars.

Toledo City Journal. 23:41-4+. Ja. 22, '38. Toledo industrial peace board. Edmund Ruffin.

Town Meeting (Bulletin of America's Town Meeting of the Air). 6, no.19:1-30. Mr. 24, '41. What should labor and industry contribute to national defense? H. E. Staasen, W. P. Reuther, and E. L. Olrich.

Town Meeting (Bulletin of America's Town Meeting of the Air). 6, no.23:1-32. Ap. 21, '41. Why strikes in defense industries? Max Lerner, William Batt, and I. L. Sharfman.

Town Meeting (Bulletin of America's Town Meeting of the Air). 7, no.7:1-24. D. 1, '41. How should we deal with defense strikes? Howard Smith, Frank Fenton, Joseph Curran, and W. L. Batt.

Town Meeting (Bulletin of America's Town Meeting of the Air). 9, no.3:1-19. My. 20, '43. Should the Connally-Smith antistrike bill be adopted? H. W. Smith, W. P. Reuther, W. L. Ransom, and M. Starr.

United States News. 17:16. D. 1, '44. Shift in labor agencies ahead.

University of Chicago Round Table. No. 157:1-26. Mr. 16, '41. Strikes and national defense. P. H. Douglas, R. W. Stone, and the Roving Reporter.

University of Chicago Round Table. No. 194:1-25. N. 30, '41. Radio discussion of labor's responsibility in defense. C. O. Gregory, T. O. Yntema and the Roving Reporter.

Virginia Law Review. 26:769-78. Ap. '40. Refusal to bargain collectively.

Virginia Quarterly Review. 16, no.2:267-78. [Ap.] '40. Labor and responsibility. Philip Murray.

Virginia Quarterly Review. 20, no.4:481-95. [O.] '44. Labor and the war administration. George Soule.

Vital Speeches of the Day. 4:308-10. Mr. 1, '38. Dangerous counsel on labor relations. E. R. Burke.

Vital Speeches of the Day. 9:717-20. S. 15, '43. Hostages for the guilty; our future political policy. William Green.

Vital Speeches of the Day. 10:261-6. F. 15, '44. National Labor Relations Act; not just to employer, employee or public. C. A. Noone.

Yale Law Journal. 46:567-98. F. '37. National Railroad Adjustment Board: a unique administrative agency. L. K. Garrison.

References Favoring Voluntary Arbitration
Books and Pamphlets

*American Arbitration Association. Policy of the American Arbitration Association on compulsory arbitration. 3p. mim. The Association. 9 Rockefeller Plaza. New York. D. 4, '44.

Chamber of Commerce of the United States. Department of Manufacture. Adjustment of labor disputes in defense industries; Committee report. 10p. The Chamber. Washington, D.C. Ja. 24, '41.

Council for Democracy. Public and strikes. (Democracy in Action, no.6) 38p. The Council. 285 Madison Ave. New York. '41.

Gompers, Samuel. Collective bargaining. 7p. American Federation of Labor. Washington, D.C. '20.

Green, William. Freedom, not slavery. 20p. American Federation of Labor. Washington, D.C. '41.

Green, William. Labor and national defense. 14p. Rotary Club of Philadelphia. Philadelphia. Ap. 2, '41.

Green, William. We work for the future. 72p. American Federation of Labor. Washington, D.C. '41.

Hawkes, Albert W.; Carey, J. Q.; and Ruffin, E. How to stop strikes. 12p. Chamber of Commerce of the United States. Washington, D.C. Jl. 18, '41.

National Association of Manufacturers. Compulsory arbitration of labor disputes. 73p. mim. The Association. 14 W. 49th St. New York. ['38].

*Seidman, Joel. Shall strikes be outlawed? (L.I.D. pamphlet series) 32p. League for Industrial Democracy. 112 E. 19th St. New York. Ja. '38.
    Bibliography, p. 30-1.

Periodicals

American Economic Review. 28:65-81. Mr. '38. Recent experience with compulsory arbitration in Australia. W. R. MacLaurin.

American Federationist. 48:22-3. F. '41. Way to avoid strikes. William Green.

American Federationist. 48:8+. Mr. '41. A.F. of L. statement condemning no-strike bills.

American Federationist. 48:9-10+. Je. '41. Slave labor is no solution. George Meany.

American Federationist. 48:10-11. Ag. '41. Four months of defense mediation. George Meany.

American Federationist. 48:3-5+. D. '41. Free labor for victory.

Arbitration Journal. 6:93-101. Spring-Summer '42. Labor arbitration in wartime. Matthew Woll.

Arbitration Journal. 6:247-51. Autumn '42. Voluntary arbitration and the war. J. A. Padway.

Congressional Record. 87:[current file]A2102. Mediation is best remedy for strikes. Jay Franklin.

Economist (London). 146:473-4. Ap. 8, '44. Arbitration and industrial unrest.

*International Labour Review. 38:575-90. N. '38. Economic enquiries as a basis for democratic adjustment of labour disputes. J. S. Dich.

*Modern Industry. 1:56+. F. '41. Should compulsory arbitration of labor disputes be instituted in the defense industries? No. C. V. Whitney.

Nation. 152:487. Ap. 26, '41. Bill to repeal the Wagner act; Vinson bill.

New Republic. 104:846-8. Je. 23, '41. Will conscripted labor work? Michael Straight.

New Republic. 109:425. S. 27, '43. Washington notes; effects of the Smith-Connally anti-strike bill.

New York Times. p. 22. N. 26, '41. Compulsory arbitration; editorial.

*Rotarian. 58:15+. Mr. '41. Compulsory arbitration of labor disputes? No! Edward Keating.

*Rotarian. 58:27-30+. Je. '41. How to insure industrial peace; with discussion. *W. H. Davis; *H. E. Staasen; J. S. Kemper; W. Green; and W. H. Spencer.

Rotarian. 64:32-4. Ja. '44. Talk it out; four arbitration clauses. J. R. Tiffany.

Vital Speeches of the Day. 11:79-84. N. 15, '44. Establishing sound labor policies; is further labor legislation desirable? T. R. Jones.

REFERENCES FAVORING COMPULSORY ARBITRATION

*Emery, James M. National public labor relations policy for tomorrow. 13p. National Founders Association. 120 S. La Salle St. Chicago. N. 17, '43.

*American Economic Review. 31:47-55. Mr. '41. Strikes in a democracy. Domenico Gagliardo.

Congressional Record. 87:(current file)A737-8. F. 17, '41. Compulsory arbitration in defense industries? E. E. Cox.

Congressional Record. 87:[current file]A2505-6. My. 19, '41. Shall strikes continue to prevent national defense? radio address. C. E. Hoffman.

International Labour Review. 34:733-71. D. '36. Restoration of compulsory arbitration in New Zealand. E. J. Riches.

*Modern Industry. 1:57+. F. '41. Should compulsory arbitration of labor disputes be instituted in the defense industries? Yes. E. E. Cox.

Newsweek. 15:50+. F. 19, '40. Arbitration by law; compulsory labor-peace plan to go on California ballot.

*Rotarian. 58:13-15. Mr. '41. Compulsory arbitration of labor disputes? Yes! H. J. Allen.

Studies (Dublin). 25:177-203. Je. '36. Strikes and compulsory arbitration; with discussion. Cornelius Lucey.

Studies (Dublin). 29:497-512. D. '40. Conciliation and arbitration in labour disputes. Cornelius Lucey.